Countering Cyber Threats to Financial Institutions

Pierre-Luc Pomerleau · David L. Lowery

Countering Cyber Threats to Financial Institutions

A Private and Public Partnership Approach to Critical Infrastructure Protection

palgrave
macmillan

Pierre-Luc Pomerleau
School of Business
Northcentral University
Granby, QC, Canada

David L. Lowery
School of Business
Northcentral University
Panama City, FL, USA

ISBN 978-3-030-54053-1 ISBN 978-3-030-54054-8 (eBook)
https://doi.org/10.1007/978-3-030-54054-8

This Palgrave Macmillan imprint is published by the registered company Springer Nature Switzerland AG
The registered company address is: Gewerbestrasse 11, 6330 Cham, Switzerland

To the mentors and leaders in sports, in my academic studies, as well as in my personal and professional lives with whom I have had the opportunity to learn from.

—Pierre-Luc Pomerleau

This work is dedicated to our modern-day cyber professionals, the men and women serving on the cybersecurity virtual "front lines" every day—the military member, the government civil servant, or the private industry worker at every organizational level—whose diligent efforts and expertise collectively enable our modern online and interconnected society to function.

—David L. Lowery

Foreword

Two major constants in life are change and evolving technology. Growing up in the late 1950s and early 1960s, I remember when gasoline was 25 cents per gallon and new cars were well under $10,000 each. We all had rotary dial phones, party lines, and calling international was outrageously expensive at the time. If a piece of equipment broke down, we either fixed it ourselves or took it to a professional repairman for repairs so we could continue using it—a stark contrast to today's disposable society, where we quickly upgrade to the latest technology without a second thought. As a college student in the 1970s, I used a manual typewriter to write my college papers and professors would reject any work that had erasures, which often meant retyping a whole page for a single error. I could go on and on about the technology-related changes I've seen in my lifetime, but my motive here is to point out that most people alive today have very little comprehension of just how technology-dependent we all are and just how far-reaching and rapidly technology has evolved over the past fifty years… and where technology will take us tomorrow.

Few can truly appreciate just how debilitating a major breakdown in today's "connected" IT infrastructure would be to our daily lives, our national economy, and the world in general. We have insidiously become totally dependent on cell phones, computers, and the internet. Our cars, airliners, appliances, finances, global logistics—virtually everything relies on our modern internet and computers. Can you imagine waking up one morning and having no cable TV, no cell phone, no internet, no email, no ATM, and no way to access your finances at all? Traffic signals would no longer work, trains wouldn't run, air travel would come to a complete standstill, and even the modern large-scale farming equipment would sit idle! These are truly unacceptable circumstances on many levels. As such, the stakes are enormously high as the protection of our global IT, satellite networks, and computing infrastructure remains not only paramount, but increasingly complex due to a number of global geopolitical factors. This solemn-but-critical task is not for the faint of heart nor the lightweight intellectual. Modern cybersecurity solutions require a unique combination of both "left-brain" logic/deductive reasoning combined with "right-brain" creativity/imagination, however, there is no room for selfish power plays nor assumptions of righteous motivations. All would-be cybersecurity professionals are potential heroes and anyone with network access is a potential vulnerability or threat if poor cyber hygiene is used.

In closing, looking forward I anticipate one of the key components needed in future cybersecurity systems will be a more robust "resiliency component." The ability to recover a massive block of data, isolate it, and use it as a starting point to begin real-time recovery should that data or system be corrupted or compromised. Regulatory rules and network security guidelines, practices, and protocols are only the first line of an effective cyber defense perimeter. The ability to recover is the crucial defensive fallback we need in place because as long as information is power, there will be actors in every major industrial sector looking to exploit vulnerabilities and to successfully attack our cyber world.

Kailua, Hawaii, USA

Brigadier General Stanley J. Osserman, Jr.
U.S. Air Force (Retired)

Acknowledgments

Someone once told me that a Ph.D. is like a marathon and that marathons are not for everyone. At that point, achieving the doctoral academic standard became a new personal challenge of mine. I must admit that the journey to accomplish this doctorate was quite exciting and rewarding. First, I would like to thank the individual study participants. Regardless of the time of the day, these private security professionals are working with dedication to protect their individual organization's financial assets from various cyber, financial, and physical threats.

To my parents, Gilles and Christine, thank you for teaching me core values of dedication, discipline, and perseverance. Playing football throughout my childhood and early adult years taught me the importance of hard work, teamwork, and considerable efforts are the key ingredients to success. To my wife and best friend, Marie-Eve, I could not have done it without you by my side to remind me what is truly important in life. You were always there to support the family and I. To my children, Maylia and Nathan, thank you for being so patient with me over the years. I know that you did not always understand why dad was spending so much time in his office working on his computer. Later in life, you will understand better and it will be my turn to assist you in reaching your own dreams. To my friends Mathieu and Matthew, thank you for supporting me during the adversity of working full-time, lecturing, and doing a Ph.D. at the same time. To my dissertation chair, Dr. Dave Lowery, I want to thank you for your leadership and continued mentorship. Your experience, motivational skills, and work ethic were vital in my success. Also, I would like to thank my Academic Reader, Dr. Leila Sopko for her support and expertise during the dissertation process. Lastly, I would like to thank Dr. David Maimon from Georgia State University for his insight and expertise. Thank you all for everything!

Pierre-Luc Pomerleau

When I retired from the Air Force and transitioned into academia in 2018, my goal was to "pay forward" the many years of professional mentoring and support I myself had received throughout my career by teaching/mentoring the next generation of doctoral/graduate students. Pierre-Luc was one of the first handful of doctoral students I was assigned as a new dissertation committee chair. Over the next year, we meticulously developed Pierre-Luc's research plan, garnered university approval, analyzed the data he collected, and I guided him as he formulated his key conclusions—all in Pierre-Luc's one speed: "full afterburner"! It is a true honor and privilege to co-author this manuscript with Pierre-Luc as well as to collaborate with Georgia State University's Dr. David Maimon and a long-time mentor of my own, Air Force Brigadier General Stan Osserman, Jr. U.S. Air Force (Retired).

I'd like to also share a very special thank you to my loving wife Sarah Lowery, children Jackson, Emma, & Jessica Lowery, father Rickey Lowery, step-mother Myra Lowery, sister-in-law Leslie Lowery, maternal aunts LaRoy Bass & Wynde Brown, and fellow professor-turned-author cousins Billie Jane McIntosh & Gary McIntosh for all their support & encouragement to pursue this endeavor. Special thanks also to my own former doctoral dissertation committee: Valdosta State University's Dr. Leigh Ross Stanford, Florida State University's Dr. Hafiz Ahmad, and Dr. Kelly Gervera for their professional mentoring that allowed me to be here today.

David L. Lowery

Contents

1 **Contemporary Cybersecurity in Our Daily Lives** 1
Introduction 1
A Broad View of Cybercriminals 2
Recent Cyberattack Trends 4
Discerning Overall Cyberattack Trends with Limited Data 7
References 8

2 **Relevance of Evidence-Based Cybersecurity in Guiding the Financial Sector's and Efforts in Fighting Cybercrime** 9
David Maimon
Introduction 9
Evidence-Based Cybersecurity 11
EBCS Research in the Context of Financial Institutions Efforts in Cyberspace 13
Identify Vulnerable Targets and Increase Cybersecurity Awareness 14
Assess the Effectiveness of Security Tools and Policies 17
Configure Financial Organizations' Internet Infrastructure 19
Dissemination of Evidence-Based Cybersecurity Research 22
Conclusion 23
References 24

3 The Evolution of Cybersecurity within the American Financial Sector 29
The American Financial Sector: Tempting Targets for CyberAttackers 29
The American Economy: A Major Element of National Security 30
The Evolution of Cybersecurity within America's Financial Sector 31
Consumer Protection During the Infancy of e-Commerce (1999–2003) 32
The Payment Card Industry Data Security Standard (2004) 33
Executive Order 13636 (2013) and the Implication to "Section 9" Firms 33
The Roll-Out of the NIST Cybersecurity Framework (2014–2018) 35
DoD Cyber Strategy (2015) and Presidential Policy Directive 41 (2016) 37
America's National Cyber Strategy (2018) 38
The U.S. Financial Sector's Militarized Approach to Fighting Cybercrime (2018–Present) 39
Looking Ahead: Layered Cyber Deterrence 40
Conclusion 42
References 42

4 The Evolution of the Threats to Canadian Financial Institutions, the Actual State of Public and Private Partnerships in Canada 47
The Actual State; Protecting Financial Institutions 47
What Is the Problem? 48
The Purpose of the Study 49
Nature of Study 50
Research Questions 51
Theoretical Frameworks in Cybersecurity and Security Networks 52
A Private and Public Partnership Approach to Critical Infrastructure Protection 55
Cyber-Threat Environment 62
References 74

5 **Major Themes in the Literature of Cybersecurity and Public–Private Partnerships; A Focus on Financial Institutions** 87
Critical Infrastructure Protection 87
Legal and Organizational Barriers to Information Sharing 93
Public Safety's Role in Cybercrime and Cybersecurity Incidents 99
Public Sector (Law Enforcement) and Government Roles and Responsibilities 102
International Public and Private Partnership Initiatives 103
Private Sector 109
The Corporate and Private Security Domain 111
The Importance of Technology 112
Summary 113
References 114

6 **Research Findings; Contemporary Perceptions of Canadian Security Professionals Regarding the Challenges in Sharing Information with the Public Sector** 123
Results 124
Demographic Data 124
Theme 1: Receiving Timely Information Sharing for Prevention Purposes 127
Theme 2: Joint-Ventures—Integrated Public–Private Fusion Centers 129
Theme 3: Mechanisms to Share Information 131
Theme 4: Lack of Legal Framework for Crime Prevention 132
Theme 5: Conflicting Organizational Missions & Objectives 136
Theme 6: Interpersonal Trust Relationships 139
Theme 7: Unclear Roles, Responsibilities, and Processes in Critical Infrastructures Protection 141
Theme 8: CyberAttacks on Banks; a Potential Domino Effect 142
Theme 9: Cross-Sector Critical Infrastructure Information Sharing 144
Theme 10: Necessity to Increase Cyber-Threat Information Sharing 145
Theme 11: Governance Model to Share Information 146
Theme 12: Various Types of Security Networks Are Necessary 150

Evaluation of the Findings 151
References 155

7 **Conclusions and Implications for Practice and Future Studies on Public–Private Partnerships** 157
Implications 159
Research Question #1 159
Recommendations for Practice 162
Recommendations for Future Research 164
Research Question #2 165
Recommendations for Practice 170
Recommendations for Future Research 172
Research Question #3 172
Recommendations for Practice 175
Recommendations for Future Research 176
Research Question #4 177
Recommendations for Practice 180
Recommendations for Future Research 182
Summary of Recommendations 183
Conclusion 188
References 189

Definitions of Key Terms 197

Index 207

About the Authors

Dr. Pierre-Luc Pomerleau is a financial crime executive with over 15 years of experience with three large Canadian financial institutions. Dr. Pomerleau is also an adjunct professor in the Cybersecurity program at Polytechnique Montreal and a cybercrime research associate for Georgia State University. Pierre-Luc holds a bachelor's degree in criminology from the University of Montreal and an MBA from the University of Sherbrooke. He pursued his Ph.D. in Business Administration with a specialization in Homeland Security & Leadership Policy at Northcentral University. He also holds the CPP, PSP, PCI, CFE, CAMS, CCCI, and CFCI professional certifications. In October 2016, Pierre-Luc was awarded an honorary diploma by the University of Montreal School of Criminology for his exemplary contribution to the advancement of society. From 2015 to 2018, Pierre-Luc was the President of the Montreal ACFE Chapter. He has experience leading teams within the fraud & risk management landscape with a concentrated focus in Corporate Security, internal investigations, payment & online fraud, data analytics, crisis management, third-Party risk Management, and anti-money laundering.

Dr. David L. Lowery is a professor of Homeland Security for Northcentral University. A retired U.S. Air Force lieutenant colonel with 20 years of active-duty service (1998–2018) in the combat communications-turned-cyberspace operations and human resources career fields, then-Lieutenant Colonel Lowery was a three-time Air Force unit commander and the deputy commander of a rapid-response humanitarian joint task force in the South Pacific. He also served as the Hawaii Air National Guard's Civil Defense "Island Commander" of the storm-prone Hawaiian Island of Kauai (2008–2010) and spent five years in Washington, DC working at the Pentagon & the National Guard Bureau. His last military assignment was serving as the executive officer for the Air Force's National Security Emergency Preparedness (AFNSEP) Directorate at Headquarters First Air Force (Air Forces Northern) at Tyndall Air Force Base, Florida. Dr. Lowery holds a Doctor of Public Administration (DPA) degree with a concentration in Homeland Security from Valdosta State University (2016), a Master of Science in Native American Leadership Studies from Southeastern Oklahoma State University (2020), a Master of Arts in Organizational Leadership from George Washington University (2007), a Master of Public Administration (MPA) from Valdosta State University (2000), and a Bachelor of Arts in Political Science/Pre-Law from the University of South Carolina (1998). Dr. Lowery is also a graduate of the National Defense University's Chief Information Officer (CIO) Course (2015), the U.S. Air Force's Cyber 400 "Scope Eagle" Course (2015), as well as the U.S. Air Force's Air War College (2012), Air Command & Staff College (2007), & Squadron Officer School (2003).

Dr. David Maimon is an Associate Professor in the department of Criminal Justice and Criminology at Georgia State University. He received his Ph.D. in Sociology from the Ohio State University in 2009. Since being at Georgia State University, Dr. Maimon has created an Evidence-Based Cybersecurity Group where he and his researchers seek to produce empirical evidence and provide systematic reviews of existing empirical research and provide tools in preventing the development and progression of cyber-dependent crimes.

List of Tables

Table 6.1 Study participants by bank 125
Table 6.2 Demographical information of participants 126
Table 6.3 Emergent themes from interviews 127
Table 7.1 Key features of future Canadian public-private partnerships 184
Table 7.2 Recommendations for practice on private and public partnerships 185
Table 7.3 Recommendations for future research on private and public partnerships 186

CHAPTER 1

Contemporary Cybersecurity in Our Daily Lives

Introduction

In contemporary modern society, we are all virtually surrounded by a plethora of internet-connected computing devices that are essentially "baked into" into any number of our everyday routines. These devices range from the obvious—cell phones, computers/laptops/tablets, smart televisions, smart watches, and interactive home exercise equipment—to more subtle devices such as our modern automobiles, high-tech kitchen appliances, and even the garage door opener. We activate our virtual assistants with the sound of our voice, routinely gather our daily news, communicate, date, shop, attend virtual college courses, make travel reservations, and conduct our financial affairs all online. With a few clicks of a button or verbal commands, our logistical and financial well-being is at our fingertips—in real-time from virtually anywhere—a digital connection can be made.

As Singer and Friedman (2014) point out, for all the conveniences and opportunities afforded to us with instant access—on-demand—in today's information age, unfortunately this easy access has also given rise to wide-spread "cyber anxiety." Fears of nefarious internet-enabled threats have slowly intertwined into America's national subconscious. Today's notions of digital security, physical security, financial/economic security, and even our individual identities and privacy needs all meld together

P.-L. Pomerleau and D. L. Lowery, *Countering Cyber Threats to Financial Institutions*,
https://doi.org/10.1007/978-3-030-54054-8_1

into a pervasive sense of collective vulnerability. Any number of collective vulnerabilities can affect us all—ranging from power plants, financial institutions, transportation systems, and the availability of consumable commodities.

While some degree of cyber-threat awareness and the practice of good cyber-hygiene/digital security is becoming more common place, cybersecurity is "one of those areas that has been left to only the most technically inclined to worry [about]…anything related to the digital world of zeroes and ones [is] an issue for computer scientists and the IT help desk…some threats are overblown, while others are ignored" (Singer and Friedman, 2014, pp. 5–6).

A Broad View of Cybercriminals

Unfortunately, cyber-enabled criminal activity is continuously evolving and is extremely unlikely to diminish anytime soon. Nation-state actors and individual hackers alike can make hundreds, thousands, or even millions of people unsuspecting victims using stolen personal identities to generate fraudulent identities or access stolen credit card data to generate fake financial transactions. According to the 2018 McAfee Annual Cybersecurity Report written by Lewis (2018), McAfee; the American-based global computer security company, suggests a good estimate is a full two-thirds of people operating online today—more than two billion users—have had their personal/financial information stolen or compromised. Thus, cybercrime is an incredibly important topic that can potentially impact everyone and cause significant disruptions to many aspects of our daily lives.

According to both Buono (2014) and Lewis (2018), for those higher-end and technically-savvy cybercriminals who have the technical knowledge and capabilities to be successful in their nefarious cybercrimes, the perceived rewards often outweigh the perceived risks of getting caught and subsequently punished. This perceived "low risk" activity is aided by the relatively high degree of anonymity afforded in cyberspace—a medium through which crimes can be committed that would never be possible in the physical off-line world (Buono, 2014). This unique combination of factors makes cybercriminal activities a lucrative industry—with a smart (and lucky) cybercriminal making potentially hundreds of thousands or even millions of dollars with only a minimal chance of arrest or jail time. Even if a cyber-perpetrator is eventually identified as being behind a successful cyberattack, law enforcement officials can find themselves hamstrung by geopolitical or international boundaries that make criminal arrests and overall enforcement incredibly difficult (Lewis, 2018). This is why cybersecurity-minded organization focus their primary efforts on continuous risk mitigation and preventative measures. This dynamic also explains why malicious cybercrimes continue to persist at such a large scale and why cybersecurity is such a critically important component of all modern e-commerce worldwide.

Just as contemporary IT-related technologies are continuously evolving at a lightning-fast pace, so too are high-tech cybercriminals. As the IT Industry has collectively moved toward cloud computing, enhanced encryption methodologies, and artificial intelligence (AI)-enabled software capabilities, so too have those same high-tech cybercriminals moved to take advantage of potential vulnerabilities within each platform or new capability (Ashford, 2018; Cowley, 2018; Lewis, 2018). While there is a natural inclination for public organizations and private industries alike to seek out the most cutting-edge and high-performance IT system-based capabilities possible—with the expectation that these "box solutions" will help protect their respective organizations from cyberattacks, this is seldom the case.

An organization's cyber-defenses are only as good as its weakest link…and this often ends up not being a technical deficiency, but rather unsuspecting "flesh and blood" employees who fail to maintain even the most basic of cyber-hygiene protocols or mistakenly click on a phishing link hidden in a harmless looking email. Beyond ignorance, potential insider threats are another distinct challenge for organizations because of the increased difficulty in detecting "in-house" activities when so much of modern cybersecurity efforts are outward-focused beyond the organization's IT firewalls. Clearly, the ever-evolving challenges of cybersecurity—the mitigation of cyber-vulnerabilities through the comprehensive prevention, detection, and protective response to unauthorized activities—is by no means exclusively an American problem, but rather a worldwide problem. Cybersecurity threats and mitigation efforts span to virtually every corner of the globe. Every modern governmental organization, financial institution, and business organization with any type of online presence, e-commerce activities, or a public interest shares in the collective threats of faceless cyber-enabled threats by disreputable actors.

Recent Cyberattack Trends

In July 2019, Internet Society's Online Trust Alliance (OTA) released its 11th Annual *Cyber Incident & Breach Trends Report*, which provides a global overview of publicly released cyberattack incidents and offers key mitigation steps public and private organizations alike can take to reduce cyber vulnerabilities to their own networks, thus limiting potential damage. This most recent OTA annual trends analysis reported a total of two million reported cyber incidents in 2018 and detailed a rapidly shifting landscape of cyber incidents with increases in some cyberattack types, which notable drop-offs of other attack types (Olmstead, 2019).

OTA described the most prevalent forms of cyberattacks in 2018 as being crypto-jacking (1.3 million) and ransomware (500,000), followed by network security data breaches (60,000), supply chain website infections (60,000), and corporate business email compromises (20,000) (Olmstead, 2019). While ransomware was on the decline, the total dollar value of these attacks that were successful continued to drive an increased net financial impact. The largest area of statistical "growth" in cyberattacks was in the area of Distributed Denial of Service (DDoS) attacks. While 2018 DDoS attacks were primarily focused on the banking, education, email services, and software service industries (Online Trust Alliance, 2019), these attacks were also felt by a variety of major online retailers as well—especially on traditionally high-volume online sales days such as "Black Friday" and "Cyber Monday" (Ashford, 2018). Additionally, OTA's analysis found aggregate 2018 cyber-related "incidents" to be 95% preventable, exposed more than 5 billion records, generated an $8 billion (USD) ransomware impact, and attributed to more than $12.5 billion (USD) in direct global losses (Olmstead, 2019; OTA, 2019). A similar 2018 cyber study conducted jointly by McAfee, partnered with the Center for Strategic and International Studies (CSIS), a major American-based cybersecurity think tank, concluded cyberattack-enabled cybercrimes is one of the most rapidly-growing and lucrative industries worldwide. The McAfee-CSIS Study found at least $445 billion (USD) were lost in 2017 (Lewis, 2018).

Generally speaking, cyberattacks include a variety of nefarious IT-related threats ranging from computer viruses to data breaches to security control breaches to complete systems failure. According to Melnick (2018), the ten most common types of cyber threats include:

1. *Denial-of-Service (DoS) & Distributed Denial-of-Service (DDoS) Attacks*: One of the more straightforward cyberattacks is a DoS attack, which is an attack seeking to overwhelm an IT system's resources so that it cannot perform its primary role of responding to online service requests. A DDoS attack operates much in the same manner, but is coordinated from a larger number of machines (usually infected with malicious software controlling system resources that are controlled by the attacker) and launch a multipronged DoS attack. Unlike more complex cyberattacks, DoS/DDoS attacks are not intended to garner system access for the attacker—but rather block routine e-commerce or data provision activities.
2. *Man-in-the-Middle (MitM) Attack*: In this type of cyberattack, an attacker attempts to "hijack" a current online session between an authenticated (or 'trusted') client providing proper access credentials and a specific network server/application. By substituting its internet protocol (IP) address in lieu of the validated/trusted client, the attacking computer gains access to the otherwise secure data because the IP server believes it is still communicating with the original authenticated client's server. As such, data that would be readily available to the real client/system user is made available to the attacker.
3. *Phishing & Spear-Phishing Attacks*: This type of attack is based on email spoofing and involves a certain degree of social engineering and trickery by creating false and misleading email messages. These false messages are intended to fool a computer user into thinking these are legitimate/trusted correspondences and clicking on embedded hyperlinks, which loads hidden malware onto the victim's computer, the system log-on credentials, and/or steals sensitive information stored on that victim's computer or network. Taking this type of attack one step further, spear phishing is a higher-level type of phishing activity that involved a customized message to a specific target with specific tailored messages—ultimately seeking to gain the same access to the user's personal information and data systems.
4. *"Drive-by" Download Attacks*: This type of cyberattack doesn't involve clicking on improper links to enable an attack—instead, it involves taking advantage of the vulnerabilities into insecure

websites and planting malicious scripts into the website's coding. This is also a common tool used to distribute malware.

5. *Password Attack*: This type of attack involved accessing a user's password to gain access to a particular IT system. An individual's password may be obtained by looking around their desk (hidden written-down passwords or clues), social engineering, "sniffing" the network, using a password database, and plain old guessing. This is why contemporary passwords are now required to be lengthier, more complex in nature, and use a combination of alphanumeric characters—to prevent this type of password acquisition from occurring.
6. *SQL Injection Attack*: A common challenge with database-centered websites, a SQL attack occurs when a hacker executes a database query via the input data from the client to the supporting server. SQL commands are then inserted, allowing the attacker to potentially gain greater access to the database—including sensitive data that could be exploited.
7. *Cross-Site Scripting (XSS) Attack*: An XSS attack uses a third-party's website to insert malicious scripts into a user's web browser.
8. *Eavesdropping Attack*: Eavesdropping occurs through the monitoring and interception of specific online network traffic. By eavesdropping, an attacker may be able to gain access to non-encrypted data ranging from passwords, credit card numbers, and other private information that a user may be transmitting online.
9. *Birthday Attack*: Birthday attacks are based on hash algorithms used for system verification to discern authentic digital signatures, messages, and attachments. The "birthday" reference refers to the likelihood of finding two different messages that generate the same hashing function identifiers.
10. *Malware Attack*: Malware is unwanted software installed on one's IT system. Malicious programming often has the ability to attach itself to legitimate program coding and begin to propagate itself—causing a variety of system problems as the propagation continues. There are a broad array of malware types ranging from macro-viruses to executable (.exe), to file infectors, to system file, from Trojans, from worms, or from ransomware (Melnick, 2018).

Discerning Overall Cyberattack Trends with Limited Data

It is important to keep in mind that these annual cyberattack statistics are most likely a significant ***underestimation***, based on the fact many cyberattacks are not publicly reported by the impacted organization (Olmstead, 2019). When searching for aggregate nation or worldwide levels, presenting an accurate and comprehensive snapshot of an ever-evolving cyberspace landscape and accurately identifying specific attack trends is an extremely difficult task due to a lack of consolidated reporting mechanisms (Cowley, 2018). While by no means an impossible task, this challenge is akin to having a 2000-piece puzzle dumped out into a pile on a large table and someone being asked to assemble the puzzle pieces—before one realizes the product box's "finished product" reference photo is not available and a double-handful of random puzzle pieces have been removed for good measure.

Let's continue with this puzzle analogy for a moment to discuss cyber-attack reporting used to ascertain certain trends and overall cyberattack venues. Without a photo of the finished product to refer to and only a general idea of what the final picture may look like, the puzzle assembler has no choice but to sort the individual puzzle pieces by shape and color. As the puzzle assembler proceeds with this process, he or she must search for discernible characteristics—colors, patterns, and shapes—and segregate the puzzle pieces accordingly before further sense can be deductively made by the jumble of puzzle pieces that lay before them.

Parlaying this puzzle analogy into the analysis of contemporary cyber-attack incidents, the "on-hand" puzzle pieces are most often regional-based vendor-specific user data, rather than global-level aggregate data. Some cybersecurity-related vendors readily share their organization's cyberattack/cybercrime data much more readily than others and unsuccessful cyberattack diagnostic data is much less likely to be reported (and thereby provided for analysis) than actual successful attacks. As such, these underreported attacks and organizational "gaps" in cyberattack report data represent the missing puzzle pieces in the analogy above. Can one still assemble most of the data and offer an aggregate "big picture" perspective without every single puzzle piece? Absolutely, however the fewer cyberattack data elements (or missing puzzle pieces), the more complete analysis (or puzzle) can be created. Additionally, even if it is not holistically complete, comprehensive cyberattack data details provide a granular view of technical boundaries (i.e., hardware/software/system-related limitations) that can then be used to define distinctive "gaps and seams" in cyberattack vectors—much like the distinctive "edge" pieces of a puzzle can define the parameters or outer edges of the entire puzzle.

References

Ashford, W. (2018). *E-commerce sites warned of heightened DDoS threat*. Retrieved from https://www.computerweekly.com/news/252453494/E-commerce-sites-warned-of-heightened-DDoS-threat.

Buono, L. (2014). Fighting cybercrime through prevention, outreach, and awareness raising. *Springerlink.com*. Retrieved from https://link.springer.com/article/10.1007/s12027-014-0333-4.

Cowley, S. (2018). Banks adopt military-style tactics to fight cybercrime. *The New York Times*. Retrieved from https://www.nytimes.com/2018/05/20/business/banks-cyber-security-military.html.

Lewis, J. (2018). McAfee-CSIS report: Economic impact of cybercrime—No slowing down. *McAfee.com*. Retrieved from https://www.mcafee.com/enterprise/en-us/assets/reports/restricted/rp-economic-impact-cybercrime.pdf.

Melnick, J. (2018). Top 10 most common types of cyber attacks. *Netwrix.com*. Retrieved from https://blog.netwrix.com/2018/05/15/top-10-most-common-types-of-cyber-attacks/.

Olmstead, K. (2019). Internet Society's Online Trust Alliance 2018 cyber incidents & breach trends report. *The Internet Society*. Retrieved from https://www.internetsociety.org/blog/2019/07/internet-societys-online-trust-alliance-2019-cyber-incidents-breach-trends-report/.

Online Trust Alliance. (2019). *2018 cyber incident & breach trends report*. Retrieved from https://www.internetsociety.org/resources/ota/2019/2018-cyber-incident-breach-trends-report/.

Singer, P., & Friedman, A. (2014). *Cybersecurity & cyberwar: What everyone needs to know*. New York, NY: The Oxford University Press.

CHAPTER 2

Relevance of Evidence-Based Cybersecurity in Guiding the Financial Sector's and Efforts in Fighting Cybercrime

David Maimon

Introduction

During the early 1970s through the early 1990s, violent crime rates in the United States increased dramatically (Kelling & Sousa, 2001). During the peak years (1990–1992) those rates reached to 758 violent crime incidents per 100,000 inhabitants (Uniform Crime Report 1995). Given the increasing crime rates trends annually reported by the Federal Bureau of Investigation (FBI) during this era—not to mention a steady intensity in public outcry—demanding public order and safety to be restored (Weisburd & Braga, 2006), police operations were subjected to rigorous scientific attention and evaluations. However, many of the scientific evaluations performed during those years found police efforts to be generally ineffective in reducing crime (Greenwood et al., 1975; Kelling, Pate, Dieckman, & Brown, 1974; Levine, 1975; Wellford, 1974).

Levine (1975) and Welford (1974), for example, assessed the relationships between police workforce and crime and found that increase in police workforce did not translate to reduction in robbery and murder rates. Similarly, Kelling and associates (1974) showed that random preventive patrol did not prevent crime, and Spelman and Brown (1984) reported that rapid response to calls for service rarely resulted in arrests.

P.-L. Pomerleau and D. L. Lowery, *Countering Cyber Threats to Financial Institutions*,
https://doi.org/10.1007/978-3-030-54054-8_2

Finally, Greenwood and colleagues found that routine follow-up investigations by police detectives rarely solved crimes (Greenwood et al., 1975). These and other studies convinced police professionals that there is a need for a change in the then prevalent (and traditional) policing practices, and opened the door to close collaborations between criminologists and police professionals (Weisburd & Braga, 2006).

In one of the most celebrated collaborations between criminologists and police departments in the United States, Sherman, Gartin, and Buerger (1989) discovered that large proportion of crime tend to be concentrated in a small number of specific geographic locations, which were in turn identified as criminal "hot spots" (Sherman et al., 1989). Building on this key finding, which was subsequently replicated across the United States and Europe (Weisburd, 2015), Sherman and Weisburd (1995) replicated Kelling's (1974) research with a laser focus on crime hot spots. Sherman and Weisburd's research identified a correlational increase in "hot spot" police patrols equated to discernibly less criminal activity calls—as compared to control "hot spots" locations where police presence/patrols had not changed (Sherman & Weisburd, 1995).

This and other similar encouraging studies (see Weisburd & Braga, 2019) for a review of some of these studies) pushed police departments around the United States to diversify their policing tool kits and deploy more focused policing strategies in areas that historically generated high levels of crime (see Braga, Turchan, Papachristos, & Hureau, 2019 for a modern review of sixty-five local law enforcement empirical studies that revisited and further retested the effectiveness of this approach). Kelling and Sousa (2001) concluded the adoption of "hot spot" policing practices has been one of the major factors responsible for the sharp decline in the United States' national-level violent crime rate. A distinct and discernible drop in annual criminal statistics began in the mid-1990s to a rate of 368.9 violent crimes per 100,000 inhabitants in 2018 (Uniform Crime Report, 2018).

Fast forward forty years and history seems to be repeating itself—only this time the local-level criminal activities of the United States during the 1970s–1990s is now occurring within the cyberspace realm. Cyber-dependent crimes are illegal activities that can only be performed using a computer, computer networks, or other forms of information communication technology, while cyber-enabled crimes are all those offenses in which computers are used in a supporting capacity (McGuire & Dowling, 2013). Unfortunately, it is not possible to disclose an exact rate of various cybercrime types (neither cyber-dependent nor cyber-enabled crimes) in the United States due to a wide range of reasons including: the absence of a reliable single portal that collects information on victims of crime, unawareness of victims to their victimization, lack of reporting, and numerous "cyber experts" reports—which often aims to deflate and sell their products (McQuade, 2006). Still, we know that the costs of cybercrime to victims increase rapidly. According to the Internet Crime Complaint Center (IC3) (2020), the annual aggregated monitory losses to cybercrime victims in the United States has risen from $1.5 billion in 2016 to $3.5 billion in 2019. Unfortunately, these costs do not include the costs of many data breaches, DDoS attacks, malware infestations and other types of cybercrime that are experienced by individuals and organizations yet are not reported to the IC3. Therefore, it comes as no surprise that Americans nowadays are more worried to become the victim of cybercrime than the victims of any other type of crime (Chapman University, 2014).

In this climate of an ever-evolving transnational crime, the operation of cybersecurity companies that offer wide range of services to reduce individuals and organizations' cybercrime risk is expected. Numerous cybersecurity services and tools aimed at identifying, visualizing, and remediating cyberattacks are offered for sale by eager vendors. However, in the absence of objective scientific research which studies how cybersecurity tools and policies, as well as law enforcement efforts in cyberspace influencing cybercrime, it is impossible to tell how successful these approaches are in preventing this phenomenon. Therefore, information security teams in both private and public sector governmental organizations alike should be leveraged to allow collaborative innovation between technical, law enforcement, and social scientists in their ongoing efforts to mitigate modern-day cybercrimes. To aid guide these efforts, the evidence-based cybersecurity approach should be adopted in the context of information security teams' workflow.

Evidence-Based Cybersecurity

Consistent with the National Institute of Standard and Technology (National Institute of Standards of Technology, 2018), cybersecurity is defined in this work as "the process of protecting information by preventing, detecting, and responding to attacks." Evidence-Based Cybersecurity (EBCS) is an approach calling for moving beyond cybersecurity experts' political, financial, social background, and personal experience when deciding on the implantation of cybersecurity policies and tools, to a model in which tools' adoption and policy enforcements decisions are made based on scientific studies findings. Following the footsteps of the successful paradigms of "evidence-based medicine" (Sackett & Rosenberg 1995) and "evidence-based policing (Sherman 1998) (to name a few), the EBCS notion suggests that the best scientific evidence should be used to guide cybersecurity practices by evaluating tools, policies and practices in cyberspace while seeking to find a good tradeoff in terms of security teams' investments—to include convenience, time, money, and collective efforts (Schneier, 2008). Scientific evidence should support the ongoing methodical quest to differentiate between unsystematic "experiences" and "common notions" as the basis for cybersecurity practices, and systematic facts observed in the process of testing research hypotheses using rigorous research designs should guide guardians' decision-making in cyberspace.

This Evidence-Based Cybersecurity Approach calls for strengthening the rigor of scientific research that is conducted in online security and cybercrime. As present-day cybersecurity practitioners are typically not well versed in the art of scientific research, and since the Cybersecurity Discipline is populated with scholars who are trained to build security tools, the vast evidence that is published in professional outlets regarding the effectiveness of security tools and policies leave something to be desired. For this to change, cybersecurity professionals and scholars should partner with researchers from a wide range of academic disciplines (including criminology, sociology, psychology computer science, computer information systems and engineering to name a few) to find the answers to questions that may improve security professionals' operations in cyberspace. Importantly, this author suspects that although past cybersecurity research has been focused on technical aspects of tools, the focus of future research should shift to the humans who operate within the cybercrime ecosystem (Maimon & Louderback, 2019). Indeed, several long-established academic scholars suggested that the interactions among cyber criminals, enablers (i.e., individuals who support the online criminal operations; Moore, Clayton, & Anderson, 2009), targets, and guardians (i.e., official law enforcement agencies and system administrators) form a unique ecosystem, in which the activities of each actor influence the behaviors of other actors (Kraemer-Mbula, Tang, & Rush, 2013; Moore et al., 2009).

As such, rigorous scientific research designs including field experiments, longitudinal surveys and observations, should be deployed with the aim of generating evidence which could: (a) identify online threats and vulnerabilities and educate targets of cybercrime; (b) guide policy development and guardians' efforts to secure cyberspace, and (c) drive the design and configuration of computing environments that can mitigate effectively the consequences cybercrime events.

In addition to strengthening the rigor of interdisciplinary cybersecurity research, a crucial component of EBCS is the translation of research findings into a format that is accessible and easy to digest for cybersecurity professionals in the field. A Chief Information Security Officer (CISO) and his/her team who debate between the deployment of different tools and policies in effort to reduce their organizations risk of cybercrime should have access to research findings, which provide clear picture regarding the effectiveness of the tool/policy in achieving its goals in order to guide their decision-making process. The overarching goal of the EBCS is to allow cybersecurity practitioners with easy access to relevant scientific research, which then could be used in their efforts to address cybercrime and cybersecurity problems which are of relevance to their organization.

In the following few pages, several examples of modern EBCS research conducted by cybersecurity professionals within the American Financial Sector will be highlighted—largely in order to emphasize the need in the development of an efficient and accessible dissemination platform, which will allow both practitioners and scholars alike to collaborate, share, distribute, and consume this shared cybersecurity-related research.

EBCS Research in the Context of Financial Institutions Efforts in Cyberspace

According to Borghard (2018), cyber-threats against financial institutions pose considerable risks to the stability of national and global economy. Similarly, Bouveret (2018) identified the major risks to financial institutions as diverse, including DDoS attacks, data breaches, and fraud. Carter (2017) added that the proliferation of easy to use malware and the easy access to hackers for hire services on online dark markets—coupled with the potential interest of individual nation-states (as well as other nefarious actors) in disrupting the financial sectors of competitor/near-peer nation-states—further increase financial institutions risk to become the victims of cybercrime. Therefore, a summer 2019 industry-wide annual report disclosed that the Financial Sector was one of the three most negatively-impacted/affected industries to experience data breaches over the past twelve months was not surprising—alongside the Healthcare and Professional Sectors (Verizon, 2020).

Due to the inherent risk posed to the stability of their operational IT financial systems and the ever-improving capabilities/ingenuity of their potential cybercriminal adversaries (Borghard, 2018), cybersecurity expenditures by financial institutions worldwide have increased significantly over the past five years. Investments by American financial institutions alone are estimated to reach $68 billion by the end of 2020 (Carter, 2017). This author suggests that adopting the Evidence-Based Cybersecurity Approach could guide a more cost-effective expenditures on security solutions and policies by CISO at individual financial institutions, in the face of the risks faced by their organizations and teams. Below, this author intends to demonstrate the utility of this approach in the context of financial organizations' efforts (1) to identify vulnerable legitimate users of their network and increase awareness among them, (2) to assess the effectiveness of security policies and tools in achieving their goals, and (3) to configure their network in a way that could mitigate the consequence of data breaches.

Identify Vulnerable Targets and Increase Cybersecurity Awareness

Manipulating insiders remain the number one vector of compromising banks. Alvarez (2017) reports that 58% of attacks on financial institutions originated in the company employees, while over 90% of these employees were unwitting pawns in the attack and were manipulated by malicious actors (through wide range of social engineering approaches). Therefore, CISO and their cybersecurity teams within individual financial organizations should devote considerable efforts to identifying vulnerable users of their network, as well as educate their respective organization's entire workforce population with security policies and cyber hygiene practices (Carter, 2017).

To emphasize this point, consider Cranor's (2008) "Human in the Loop" framework, which seeks to support the timely identification and mitigation of human threats to major cybersecurity activities. According to her model, cybersecurity failures are the outcome of the computer user's traits (i.e., personal variables, intentions, and capabilities) and communication impediments which are embedded in the security professional messages to the user, which in turn, leads to insecure human behavior in cyberspace. Therefore, this author suggests it is important to identify personal variables, intentions and capabilities among organizational users which could allow determining whether security messages will result in expected security behavioral outcomes or not. Moreover, identifying social clusters within an organization which are likely to expose an organization to various attackers and attacks are key (Maimon et al., 2013).

Identification of vulnerable users could be done using both survey and experimental research designs. For example, Maimon et al. (2013) leveraged a survey research design to understand how organizational social clusters influence the organization probability to experience cyber-dependent crimes from various countries around the globe. Analyzing the events logs from an intrusion detection system (IDS), which had been installed in a large American academic university, they found a positive association between the number of network's foreign users and the volume of cyber-dependent crimes recorded on the network from these users' countries of origin. Simulation of phishing attacks on organizational listserve may further explore vulnerable users of the system.

Email phishing attacks are one of the most popular attack methods in cyberspace (Willems, 2019). Hackers vastly use a variety of phishing scams in order to gain access to a computer network and install malwares that consistently steal information from individuals, corporations, or governments. Understanding what type of departmental and individual characteristics make an individual increasingly vulnerable to phishing scams, is of paramount value for financial institutions.

In addition to identifying vulnerable users, it is key to examine whether educational and awareness programs, which incorporates simulated harm to program participants' computers, influences financial institutions' computer users' probability to adopt online self-protective behaviors as well as their probability to become the victims of online crime. Similar to practices taken by public health organizations (Mulligan & Schneider, 2011), some cybersecurity policies aim to educate and "nudge" legitimate users of the network to engage in cautious online behaviors and adopt online self-protective behaviors—such as using a secure VPN connection, and avoiding opening emails and links which were sent from unfamiliar sources (Maimon et al., 2017) while using the organization's IT network services.

Public awareness campaigns regarding the consequences of cyber-dependent crimes, as well as advertisements of a list of rules to follow, are common practices taken by CISO's in computing environment in aim to make their organization's network users aware of the accepted behavioral norms while operating on the company's network, and prevent them from claiming ignorance of these expectations (Hartel et al., 2010; Morris, 2004). A common notion in the cybersecurity field suggests that creating an environment in which people are encouraged to comply with normative standards of behaviors reduces the probability that a situation conducive to crime will emerge. This in turn reduces the probability of criminal events. Accordingly, both Willison and Siphonen (2009) and Morris (2004) suggested that education of staff and employees regarding organizational security practices assist compliance and may reduce the risk of cyber-dependent crimes.

A recent review of academic literature focusing on cybersecurity awareness and related organizational training programs indicates that their effectiveness in improving information security practices and promoting a sustainable society has not had the desired impact (Braga et al., 2019). As such, these scholars concluded that security education and awareness programs should be targeted, actionable, and provide feedback to users in order for them to be effective. This author concurs with Braga et al. (2019) and proposes regular and comprehensive operational testing of the effectiveness of tailored-cybersecurity awareness and training efforts in an attempt to reduce risky online behaviors and victimization in following experimental research designs.

One potential design should include the implementation of cybersecurity training among a selected sample of employees, customers, and contractors within a given financial institution, and then conduct a detailed assessment of these subjects' vulnerability to cybersecurity risks before and after the implementation of the awareness program. Cybersecurity risk could follow previous operationalization of the concept (for example: Ganin et al., 2017), or be measured using other innovative and more relevant operationalization. Comparison of the selected treatment group vulnerability assessment should be done also to an assessment performed to a control group within the organization, which was not exposed to the awareness program.

Assess the Effectiveness of Security Tools and Policies

Antivirus software, firewalls and intrusion detection/prevention systems are commonly used by large organizations to prevent the progression of cyber-dependent crimes (Bace & Mell, 2001; McHugh, Christie, & Allen, 2000; Willems, 2019). These are just but a few of the many cybersecurity tools available to detect attacks and security violations, prevent them from developing, and provide useful information for IT security managers who are responsible for recovering from cyber-dependent crimes (Willems, 2019). Similarly, one important policy often incorporated into contemporary corporate computing environments is the implementation of surveillance means in employees' computer systems (Eivazi, 2011; West & Bowman, 2016). But despite the growing number of public and private organizations in general, and financial institutions in particular, that implement these tools and policies on their computing environments, the effectiveness of these strategies in preventing and mitigating the occurrence of malicious cyber activities is still relatively unclear.

Several key approaches are employed by scholars when evaluating these tools' performances. The typical evaluations conducted by commercial and scholarly research laboratories are based on a variety of in-depth scans of collected or synthesized malicious traffic samples (Algaith et al., 2016; AV Comparatives, 2013; Garg, Vidyaraman, Upadhyaya, & Kwiat, 2006; Gashi, Stankovic, Leita, & Thonnard, 2009; Noureldien & Osman, 2000; Seeberg & Petrovic, 2007; Surisetty & Kumar, 2010). While this approach may test the tools' accuracy, it fails to consider computer users' (both legitimate and illegitimate) actual behaviors with their computers and the computer network, and do not assess the effectiveness of this security tool in preventing the development of cyber-dependent crimes.

An alternative approach for evaluating antivirus software performance is through the use of an on-demand detection tools that can detect both the presence of threats on the scanned computer and the availability of antivirus software (AV Comparatives, 2011). Although informative, these studies are subject to sample selection bias because the samples they employ include computer users who bought the scanning service only. Another approach for assessing the effectiveness of *antivirussoftware* employs computer users' self-reports on security incidents they experienced with their computers, as well as reports on the presence of antivirus software on their computers (Eurostat, 2011). Unfortunately, these studies draw on survey methodology and may include multiple inaccuracies.

Following the common methodological and scientific practices of both the modern-day criminological and medical fields, we believe that the implementation of randomized field trials is most conducive for assessing the effectiveness of security tools and policies in preventing, detecting and mitigating cybercrime against financial institutions and their computer and network users. Lévesque, Nsiempba, Fernandez, Chiasson, and Somayaji (2013) and Lévesque, Fernandez, Batchelder, and Young (2016) studies help demonstrate this point. In their earlier research study, Lévesque et al. (2013) recruited 50 participants from the University of Montreal's main campus, provided them with new laptops, and monitored these participants' real-world computer usage using various diagnostic tools over a period of four months in effort to evaluate antivirus products in real-world environment. The scholars also conducted monthly interviews with the participants and administered questionnaires among them. Lévesque et al. (2013) reported that during the four months of the experimental period, 38% of the study's participants were exposed to malware (i.e., almost one out of two newly installed laptops would have been infected with malware within four months if the computers had no antivirus software installed). In addition, Lévesque and her team explored the proportion of malware infections that went undetected by the antivirus software during the experimental period. They reported that 20% of the study's computers were infected by some form of malicious software that was not detected by the antivirus software that was installed on the machine.

In their second research initiative three years later, Lévesque et al. (2016) reported a large-scale cohort study that was aimed to test the effectiveness of different antivirus products in detecting and preventing malware infections. Using data collected from millions of computers that had the *Microsoft Malicious Software Removal Tool* and the *Microsoft Windows Defender* installed, these scholars reported results from a natural experiment: malware infection was the outcome, and being protected by a third-party antivirus product was the exposure measure. Specifically, by monitoring close to 27 million *Windows 10* IT systems for a period of four months, the scholars were able to differentiate between systems that were protected by a third-party antivirus products (the treatment group) and systems that were protected by Microsoft Windows Defender (Microsoft's default antivirus software), the control group.

Using this data, they tested the probability of these computers to get infected with a malware. Lévesque's research team found that 1.22% of the computer systems in the experimental group were infected by malware during the experimental period. In contrast, 14.95% of the computer systems in the control group could have been infected by malware if no antivirus product were protecting the system. A comparison of the effectiveness of the ten most prevalent antivirus products (more than 90% of the systems were protected by third-party software) revealed that the effectiveness of these products in detecting malicious software ranged from 90 to 98%. This particular research effort of Lévesque's team provided substantial evidence regarding the effectiveness of antivirus software in the wild. Future cybersecurity-related research following in Lévesque's footsteps should strongly consider deploying similar field experiment designs along with a refined focus on employees of financial institutions and identify a list of available tools and security-related policies. This will assist with the fundamental protection financial organizations from cybercrime and assess the effectiveness of the tools in achieving its goals.

Configure Financial Organizations' Internet Infrastructure

Although governments around the globe protect their private sectors from physical threats, financial institutions carry the heavy lift of the defensive efforts while protecting their networks against sophisticated criminal actors and foreign sovereign states attacks (Borghard, 2018). Detection of system trespassers and Advanced Persistence Threats (APT) on any given IT network or individual IT system are crucial in this process for mitigating the consequence of such events. Generally speaking, system trespassing (i.e., the unauthorized use of a computer system) and invasion of computer privacy have become common global problems.

An industry-wide 2018 annual report by Risk Based Security suggests that over 5 billion records were exposed in Calendar Year 2017 as a result of 6515 trespassing incidents reported by governmental and private organizations around the world (Risk Based Security, 2018). The average cost of each data breach to these large organizations in the United States was estimated to be around $8.19 million in 2019, while the average total cost of a data breach to a financial institution was estimated at $5.86 million at the same year (Ponomon Institute, 2020). In an effort to address this pressing issue, financial organizations invest substantial funds in building fortress-computing environments that are designed to harden system trespassers' access to the organizations' computer networks.

To date, there has not been enough attention devoted for the design of security measures and forensic tactics that allow faster detection and mitigation of system trespassing events. This is very unfortunate, because IT security teams in financial organizations are responsible for providing prompt response to the presence of hackers on the system by detecting the event and blocking trespassers' access to the organization. Therefore, it is imperative to initiate scientific research that supports the development of forensic, deception, and hunt tactics that reduce the time passing from the initiation of a trespassing event by illegitimate user on the system and the detection of this event by IT security managers.

Taking an Evidence-Based Cybersecurity Approach to this common cybersecurity challenge, significant efforts should be made to generate a better understanding regarding hackers' online behaviors and responses to situational stimuli during system trespassing events initiated against different types of computing environments. Findings from such research will facilitate the design of computer systems that make attackers decision-making process during system trespassing event more predictable, and consequently, their detection by IT security teams easier to achieve. To this end, the unique experimental designs of Maimon, Alper, Sobesto, and Cukier (2014) and Maimon, Wilson, Ren, and Berenblum (2015) in conjunction with the intentional deployment of target computing platforms and networks (i.e., network "honeypots" or "bait traps") in efforts to study the behaviors and techniques of individual cyber hackers' while they attempt to further infiltrate and attacking the "baited" computing system should be employed by financial institutions to prevent cybersecurity incidents.

Indeed, most previous approaches to understanding system trespassers' online behavior have focused on single methods to isolate their etiology. However, most of these efforts fail to integrate system trespassers' decision-making process under different configuration of the computing environment. It is important to note that many past experiments do not investigate system trespassers' response to situational stimuli in the attacked computer. Maimon et al. (2014, 2015) along with Wilson, Maimon, Sobesto, and Cukier (2015) address this issue and employ rigorous randomized trials to test system trespassers' reactions to deterring cues in the attacked computer environment. These scholars found, for instance, that a generic warning banner in the attacked computer system reduced the duration of both first and repeated system trespassing incidents against the target computer (Maimon et al., 2014).

Maimon's research team also reported that the presence of a surveillance banner in an attacked computer system reduces the probability of commands being typed in the system during the first system's trespassing incidents (Wilson et al., 2015). These authors also found that the probability of commands being typed during subsequent system trespassing incidents (on the same target computer) is conditioned by the presence of a surveillance banner and by whether commands have been entered during previous trespassing incidents (Wilson et al., 2015). Finally, Maimon, Testa, Sobesto, Cukier, and Ren (2019) have recently discovered that system trespassers are more than twice as likely to enter cleaning tracks commands in attacked computers with surveillance banner and software installed on than on attacked computers with no surveillance banner and software installed on.

While this author and his team use high interaction honeypots that emulate the operation of a single computer, the development of "deception grid platform" allows the deployment of a network of hundreds to thousands of computers simultaneously on a network. This platform could emulate the complete Internet infrastructure of an organizational network including servers, switches, databases, and applications. These findings guide major financial organizations to strategically deploy target computers and "deception grids" that replicate financial organizations common servers, computers Internet infrastructure, and the initiation of a series of randomized trials to:

1. Investigate system trespassers' online behaviors during the progression of a criminal event.
2. Explore the influence of various online deterrence and surveillance means (i.e., formal and natural) on system trespassers' behaviors during the progression of a system trespassing incident.
3. Develop a list of red flags that indicate the presence of a system trespasser on the system. This list would allow more rapid detection and reaction to the development of system trespassing events on the attacked computer.

Deployment of such platforms could support exploration of system trespassers' baseline behaviors on financial institutions' computers, as well as to test the effectiveness of different security measures in mitigating the consequence of a trespassing event on the system. The collected data will consist solely of malicious traffic because it will only include users who have reached the honeypots. These data will help to characterize system trespassers' behavior once encountering different computing environments and situational stimuli on the system. Such data may also support education and evidence-based guidelines for configuration of financial institutions computing environments, which could support rapid detection and effective mitigation of system trespassing events.

Dissemination of Evidence-Based Cybersecurity Research

Next, we examine the continuous implementation of rigorous research designs aiming to generate understanding of human behavior within the cybercrime ecosystem. The overarching goal here is to improve overall cybersecurity-related practices, the Evidence-Based Cybersecurity Approach calls for effective and efficient dissemination of cybersecurity research findings to both practitioners and academics. All in all, an evidence-based approach for guiding cybersecurity practices and policies faces three key challenges including scattered empirical evaluations of tools and policies across different academic fields (and specifically Computer Science, Computer Information Science, Criminology, Law, and Political Science) and in many written languages, failure to publish program evaluations in scientific journals, and practitioners' limited access to scientific research findings.

Moving forward, cybersecurity scholars should aim to publish and present their research in international journals and at myriad of conferences, but also at industry-based conferences and professional trade publications. Concentrated efforts should be made by cybersecurity scholars to develop white papers that explain the research findings in a way that is accessible to practitioners. Additionally, keeping in mind the heavy reliance of CISOs and their teams on social media platforms for consuming cybersecurity-related contents, relevant content from rigorous empirical cybersecurity research should be discussed and disseminated over social media platforms such as LinkedIn and Twitter.

Conclusion

The cybersecurity market was identified as a "market for lemons" almost a decade and a half ago (Anderson & Moore, 2006). This term, "market of lemons," was originally coined by Akerlof (1970) to denote a market failure in which the quality of goods traded in a market is devalued in the presence of information asymmetry between buyers and sellers. In his classic example, Akerlof explained this term borrowing from the used-car market, where a buyer has less information about a car than a seller. Given what we know about the cybersecurity market, one may argue that information asymmetry exists also in this market, where cybersecurity consumers have less information about security products and services than cybersecurity vendors. In fact, some vendors may also have less information than is required to defend the security products they sell during their sales pitch. Tying this back to the present-day cybersecurity functions of the Financial Sector, CISOs in large organizations are not willing to pay high prices for cybersecurity products and are willing to "gamble" with the deployment of cheaper products on their organizational infrastructure.

One of the solutions for markets for lemon is a change in the information asymmetry between consumers and vendors. In the context of the cybersecurity area, we already have cyber insurance. The Evidence-Based Cybersecurity Approach is a very strong contender to lead the way in generating empirical evidence around cybersecurity tools and policies by conducing rigorous scientific research regarding the effectiveness of security tools and policies in the wild. Findings from these studies should be then disseminated in an efficient manner among practitioners and policymakers, who may then use those findings to guide their decision-making process regarding the implementation of security technologies. Security officers in financial institutions should consider the adoption of this approach in the context of their workflow and their quest to identify online threats and vulnerabilities against their organizations, educate employees, and customers regarding the risks of cybercrime, develop, deploy, and enforce security posture in their organizations, and design computing environments that can mitigate attacks effectively. Importantly, although the focus in this chapter was in the application of the EBCS approach in the context of financial organizations and their attempts to strengthen their security posture in cyberspace, this author believes that this approach is also very relevant in the context of other industries including government, universities, and health organizations.

References

Akerlof, G. A. (1970). The market for "lemons": Quality uncertainty and the market mechanism. *Quarterly Journal of Economics, 84*(3), 488–500.

Algaith, A., Gashi, I., Sobesto, B., Cukier, M., Haxhijaha, S., & Bajrami, G. (2016). Comparing detection capabilities of antivirus products: An empirical study with different versions of products from the same vendors. In *2016 46th Annual IEEE/IFIP International Conference on Dependable Systems and Networks Workshop* (pp. 48–53). IEEE.

Alvarez, M. (2017, April). *Security trends in the financial services sector*. IBM X-Force Research. Retrieved from https://www-01.ibm.com/common/ssi/cgi-bin/ssialias?htmlfid=SEL03129USEN&.

Anderson, R., & Moore, T. (2006). The economics of information security. *Science, 314*(5799), 610–613.

AV Comparatives. (2011). *On demand detection of malicious software*. Retrieved from https://www.av-comparatives.org/images/stories/test/ondret/avc_od_feb2011.pdf.

AV Comparatives. (2013). *File detection test of malicious software* (Technical Report, AV Comparatives). Retrieved from https://www.av-comparatives.org/wp-content/uploads/2017/03/avc_sum_201312_en.pdf.

Bace, R., & Mell, P. (2001). *NIST special publication on intrusion detection systems*. Mclean, VA: Booz-Allen and Hamilton Inc.

Borghard, D, E. (2018). *Protecting financial institutions against cyber threats: A national security issue*. Retrieved from https://carnegieendowment.org/2018/09/24/protecting-financial-institutions-against-cyber-threats-national-security-issue-pub-77324.

Bouveret, A. (2018). *Cyber risk for the financial sector: A framework for quantitative assessment*. Washington, DC: International Monetary Fund.

Braga, A. A., Turchan, B., Papachristos, A. V., & Hureau, D. M. (2019). Hot spots policing of small geographic areas effects on crime. *Campbell Systematic Reviews, 15*(3), e1046.

Carter, W. (2017). *Forces shaping the cyber threat landscape for financial institutions*. Retrieved from https://www.csis.org/programs/technology-policy-program/cybersecurity-and-governance/financial-sector-cybersecurity-0.

Chapman University. (2014, October 21). Survey shows what Americans fear most. *ScienceDaily*. Retrieved from www.sciencedaily.com/releases/2014/10/141021125937.htm.

Cranor, L. F. (2008). A framework for reasoning about the human in the loop. In *Proceedings of the Conference on Usability, Psychology, and Security*. USENIX Association.

Eivazi, K. (2011). Computer use monitoring and privacy at work. *Computer Law & Security Review, 27*(5), 516–523.

Eurostat. (2011). *Nearly one third of internet users in the EU27 caught a computer virus*. Retrieved from: http://epp.eurostat.ec.europa.eu/cache/ITY_PUBLIC/4-07022011-AP/EN/4-07022011-AP-EN.PDF.

Ganin, A. A., Quach, P., Panwar, M., Collier, Z. A., Keisler, J. M., Marchese, D., & Linkov, I. (2017). Multicriteria decision framework for cybersecurity risk assessment and management. *Risk Analysis,* 40(4), 183–199.

Garg, A., Vidyaraman, S., Upadhyaya, S., & Kwiat, K. (2006). Usim: A user behavior simulation framework for training and testing IDSes in GUI based systems. In *Proceedings of the 39th Annual Symposium on Simulation* (pp. 196–203). IEEE Computer Society.

Gashi, I., Stankovic, V., Leita, C., & Thonnard, O. (2009). An experimental study of diversity with off-the-shelf antivirus engines. In *Eighth IEEE International Symposium on Network Computing and Applications, 2009. NCA 2009* (pp. 4–11). IEEE.

Greenwood, P. W., Chaiken, J. M., Petersilia, J. R., Prusoff, L. L., Castro, R. P., Kellen, K., & Wildhorn, S. (1975). *The criminal investigation process: Volume III: Observations and analysis*. Retrieved from https://www.rand.org/pubs/reports/R1778.html.

Hartel, P. H., Junger, M., & Wieringa, R. J. (2010). *Cyber-crime science=crime science+information security*. CTIT, University of Twente, Technical Report TR-CTIT-10-34.

Internet Crime Complaint Center. (2020). *2019 Internet Crime Report*. Retrieved from https://pdf.ic3.gov/2019_IC3Report.pdf.

Kelling, G. L., & Sousa, W. H. (2001). *Do police matter? An analysis of the impact of New York City's police reforms*. New York: CCI Center for Civic Innovation at the Manhattan Institute.

Kelling, G. L., Pate, T., Dieckman, D., & Brown, C. E. (1974). *The Kansas City preventive patrol experiment*. Washington, DC: Police Foundation.

Kraemer-Mbula, E., Tang, P., & Rush, H. (2013). The cybercrime ecosystem: Online innovation in the shadows? *Technological Forecasting and Social Change, 80,* 541–555.

Lévesque, F., Nsiempba, J., Fernandez, J. M., Chiasson, S., & Somayaji, A. (2013). A clinical study of risk factors related to malware infections. In *Proceedings of the 2013 ACM SIGSAC Conference on Computer & Communications Security* (pp. 97–108). ACM.

Lévesque, F. L., Fernandez, J. M., Batchelder, D., & Young, G. (2016). Are they real? Real-life comparative tests of antivirus products. In *Virus Bulletin Conference* (pp. 1–11).

Levine, J. P. (1975). The ineffectiveness of adding police to prevent crime. *Public Policy, 23*(4), 523–545.

Maimon, D., Alper, M., Sobesto, B., & Cukier, M. (2014). Restrictive deterrent effect of a warning banner in an attacked computer system. *Criminology, 52,* 33–59.

Maimon, D., Becker, M., Patil, S., & Katz, J. (2017). Self-protective behaviors over public WiFi networks. In *The {LASER} workshop: Learning from authoritative security experiment results* ({LASER} 2017) (pp. 69–76).

Maimon, D., Kamerdze, A., Cukier, M., & Sobesto, B. (2013). Daily trends and origin of computer-focused crimes against a large university computer network: An application of the routine-activities and lifestyle perspective. *British Journal of Criminology, 53*(2), 319–343.

Maimon, D., & Louderback, E. R. (2019). Cyber-dependent crimes: An interdisciplinary review. *Annual Review of Criminology.*

Maimon, D., Testa, A., Sobesto, B., Cukier, M., & Ren, W. (2019). Predictably deterrable? The case of system trespassers. In *International Conference on Security, Privacy and Anonymity in Computation, Communication and Storage* (pp. 317–330). Cham: Springer.

Maimon, D., Wilson, T., Ren, W., & Berenblum, T. (2015). On the relevance of spatial and temporal dimensions in assessing computer susceptibility to system trespassing incidents. *British Journal of Criminology, 55*(3), 615–634.

McGuire, M., & Dowling, S. (2013). *Cyber-crime: A review of the evidence summary of key findings and implications* (Home Office Research Report 75, Home Office, United Kingdom). Retrieved from https://assets.publishing.service.gov.uk/government/uploads/system/uploads/attachment_data/file/246749/horr75-summary.pdf.

McHugh, J., Christie, A., & Allen, J. (2000). Defending yourself: The role of intrusion detection systems. *IEEE Software, 17*(5), 42–51.

McQuade, S. C. (2006). *Understanding and managing cybercrime.* Boston: Pearson/Allyn and Bacon.

Moore, T., Clayton, R., & Anderson, R. (2009). The economics of online crime. *Journal of Economic Perspectives, 23,* 3–20.

Morris, S. (2004). *The future of netcrime now: Part 1–threats and challenges.* Washington, DC: Home Office Crime and Policing Group, Technical Report, 62(04).

Mulligan, D. K., & Schneider, F. B. (2011). Doctrine for cybersecurity. *Daedalus, 140*(4), 70–92.

National Institute of Standards of Technology. (2018). *Framework for improving critical infrastructure cybersecurity version 1.1* (No. NIST Cybersecurity Framework). Retrieved from https://nvlpubs.nist.gov/nistpubs/CSWP/NIST.CSWP.04162018.pdf.

Noureldien, N. A., & Osman, I. M. (2000). On firewalls evaluation criteria. In *TENCON 2000. Proceedings* (Vol. 3, pp. 104–110). IEEE.

Ponomon Institute. (2020). *Cost of a data breach report 2019*. Retrieved from https://www.ibm.com/downloads/cas/ZBZLY7KL?_ga=2.179203949.852457783.1582652774-115077265.1582652774&_gac=1.247196336.1582652774.EAIaIQobChMIqdGmgKHt5wIVWgOzAB065weiEAAYASAAEgJTKvD_BwE.

Risk Based Security. (2018). *2018 ends as the second most active year for publicly disclosed breaches*. Retrieved from https://pages.riskbasedsecurity.com/2018-ye-breach-quickview-report.

Sackett, D. L., & Rosenberg, W. M. C. (1995). On the need for evidence-based medicine. *Journal of Public Health, 17*(3), 330–334.

Schneier, B. (2008, June). The psychology of security. In *International conference on cryptology in Africa* (pp. 50-79). Berlin, Heidelberg: Springer.

Sherman, L. W. (1998). *Evidence-based policing*. Washington, DC: Police Foundation.

Sherman, L. W., Gartin, P. R., & Buerger, M. E. (1989). Hot spots of predatory crime: Routine activities and the criminology of place. *Criminology, 27*(1), 27–56.

Sherman, L. W., & Weisburd, D. (1995). General deterrent effects of police patrol in crime “hot spots”: A randomized, controlled trial. *Justice Quarterly, 12*(4), 625–648.

Seeberg, V. E., & Petrovic, S. (2007). A new classification scheme for anonymization of real data used in IDS benchmarking. In *The Second International Conference on Availability, Reliability and Security, 2007. ARES 2007* (pp. 385–390). IEEE.

Spelman, W., & Brown, D. K. (1984). *Calling the police: Citizen reporting of serious crime*. Washington, DC: U.S. Department of Justice, National Institute of Justice.

Surisetty, S., & Kumar, S. (2010). Is McAfee security center/firewall software providing complete security for your computer? In *Fourth International Conference on Digital Society, 2010. ICDS'10* (pp. 178–181). IEEE.

Uniform Crime Report. (1995). *Crime in the United States 1995*. Retrieved from https://ucr.fbi.gov/crime-in-the-u.s/1995.

Uniform Crime Report. (2018). *Crime in the US*. Retrieved from https://ucr.fbi.gov/crime-in-the-u.s/2018/crime-in-the-u.s.-2018/topic-pages/violent-crime.

Verizon. (2020). *2019 data breach investigations report*. Retrieved from https://enterprise.verizon.com/resources/reports/2019-data-breach-investigations-report.pdf.
Weisburd, D. (2015). The law of crime concentration and the criminology of place. *Criminology, 53*(2), 133–157.
Weisburd, D., & Braga, A. A. (Eds.). (2006). *Police innovation: Contrasting perspectives*. Cambridge: Cambridge University Press.
Weisburd, D., & Braga, A. A. (Eds.). (2019). *Police innovation: Contrasting perspectives*. New York: Cambridge University Press.
Wellford, C. R. (1974). Crime and the police: A multivariate analysis. *Criminology, 12*(2), 195–213.
West, J. P., & Bowman, J. S. (2016). Electronic surveillance at work: An ethical analysis. *Administration & Society, 48*(5), 628–651.
Willems, E. (2019). The antivirus companies. In *Cyberdanger* (pp. 65–83). Cham: Springer.
Willison, R., & Siponen, M. (2009). Overcoming the insider: Reducing employee computer crime through Situational Crime Prevention. *Communications of the ACM, 52*(9), 133–137.
Wilson, T., Maimon, D., Sobesto, B., & Cukier, M. (2015). The effect of a surveillance banner in an attacked computer system additional evidence for the relevance of restrictive deterrence in cyberspace. *Journal of Research in Crime and Delinquency, 52*(6), 829–855.

CHAPTER 3

The Evolution of Cybersecurity within the American Financial Sector

The American Financial Sector: Tempting Targets for CyberAttackers

Intuitively, banks and other key financial institutions are quite often major targets of cybercriminals, via cyberattacks, across the globe. Generally speaking, financial institutions are tempting target because, quite simply, this is where the money is kept. However, the collective impact of U.S. banking institutions extends well beyond the mere management of monetary currency inventories. Networked banking systems enable billions of financial e-transactions and monetary transfers, loans, and payments every day through a vast array of financial services networks.

Collectively speaking, America's financial institutions form the backbone of the global financial system—which is heavily reliant on information technology (IT) systems. These financial IT systems orchestrate virtually every aspect of financial operations—from executing billions of dollars in daily transactions to generating financial audit reports to managing consumer services. Because of the criticality of these operations, the integrity and security of the financial data contained on these IT systems is paramount. To maintain this essential data security, highly robust and resilient IT systems and well-maintained/secured networks are required. So long as the financial sector's institutional financial data and its supporting infrastructure remains both secure and operational from cyberattacks, this only strengthens and reenforces the global financial

P.-L. Pomerleau and D. L. Lowery, *Countering Cyber Threats to Financial Institutions*,
https://doi.org/10.1007/978-3-030-54054-8_3

system as a whole (Zheng & Carter, 2015). As the Center for Strategic and International Studies (2020) explains, for the would-be cybercriminals, banking institutions offer "multiple avenues for profit through extortion, theft, and fraud," (p. 1) while sovereign nation-state actors and hacktivists also intentionally "target the financial sector for political and ideological leverage" (p. 1).

The American Economy: A Major Element of National Security

Because American financial institutions play such an out-sized and critical role in the world's overarching Global Financial System, the U.S. economy makes an extremely tempting target—and can therefore be vulnerable to nefarious cyber-related economic/financial-related criminal activities. However, keep in mind that threats to America's economy are not just solely limited to would-be cybercriminals seeking financial e-commerce-related treasure. The key elements of the U.S. economy—including both the financial sector and key infrastructure components—can also be susceptible to a variety of offensive cyberspace operations by any number of America's nation-state competitors. Non-state national security-related actors, such as terrorist organizations, could also seek to do the United States harm (Borghard, 2018).

Borghard (2018) effectively illustrates her point by pointing to public congressional testimony on February 13, 2018 to a Congressional committee by the directors of National Intelligence, the National Security Agency, the Central Intelligence Agency, and the Federal Bureau of Investigation all warned that cyberattacks perpetrated by foreign adversaries as being one of the most significant concerns to national security. In his opening remarks, the Director of National Intelligence, former U.S. Senator Dan Coats, bluntly told his former congressional colleagues that America is "under attack" by "entities using cyber to penetrate virtually every major action that takes place in the United States" (p. 1). Coats also added there many federal agencies involved in preventing further cyberattacks from happening against the United States with significant support nowadays also coming from the private sector. "We can't as a government direct them what to do" stated Coates, "but we're spending every effort to work with them to provide answers" (CBS News, 2018, p. 1). By sharing real-time risk assessment and warnings about potential newly emerging cybersecurity threats across the American financial sector, both the federal government and individual financial institutions ensure a higher degree of cybersecurity situational awareness and collective mitigation posturing.

The Evolution of Cybersecurity within America's Financial Sector

Early Federal Legislation (1970–1991)

According to Zheng and Carter (2015), the early foundations of IT-related security requirements for America's financial sector began in October 1970 with the passage of the *Bank Secrecy Act* (BSA) and, later, in December 1991 with the subsequent passage of the *Federal Deposit Insurance Corporation Improvement Act* (FDICIA). These two early federal laws largely focused on the monitoring and operational assurance of financial transactions by requiring financial institutions to ensure the data and physical security of their individual information systems. This was seen as a necessary industry-wide standard in order to ensure the fundamental integrity of each individual financial transaction, customer account identification, and to provide an avenue for identifying suspicious or fraudulent financial transactions.

Because the BSA was originally signed into federal law decades before the modern internet took shape, it should be noted the contemporary term of "cybersecurity" was not used in the original statutory verbiage. Despite this omission, the core concepts of contemporary cybersecurity are still plainly articulated as industry-wide compliance requirements. This includes the requirements to (a) maintain strict physical and data security of the individual financial systems, (b) log customer information, and (c) analyze account transactions for suspicious activity. The BSA also mandated American financial institutions report suspicious financial activities to a nation-wide Financial Crimes Enforcement Network (Zheng & Carter, 2015; Federal Financial Institutions Examination Council, 2014).

Twenty-one years later, in December 1991 the U.S. Congress passed the FDICIA as a modernization amendment to the September 1950 Federal Deposit Insurance Act (FDIA). This legislation required the establishment of "operational and managerial standards" relating to "internal controls, information systems, and internal audit systems" (Cornell University Legal Information Institute, 2020, ii. Section 39a).

Four years later, a subsequent requirement was added for American financial depository institutions to have adequate internal controls and IT-related capabilities that were appropriated-sized based on the nature and scope of the institution's financial activities (Zheng & Carter, 2015).

Consumer Protection During the Infancy of e-Commerce (1999–2003)

The next three major American legislative advancements in the realm of evolving cybersecurity threats came about with the *Gramm-Leach-Bliley Act* (GLBA) in November 1999, the *Sarbanes-Oxley Act* (SOX) in July 2002, and the *Fair and Accurate Credit Transactions Act* (FACTA) in December 2003. All three of these pieces of federal legislation came about at a time when online banking was still a relatively new concept in its technical infancy, but was rapidly expanding nation-wide. Collectively, these three pieces of federal legislation sought to ensure a variety of personal consumer and financial data-related protections by mandating a variety of IT system-related security enhancements that we now know as cybersecurity-related activities today.

Signed into law in late 1999, the GLBA codified personal data security requirements as a way to protect American consumers by guarding against unauthorized disclosures of personal consumer data through a robust series of data safeguards that included multilayer accessibility of IT data systems, the monitoring of network activity, appropriately responding to suspicious activities/policy violations, and implement measures to detect/prevent malicious code (Federal Financial Institutions Examination Council IT Examination Handbook, n.d.). As a result, at least in part, of the national headline-grabbing financial accounting scandal of Enron financial accounting scandal in late 2001, the U.S. Congress passed the SOX in the summer of 2002. The SOX mandated the use of accurate audit and regulatory reporting systems, which drove financial institutions to conduct annual security assessments of their own IT security systems and internal data (Stults, 2004).

Congress passed the Fair and Accurate Credit Transactions Act (FACTA) in December 2003 as a way to prevent a surging problem not only within America's e-commerce sector, but world-wide: consumer identity theft. Extending well beyond America's traditional banking institutions, this law also required any American business entity considered a "creditor" to adhere to strict protocols to providing, acquiring, or sharing credit reports/histories of individual American consumers (Federal Trade Commission, 2013). The FACTA also drove specific IT compliance requirements to identify suspicious activities, possible data breaches, and a legal requirement to notify U.S. consumers of situations where their personal data may have been compromised (Zheng & Carter, 2015).

The Payment Card Industry Data Security Standard (2004)

In December 2004, the big five global credit card companies—American Express, Discover, MasterCard, Visa, and JCB International—collectively used their dominant positions in both the American and worldwide marketplaces to proactively establish a new industry-wide financial credit security standard known as the Payment Card Industry Data Security Standard (PCI-DSS) (Zheng & Carter, 2015; Williams, Chuvakin, & Bradley, 2007). Unlike the prior legislatively mandated actions taken by the U.S. Federal Government, this is a key example of the industry leaders within the American Financial Sector proactively huddling together and effectively driving the establishment of a new common data security standard across their respective market sector. Generally speaking, PCI-DSS drove strong data security enhancement measures, which included the establishment of six core system control objectives and fourteen software protection features, to govern the processing of credit card financial transactions in real-time (PCI Security Standards Council, 2020).

Executive Order 13636 (2013) and the Implication to "Section 9" Firms

On February 12, 2013, then-U.S. President Barack Obama signed *Executive Order #13536: Improving Critical Infrastructure Cybersecurity*, which enabled the Federal Government to prioritize its efforts to assist our America's most critical infrastructure entities. Identified as "Section 9" entities, the executive order defined these entities as "critical infrastructure where a cybersecurity incident could reasonably result in catastrophic regional or national effects on public health or safety, economy security, or national security" (Obama, 2013, pp. 1–2). Generally speaking, Section 9 entities perform critical functions within the U.S. economy, but are reliant on the operational security and resiliency of America's existing cyber infrastructure to perform those functions (Krebs, 2019).

By prioritizing federal funding and services support to Section 9 entities within the American Economy, which includes the U.S. Financial Sector, it is considered an effective and efficient way to mitigate national risk overall. *Executive Order #13636* also designated the U.S. Department of Homeland Security (DHS) as the executive agent to implement this order, thereby giving DHS a central orchestrating role in directly supporting a wide array of voluntary Section 9 cybersecurity risk management efforts "by offering programs, sharing information, and providing technical assistance to help organizations reduce their individual risk" (Krebs, 2019, p. ii).

One of the major deliverables that came about as a direct result of this executive order was the establishment of the National Risk Management Center (National Risk Management Center, 2018), which launched in the fall of 2018. The NRMC works in close coordination with the Section 9 entities, other key private sector organizations, and major stakeholders in the critical infrastructure community to:

> Identify, analyze, prioritize, and manage the most strategic risks to our National Critical Functions — the functions of government and the private sector so vital to the United States that their disruption, corruption, or dysfunction would have a debilitating impact on security, national economic security, national public health or safety, or any combination. (National Risk Management Center, 2018, p. 1)

One of the key primary functions of the NRMC is known as the "Pipeline Cybersecurity Initiative," which collaboratively works directly with pipeline asset owners and operators to include an in-depth review and evaluation of the control system's network design, configuration, and interdependencies (National Risk Management Center, 2018, p. 1).

An illustrative example of this federal-private partnership focused on joint resiliency collaboration began in October 2018, when DHS kicked off a long-term active partnership with America's Oil & Natural Gas Sector to manage long-term risk in this critical infrastructure sector. As DHS Undersecretary Christopher Krebs explained the "NRMC is DHS's effort to secure tomorrow's infrastructure, providing a central point of entry for working with industry to manage long-term strategy risk across our critical infrastructure sectors" before adding this collaborative effort is a:

> Key milestone in the partnership between the federal government and the oil and natural gas industry, as we launched the pipeline cybersecurity initiative that partners DHS' NPPD [National Protections and Programs Directorate] cybersecurity resources, DOE's [Department of Energy] expertise, with TSA's [Transportation Security Administration] regular and ongoing assessments of pipeline security to get a broader understanding of the risks the sector faces. Collaborative efforts like this allow us to better understand the threat landscape and direct more targeted and prioritized risk management activities. (Department of Homeland Security, 2018, pp. 1–2)

Assistant U.S. Energy Secretary for Electricity Bruce Walker explained "boosting public and private investments to improve the country's critical energy infrastructure and technology is paramount to ensuring a reliable and resilient electric grid" (Randolph, 2018, p. 1). Walker added that since the Department of Energy was the lead federal interface with the American Energy Sector, "we are prioritizing work with our federal partners, the oil and gas industry, and the electric industry to incentivize these crucial and necessary investments" (Randolph, 2018, p. 1).

The Roll-Out of the NIST Cybersecurity Framework (2014–2018)

The American-based National Institute of Standards and Technology (NIST) is a U.S. Department of Commerce physical sciences laboratory chartered to promote technical innovation and industrial competitiveness. Originally established as the "National Bureau of Standards" by an act of the U.S. Congress in 1901, this Gaithersburg, Maryland-based organization was tasked with boosting the American Economy's then-lagging Industrial Sector. The organization was ultimately credited to assist the sector effectively compete globally with the United Kingdom, Germany, and other international economic rivals of the day. Today, NIST's activities include a wide array of technology-related research endeavors and serves as a technical authority on the establishment and maintenance of technical standards in the fields of cybersecurity/information technology, engineering, and nanoscale technologies (National Institute of Standards and Technology, 2018a).

One of the NIST's key technological standardization frameworks is the NIST Cybersecurity Framework, officially known as "*Framework for Improving Critical Infrastructure Cybersecurity.*" The original version of the NIST Framework, commonly referred to as "Version 1" was released in February 2014 and was subsequently superseded by an updated "Version 1.1" in April 2018. This framework serves as a set of detailed guidelines and industry best practices as a way to assist governmental and private organizations alike with effectively reducing and mitigating potential cybersecurity risks. Originally designed to be versatile, the framework was constructed around the fundamental premise that recommended guidelines, standards, policies, procedures, and protocols can only be effective if implemented across the organization as a whole—not just by the organization's internal IT department (National Institute of Standards and Technology, 2018b).

As a functional construct, the NIST Cybersecurity Framework is transportable between various industries and is intended to facilitate active, cyber hygiene awareness, and cybersecurity-minded communications organization-wide. Delving a bit deeper into the NIST Cybersecurity Framework, it can serve as a foundational baseline for an organization's cybersecurity policies or enhance existing policies and procedures. Central to this framework are five core continuous functions: to *Identify, Protect, Detect, Respond*, and *Recover.* Collectively, these five distinct operational pillars form the essential components of a holistic cybersecurity program that revolve around the three basic types of cyber threats: *perimeter threats* (i.e., firewalls and anti-virus protection), *intranet threats* (i.e., portable data devices and network protection), and *human security* (i.e., poor cyber hygiene practices and potential insider threats) (National Institute of Standards and Technology, 2018a).

It should be noted that collectively speaking, the third element of the cyber threat "triad" poses the most significant vulnerabilities—the human cybersecurity risks—for a multitude of potential reasons. Whether due to unintended human error, deliberate covert actions (i.e., unauthorized disclosure of sensitive information), or concerted technical modifications of existing cybersecurity-related IT system functions, unauthorized changes, activated email-embedded phishing hyperlinks, or inadvertent HTML-enabled system loaded malware, any of these actions can negatively impact a major IT system or network through a significant decrease in system-level functionality and data security (National Institute of Standards and Technology, 2018a). Additionally, beyond the NIST Cybersecurity Framework, NIST also provides *NIST Special Publication 800-30*, an overarching cyber risk assessment framework for conducting risk assessments of individual organizational-level networks based on federal information systems assessment standards (National Institute of Standards and Technology, 2012).

DoD Cyber Strategy (2015) and Presidential Policy Directive 41 (2016)

In April 2015, the U.S. Department of Defense (DOD) formally laid out its own *DoD Cyber Strategy* (2015) for defending the national security interests of the United States within the cyberspace domain. Rather than continuing to focus on risk mitigation-centered data sharing, this new framework focused on three core strategic goals for its cyber mission is to "defend the nation against cyberattacks of significant consequence" (p. 3) (Department of Defense, 2015). Extending well beyond its own heavily firewalled military networks, this new DoD strategy called for collaborative cyber-centric partnerships with the private sector in order to facilitate intelligence gathering and cyber-threat warning capabilities. Within the DoD, the Cyber National Mission Force was established with the responsibility of serving as the departmental focal-point for the major public–private partnership efforts necessary to adequately defend America's critical infrastructures in cyberspace (Borghard, 2018).

Just over a year later, in July 2016, *Presidential Policy Directive-41* (PPD-41) laid out the principle actors for a major federal response to cyber-related incidents occurring either in the public or private sectors. It is important to note this directive stressed an overall unity of effort between the two distinct sectors in order to ensure the overarching strategic importance of providing proper security and resiliency for America's critical infrastructures. PPD-41 succinctly stated, "the private sector and government agencies have a shared vital interest in protecting the Nation from malicious cyber activity and managing cyber incidents and their consequences" (Obama, 2016, p. 1).

America's National Cyber Strategy (2018)

On September 20, 2018, the White House released U.S. President Donald J. Trump's newly signed *National Cyber Strategy of the United States of America* (2018). In a formal statement, President Trump said the United States "cannot ignore the costs of malicious cyber activity — economic or otherwise — directed at America's Government, businesses, and private individuals" (White House, 2018, p. 1). In his own White House Press Conference following the release of the new American Cyber Strategy, U.S. National Security Advisor John Bolton remarked "we will identify, counter, disrupt, degrade, and deter behavior in cyberspace that is destabilizing and contrary to national interests, while preserving the United States' overmatch in and through cyberspace" (Lyngaas, 2018, p. 1).

Overall, this new national-level American cybersecurity strategy made several major enhancements that gave governmental agencies and their law enforcement organizations greater operational abilities to aggressively respond to cybercrime and nation-state attacks. This strategy specifically spotlighted DHS' active cultivation of domestic cyber defense roles. It also highlighted enhanced international offensive cyber stances authorized for the U.S. DoD to take—allowing the DoD to respond more quickly and proactively in response to international cyberattacks (Trump, 2018).

America's new national cyber strategy also succinctly outlined four "pillars of priority" which included: (1) protect the American People, the [American] Homeland, and the American Way of Life, (2) Promote American Prosperity, (3) Preserve Peace through Strength, and (4) Advance American Influence [through building international cyber-capacities with U.S. international allies to go after "threats of mutual interest"] (Trump, 2018). Furthermore, this new cyber strategy also made one central message crystal clear: America will not sit ideally by and watch when attacked in cyberspace (Trump, 2018). Several core "Section 9" areas were also included on a list of areas/functions where the United States would respond offensively within cyberspace—ranging from the protection of critical infrastructural and intellectual property to space exploration (Trump, 2018). Additionally, this strategy also added upon many foundational/apolitical policies of the two previous presidential administrations [of former U.S. Presidents George W. Bush (2001–2009) and Barack Obama (2009–2017)] in areas such as enhancing America's cybersecurity workforce and strengthening critical infrastructure. This included the U.S. Financial Sector and the operation of America's electrical grids—components that literally impact the lives of every single American (Arampatzis, 2018).

The U.S. Financial Sector's Militarized Approach to Fighting Cybercrime (2018–Present)

By the fall of 2018, armed with a new national-level cyber strategy, significantly enhance cooperation/collaboration with both DHS/DoD, and formal U.S. Treasury Department guidance declaring ongoing cyberattacks to be one of the greatest risks to the country's financial sector, American financial institutions have responded to calls to increase their own internal cybersecurity mitigation efforts with an increasingly militarized approach. According to Cowley (2018), "former government cyber-spies, soldiers, and counterintelligence officials now dominate the top ranks of [American] banks' security teams. They've brought to their new jobs the tools and techniques used for national defense: combat exercises, intelligence hubs modeled on those used in counterterrorism work and threat analysts who monitor the internet's shadowy corners" (pp. 2–3).

Within the American Financial Sector, major U.S. financial institutions have actively recruited some of the best and brightest cybersecurity professionals from across the industry over the past decade to help secure and maintain their own financial networks and data systems. Due to a sizeable number of these highly-skilled cybersecurity professional recruits hailing from U.S. military-trained cyberspace/network defense backgrounds, a variety of operational network security-centric military-styled tactics, techniques, and procedures (TTPs) were also translated into the civilian sector. As these prior-military cybersecurity professionals integrated into their new civilian institutions and actively leveraging their own technical skill sets, new functional coordination entities known as "corporate fusion centers"—the civilian equivalent of a military operational command center—quickly began to dominate the financial sector's cybersecurity rapidly expanding landscape.

In tandem with the rise of financial institutional fusion centers also came the establishment of the Financial Services Information Sharing and Analysis Center (FS-ISAC). An American-based financial industry-wide consortium, FS-ISAC was created in 1999 and the organization is dedicated to reduce cyber-risk in the global financial system and connects over

7000 member financial institutions—banks, brokerages, credit unions, financial trade associations, insurance companies, investment firms, bank service providers, and payment processors—spanning 70 jurisdictions (FS-ISAC, 2018; Sedenberg & Dempsey, 2018). In 2017, FS-ISAC expanded its operational reach by establishing international regional hubs in London and Singapore as well (Financial Services Information Sharing and Analysis Center, 2018).

By leveraging its collaboration-based peer-to-peer intelligence data-sharing platform, resiliency resources, and cybersecurity experts, FS-ISAC actively seeks to anticipate, identify, and effectively mitigate emerging cyber-based threats against its vast financial network. Because a cyber-attack against one of FS-ISAC's member financial institution could affect the entire U.S. Financial Sector or even the global-level financial system, these cyber-partnerships consolidate key cyber-defense expertise, early warning and detection, and share rapid response mitigation strategies (Financial Services Information Sharing and Analysis Center, 2018).

Within this trusted peer-to-peer consortium of financial institutional fusion centers, the name of the game is the continued real-time sharing of situational awareness and identification of emerging cyber-threats. With a concerted focus that is "to the left of the boom"—a military term referring to the critical moments just before a bomb detonates—the name of the game in these military-styled civilian financial cyber-fusion centers is the proactive detection and rapid mitigation of technical vulnerabilities/cyber-hacks before they can occur (Cowley, 2018). Through the sharing and collaboration of evolving cybersecurity-related mitigation strategies, cyber-related policies, and deterrence initiatives, the overall cybersecurity of the entire network is collectively enhanced.

Looking Ahead: Layered Cyber Deterrence

Authorized as part of the Fiscal Year 2019 National Defense Authorization Act, the Cyberspace Solarium Commission (CSC) (2020) was tasked to "develop a consensus on a strategic approach to defending the United States in cyberspace against cyberattacks of significant consequences" (p. 1). The CSC's finished report was released to the public on March 11, 2020. This newly released strategy called for a future end-state of multilayered cyber-deterrence posturing, which the CSC viewed as necessary in order to reduce the overall impacts of future cyberattacks.

The CSC's (2020) public report outlined three ways to achieve a layered cyber deterrence posture though (a) the promotion of responsible international cyber behavior, (b) the denial of benefits to cyber-adversaries who have historically exploited the cyberspace domain to their advantage through increased cybersecurity and resiliency of the cyber-ecosystem, and (c) impose significant retaliatory costs to those who target America's national security interests through cyberspace. According to Homeland Security Today (2020), each of the three layered deterrent postures is dependent on continued (and further enhanced) American public/private sector cybersecurity collaborative partnerships to strategically alter how potential cyber adversaries (competitor nation-states and cybercriminal groups) fundamentally perceive the costs and benefits of leveraging the cyberspace domain to strike at American national security and economic interests around the globe.

The CSC's (2020) public report also outlined more than 80 key recommendations organized into six distinct pillars of: (a) reform the U.S. Federal Government's current cyberspace organizational structures, (b) continue to strengthen worldwide cyberspace norms among allies/partners and other nation-states, (c) continue to further enhance the country's national resiliency efforts, (d) seek to positively reshape the contours of the worldwide "Cyber Ecosystem" (p. 1), (e) continue to integrate operational cyber collaboration efforts between the U.S. Government and private sectors, and (f) further enhance America's "military instrument of National Power" (p. 1) to be employed with overwhelming effectiveness when called upon to do so.

According to Homeland Security Today (2020), these six pillars represent both the strategic and technical means by which the United States can proactively implement a layered cyber deterrence moving forward. While deterrence-backed-with-overwhelming-military-force has been the long-standing, core American national security strategy for close to a century, two key factors make this new multilayered cyber deterrence approach unique. First, this construct readily focuses on a strong, standing, and ever-resilient cybersecurity force comprised of the best and brightest cybersecurity professionals (from both the public and private sectors) partnered together for mutual cyber defense. Through constant collaboration, cyber vulnerabilities can be dramatically reduced—thus preventing cyberattackers from having opportunities to attack American interests in the cyber realm. Secondly, this new multilayered strategy seeks to "defend forward" as a pathway to significantly reduce both the severity and frequency of cyberattacks that would not generally rise to a conventional military response. The basic premise of defending forward centers around the identification of strategic centers of gravity or leverage points may need to be proactively countered/neutralized by actions that are (a) short of armed conflict and (b) consistent with international law, but still provide an appropriately measured government response from the United States (Homeland Security Today 2020).

Conclusion

As we strive to look ahead across today's cyber "lay of the land" and attempt to ascertain what future challenges might arise just over the horizon, a few core going-in assumptions remain quite clear. First, cyber-related technologies, opportunities, challenges, and threats are all-but-certain to continue to evolve at a rapid pace. Second, just as contemporary American society continues to become ever more dependent on modern infrastructures and technologies in virtually all aspects of our daily lives, so too must the physical/technical/cyber-based defensive security and overall resiliency of those critical infrastructures/technologies be continually enhanced.

Many of tomorrow's cyberspace and critical infrastructure enhancements will be readily made through continued (and further expanded) public/private sector partnerships. Specifically looking at the American Financial Sector and its associated cyber-connected infrastructure, the more the U.S. Federal Government understands the key vulnerabilities, challenges, and opportunities of the private financial sector's infrastructure, the more fidelity can be achieved against mitigating specific risks or vulnerabilities against those infrastructures. With greater and more frequent collaboration, joint partnerships and interoperable training/exercises/real-world response activities become more routine—thus, allowing all public and private sector stakeholders to be better prepared when future cyberattacks do take place.

References

Arampatzis, A. (2018). U.S. national cyber strategy: What you need to know. *Tripwire.com*. Retrieved from https://www.tripwire.com/state-of-security/government/us-cyber-strategy/.

Borghard, D. E. (2018). *Protecting financial institutions against cyber threats: A national security issue*. The Carnegie Endowment for International Peace. Retrieved from https://carnegieendowment.org/2018/09/24/protecting-financial-institutions-against-cyber-threats-national-security-issue-pub-77324.

CBS News. (2018). *Intelligence officials say U.S. "under attack," cybersecurity at-risk in 2018*. Retrieved from https://www.cbsnews.com/news/christopher-wray-mike-pompeo-dan-coats-testify-on-worldwide-threats-live-stream/.

Center for Strategic and International Studies. (2020). *The evolution of cyber-security requirements for the U.S. financial industry*. Washington, DC: CSIS. Retrieved from https://www.csis.org/programs/cybersecurity-and-governance/technology-policy-program/financial-sector-cybersecurity.

Cornell University Legal Information Institute. (2020). *12 CFR part 30, appendix A to part 30—Interagency guidelines establishing standards for safety and soundness*. Retrieved from https://www.law.cornell.edu/cfr/text/12/appendix-A_to_part_30.

Cowley, S. (2018). Banks adopt military-style tactics to fight cybercrime. *The New York Times*. Retrieved from https://www.nytimes.com/2018/05/20/business/banks-cyber-security-military.html.

Cyberspace Solarium Commission. (2020). *The United States of America cyberspace solarium commission*. Retrieved from https://www.solarium.gov/.

Department of Defense. (2015). *The Department of Defense cyber strategy*. Retrieved from https://archive.defense.gov/home/features/2015/0415_cyber-strategy/final_2015_dod_cyber_strategy_for_web.pdf.

Department of Homeland Security. (2018). *DHS and DOE meet with oil and natural gas sector coordinating council, announce pipeline cybersecurity initiative*. Retrieved from https://www.dhs.gov/news/2018/10/03/dhs-and-doe-meet-oil-and-natural-gas-sector-coordinating-council-announce-pipeline.

Federal Financial Institutions Examination Council. (2014). *Bank secrecy act anti-money laundering examination manual appendix A: BSA laws and regulations*. Retrieved from https://bsaaml.ffiec.gov/manual.

Federal Financial Institutions Examination Council IT Examination Handbook. (n.d.). *Security guidelines*. Retrieved from https://ithandbook.ffiec.gov/it-booklets/e-banking/risk-management-of-e-banking-activities/information security-program/security-guidelines.aspx.

Federal Trade Commission. (2013). *Fighting identity theft with the red flags rule: A how-to guide for business*. Retrieved from https://www.ftc.gov/tips-advice/business-center/guidance/fighting-identity-theft-red-flags-rule-how-guide-business.

Financial Services Information Sharing and Analysis Center. (2018). *Overview*. Retrieved from https://www.fsisac.com/who-we-are.

Homeland Security Today. (2020). *Cyberspace solarium commission recommends layered cyber deterrence in new report*. Retrieved from https://www.hstoday.

us/subject-matter-areas/cybersecurity/cyberspace-solarium-commission-recommends-layered-cyber-deterrence-in-new-rep.

Krebs, C. (2019). *Improving critical infrastructure cybersecurity; Fiscal year 2017 report to congress*. Retrieved from https://www.dhs.gov/sites/default/files/publications/cisa_-_improving_critical_infrastructure_cybersecurity.pdf.

Lyngaas, S. (2018). White House announces federal cyber strategy, vows to go on offensive. *Cyberscoop.com*. Retrieved from https://www.cyberscoop.com/white-house-cyber-strategy-john-bolton-announcement/.

National Institute of Standards and Technology (NIST). (2012). *NIST special publication 800-30: Guide for conducting risk assessments*. Retrieved from https://nvlpubs.nist.gov/nistpubs/Legacy/SP/nistspecialpublication800-30r1.pdf.

National Institute of Standards and Technology (NIST). (2018a). *About NIST*. Retrieved from https://www.nist.gov/about-nist.

National Institute of Standards and Technology (NIST) (2018b, April 16). *Framework for improving critical infrastructure cybersecurity—Version 1.1*. Retrieved from https://www.nist.gov/cyberframework/framework.

National Risk Management Center. (2018). *The National Risk Management Center*. U.S. Department of Homeland Security. Retrieved from https://www.cisa.gov/sites/default/files/publications/NRMC%20100%20Days%20Fact%20Sheet%2020181115_CISA%20v2.pdf.

Obama, B. (2013). *Executive order 13636: Improving critical infrastructure cybersecurity*. Washington, DC: The White House. Retrieved from https://obamawhitehouse.archives.gov/the-press-office/2013/02/12/executive-order-improving-critical-infrastructure-cybersecurity.

Obama, B. (2016). *Presidential Policy Directive 41: United States cyber incident coordination*. Washington, DC: The White House. Retrieved from https://obamawhitehouse.archives.gov/the-press-office/2016/07/26/presidential-policy-directive-united-states-cyber-incident.

PCI Security Standards Council. (2020). *PA-DSS security standards library*. Retrieved from https://www.pcisecuritystandards.org/document_library?category=padss&document=pci_pa_dss_program_guide.

Randolph, K. (2018). DOE, DHS officials discuss cybersecurity and oil, natural gas infrastructure. *The Daily Energy Insider*. Retrieved from https://dailyenergyinsider.com/news/15250-doe-dhs-officials-discuss-cybersecurity-and-oil-natural-gas-infrastructure/.

Sedenberg, M. E., & Dempsey, X, J. (2018). *Cybersecurity information sharing governance structures: An ecosystem of diversity, trust, and tradeoffs*. Retrieved from https://arxiv.org/abs/1805.12266.

Stults, G. (2004). An overview of Sarbanes-Oxley for the information security professional. *SANS Institute InfoSec Reading Room*.

Retrieved from http://www.sans.org/reading-room/whitepapers/legal/overviewsarbanes-oxley-information-security-professional-1426.
Trump, D. (2018, September 20). *National Cyber Strategy of the United States of America*. Washington, DC: The White House. Retrieved from https://www.whitehouse.gov/wp-content/uploads/2018/09/National-Cyber-Strategy.pdf.
Williams, B., Chuvakin, A., & Bradley, T. (2007). *PCI compliance: Understand and implement effective PCI data security standard compliance*. Waltham, MA: Syngress Publishing.
White House. (2018). *President Donald J. Trump is strengthening America's cybersecurity*. Retrieved from https://www.whitehouse.gov/briefings-statements/president-donald-j-trump-is-strengthening-americas-cybersecurity/.
Zheng, E, D., & Carter, A, W. (2015). *Leveraging the Internet of things for a more efficient and effective military*. Retrieved from https://csis-website-prod.s3.amazonaws.com/s3fs-public/legacy_files/files/publication/150915_Zheng_LeveragingInternet_WEB.pdf.

CHAPTER 4

The Evolution of the Threats to Canadian Financial Institutions, the Actual State of Public and Private Partnerships in Canada

The Actual State; Protecting Financial Institutions

Infrastructure protection is a shared responsibility between the government and private companies working together to improve its resilience. More specifically, cybersecurity is a *public good* that must be framed as a collective action problem between both actors (McCarthy, 2018). The private sector owns approximately 80% of the critical infrastructure in the country so its role must be important in the management of these threats (Etzioni, 2017; Vroegop, 2017). Homeland Security is the responsibility of various groups "security nodes" and actors from the public and the private sectors (Dupont, 2004). The consequences of cyberattacks on critical infrastructure can have significant economic, social and environmental impacts (Mezher, El Khatib, & Sooriyaarachchi, 2015). Cyber-threats against financial institutions now pose considerable risks to national security (Borghard, 2018). Financial institutions are diversifying, e-commerce is predominant, and attackers use a variety of deceptive techniques to generate a profit from crime (Gordon, 2018). Currently, Canadian banking security professionals have a dynamic framework structure to leverage in order to collectively combat various threats against their organization, while readily sharing information to protect the banking industry. As such, Canada's private sector is quickly adapting to the rapid changes in the cyber threat landscape in near real-time. Even

P.-L. Pomerleau and D. L. Lowery, *Countering Cyber Threats to Financial Institutions*,
https://doi.org/10.1007/978-3-030-54054-8_4

though banking security professionals share information, the specific intelligence or warnings they regularly share with the public sector is mostly organic, omitting the vast amount of data available in the private sector. This situation leaves the government with a myopic view of the actual cyber threat landscape, which inherently increases risks to critical infrastructure. As Carr (2016) argues, there is still a fundamental disjuncture between the expectations of private and public security partners regarding roles, responsibility, and authority in protecting critical infrastructure from cyber-threats. Given the rapid evolution of the cyber threat landscape and a barrage of recent cyberattacks on banks at the international level, foreign threats to the financial sector in cyberspace should be a priority and conceptualized as a national security challenge.

What Is the Problem?

In recent years, the threat landscape of financial institutions has changed, not only from a criminal and profit-oriented threat actor standpoint, but also from a state and non-state actor using cyberspace directing attacks toward financial institutions (Borghard, 2018). The cost of cybercrime in Canada is equivalent to 0.17% of its Gross Domestic Product (GDP), which represents annual losses of CAD$3.2 billion per year (Public Safety Canada, 2018). The average size and total cost of cyberattacks on the private sector have increased beyond previous years (Kaijankoski, 2015; Ponemon Institute, 2018; Rightmier, 2017) as the volume of cyberattacks against financial institutions is three times that of any other industries (Johnson, 2016). Additionally, non-state actors continue to invest in their cyber capabilities to enable cyberattacks on financial institutions and pose a risk to the national security and economic objectives of Canada (Communications Security Establishment, 2018).

According to the International Monetary Fund (IMF), bank's potential annual losses associated to cybercrime is estimated to nine percent of their net income which is a loss equivalent to US$97 billion (Bouveret, 2018; Leuprecht, 2019). The financial impact is considerable as witnessed by the numerous attacks on banks through the Society for Worldwide Interbank Financial Telecommunication (SWIFT) global transfer system or the JP Morgan Chase cyberattack in July 2014 that compromised the personal accounts of 76 million U.S. customers and two million businesses (Taplin, 2016). The problem to be addressed is why private and public partnership relationships have been ineffective in monitoring, detecting and reacting to these incidents? (Bures, 2013; Dunn-Cavelty & Suter, 2009). The probability of companies to detect hackers is low, and the perceived risk of threat actors of being caught is minimal (Boes & Leukfeldt, 2017). Due to the international nature of cybercrime, law enforcement struggles to prosecute cybercriminals and to assist banks in preventing these incidents (Holt, 2018).

Financial institutions security professionals and their teams are responsible for identifying and protecting their organization against cyberattacks while the public sector is accountable to provide security, deter, prosecute, and enforce existing law. The banking sector does not have the necessary intelligence collection authorities and capabilities to protect its network and infrastructure, while the government does possess these necessary authorities and abilities to do so—however, it does not have a banking-specific expertise of the cyber threats affecting the financial industry (Boes & Leukfeldt, 2017; Borghard, 2018). Chief executive officers and board members of numerous Canadian banks, the Canadian financial sector, policymakers, and the federal and provincial governments are all astutely aware of the critical importance of potential losses from cyberattacks (O'Donnell & Nesbitt, 2016). Mitigating this problem requires an in-depth understanding of (a) precisely what these challenges are and (b) how they can be most effectively met. Previous academic research in this area has seldomly considered the perceptions of private corporate security professionals—both corporate & information security—leading corporate security and cybersecurity teams protecting these financial institutions (Maimon, Alper, Sobesto, & Cukier, 2014; Maimon, Testa, Sobesto, Cukier, & Wuling, 2019; Testa, Maimon, Sobesto, & Cukier, 2017; Wilson, Maimon, Sobesto, & Cukier, 2015).

The Purpose of the Study

The purpose of this qualitative study was to conduct interviews with a select group of corporate security professionals (corporate and information security) representing Canada's financial institutions. The technical and operational inputs of these professionals is a key component to enabling the public and private sectors to work together, thus failing to take advantage of a valuable resource. The research focus was the collection of information allowing to understand the challenges these private security professionals face in sharing information aimed at preventing cybersecurity incidents with the public sector as well as to provide recommendations for decision-makers on how best to harden their existing cyber security protections. This study determined that the Network Security Governance Framework first proposed by Dupont (2004) and adapted by Whelan and Dupont (2017), allows to better understand the phenomenon, as well as identifying best practices for information sharing. Understanding the perspectives of private security professionals on public–private partnerships (PPPs) lead to better collaboration in preventing cyberattacks against financial institutions, increases in the overall effectiveness of cybersecurity systems, and the establishment of proper protocols to cooperate with the public sector in investigating actual cybersecurity incidents. The private security professional's perspective offers a better understanding of (a) what factors contribute to the current system not functioning and (b) to provide recommendations to improve public and private partnerships to protect the financial industry from various cyber-threats.

Nature of Study

Private and public partnership relationships have been ineffective in monitoring, detecting, and reacting to cyber-threats against financial institutions. Previous scholars did not examine the Canadian private security professional's perspective on improving this situation. This study aimed to understand the perceptions of private security professionals—Chief Security Officers (CSO) and Chief Information Security Officers (CISO)—working for financial institutions as to what they believe need to be implemented to enable the public and private sectors to work together to better protect financial services. The findings of this study with Canadian security professionals would also be applicable to other nations in the world.

The research method for this qualitative study was phenomenology. This method allows confronting assumptions, traditions, languages, and cognition to understand better the existential, complex, more nuanced everyday lived experiences (Van Manen, 2014) as well as to explain the phenomenon through the participants commonly shared experiences (Merriam & Tisdell, 2016). The data collection process consisted of semi-structured interviews with participants to get their perspective on this topic. These interviews allowed participants to describe their challenges in sharing information with the public sector. Phenomenology is the study of people's experiences, their everyday-life interactions in the real world as well as the discovery of knowledge by reference to the things and facts themselves (Merriam & Tisdell, 2016; Moustakas, 1994; Vagle, 2018). The researcher used the NVivo software to analyze the qualitative data from interviews using the constant comparison analysis technique. This analysis allowed identifying general concepts and themes as well as to propose recommendations to decision-makers to improve information sharing between private and public partnerships in protecting critical infrastructure such as the financial institutions.

Research Questions

The Federal government is responsible and accountable for the response and the provision of national security (Carr, 2016). Private companies operate and own most of the critical infrastructure in Canada. Comprehensive, proactive and rigorous use of cybersecurity best practices are required at the local, national, and international levels to manage cyberattacks effectively (Shackelford, 2013). Therefore, it requires a robust and strategic relationship between the public and private sectors regarding the responsibility of providing security (Carr, 2016). In this context at the local and national level, it would be difficult for the government to manage a critical cybersecurity incident without the assistance of the private sector. The research questions this study answered are:

RQ1. From the Canadian financial institution's senior security professional's perspectives, what are the best practices information-sharing PPPs should implement to become more efficient and proactive in preventing, detecting, and responding to critical cyberattacks and to increase the resilience of the financial industry?

RQ2. From the Canadian financial institution's senior security professional's perspectives, how does the private sector perceive its relationship with the public sector regarding the efficiency with the current information-sharing mechanisms to prevent, detect, and respond to cyberattacks on the financial industry?

RQ3. From the Canadian financial institution's senior security professional's perspectives, how do private security professionals perceive the power structure, the accountability for national security, and their loyalty and ownership relationship with the public sector concerning cybersecurity information-sharing issues associated with critical infrastructure protection?

RQ4. From the Canadian financial institution's senior security professional's perspectives, to what extent should financial institutions share cyber-threat information with the public sector to protect the financial industry against cyberattacks and what type of governance model should be implemented to do so?

Throughout the existing literature on information sharing between public and private partnerships (PPPs), many contemporary authors define the basic premise of what specifically constitutes a public and private partnership. These partnerships exist as there is a common need among organizations to share information to prevent a wide variety of criminal activities. Specific information sharing between organizations may focus on attackers, victims, incidents or vulnerabilities. By assisting one another in the collective pool of mitigating risk and sharing information, organizations can decrease time to a major event or newly discovered vulnerabilities and then decide the appropriate course of action (Kolini & Janczewski, 2017). Heldeweg and Sanders (2014) define a public and private partnership as "a legally structured partnership between one or more public authorities and one or more corporate entities governed by private law, which focuses on the development and execution of a common strategy for the realization of a policy project" (p. 11).

Theoretical Frameworks in Cybersecurity and Security Networks

Three key theoretical frameworks allow to better understand the relationship of security stakeholders that are members of public and private partnerships in information sharing. The first theory is the Security Network Framework Theory. Developed by Dupont (2004), this theory focuses on the importance of security governance and the necessity of relying on security networks to manage security. Dupont (2004) claims there are four types of security networks; local security networks, institutional security networks, international security networks, and virtual security networks. He defines a security network as: "A set of institutional, organizational, communal or individual agents or nodes that are interconnected to authorize and ensure the security and safety to the benefit of internal or external stakeholders" (Dupont, 2004, p. 78). According to Dupont (2004), the Security Network Framework should be used to interpret the complex relationship of accountability regarding security as well as to reduce the gap between the responsibility of the state and the overall responsibility of private actors. The Network Security Governance Framework primarily focuses on how institutional security networks work together to adapt to evolving threats and to implement governance mechanisms to manage relations, cultures, and interpersonal relationships (Whelan & Dupont, 2017). Whelan and Dupont (2017) revisit Dupont's (2004) Security Network Framework (Local, institutional, international, and virtual) as each of the four types of networks may also operate at the subnational, national, or transnational levels (Whelan & Dupont, 2017). The two authors propose a typology of networks to improve security network research, and they categorize these types of networks as the information exchange networks, knowledge generation networks, problem-solving networks and the coordination networks (Whelan & Dupont, 2017).

The second framework is known as the Critical Theory in International Relations and Security Studies. According to McCarthy (2018) and Stevens (2018), this theory views cybersecurity through the paradigm of an assemblage of sociotechnical practices and politics at-work. Choucri (2012) argues that the global and nontransparent interconnections that are possible through cyberspace challenged the traditional international relations and power politics concerning national security, borders, and boundaries as many features of cyberspace reshaped the International Relation's Theory. McCarthy (2018) claims that a considerable number of studies in Security Studies and International Relations, from a variety of perspectives, demonstrate the importance of domestic social forces in constituting the national security interests of states, while in contrast to the public goods approach, the state is perceived as an institution mediating between different social forces within society. McCarthy (2018) and Stevens (2018) advocate Critical theory is interdisciplinary, it recognizes the public and private divide as an outcome of liberal orders. It also takes into consideration the private sector's accountability in cybersecurity since this approach is committed to the democratization of science and technology as a vehicle for greater social and political equality. Besides, Critical theory offers the possibility to analyze cybersecurity as an assemblage of s*ociotechnical* practices and politics (Stevens, 2018). Stevens (2018) defines cybersecurity as "a mean not only of protecting and defending society and its essential information infrastructures, but also a way of prosecuting national and international policies through information-technological means" (p. 1). Cybersecurity represents a complex configuration of actors, organizations, and institutions (Choucri, 2012; Collier, 2018). Cybersecurity management is a shared responsibility between governments, security agencies, the military, the private sector, which owns and operate infrastructures as well as its citizens (Stevens, 2016). For Stevens (2016), security is always political as it is foundational to politics. The author argues there are four logics which are assemblage, real-time due to speed and acceleration, the event, and the end of the world or what the author described as the *eschaton*, or the fact the security assemblage represents different temporal characteristics to the chronopolitics of cybersecurity (Stevens, 2016). For Stevens (2016), an assemblage consists of "a mere thing that just is but an assemblage of things, both human and nonhuman, that becomes" (p. 181). This assemblage is in a constant state of change as the cybersecurity function operates in a temporality of continual change to maintain and to modify its character due to continuous changes in the information-technological networks (Stevens, 2016). Within this framework, an entity characterized as a cybersecurity assemblage needs to change to persist in time and space as these two concepts are essential components of the sociotemporality of cybersecurity (Stevens, 2016). Also, the security assemblage must enroll new actors in time in appropriating each of the temporalities, or it will lose its identity and its efficiency (Stevens, 2016).

The third and final framework is known as the Securitization Theory. Developed by Wæver (1995), it explains how the securitization process strongly depends on organizational power and political influence. Buzan, Waever, and De Wilde (1998) work is also crucial to the development of this framework. Securitization is "the move that takes politics beyond the established rules of the game and frames the issue either as a special kind of politics or as above politics" (p. 23) and desecuritization is the reverse process which consist of the "shifting of issues out of the emergency mode and into the normal bargaining process of the political sphere" (Buzan et al., 1998, p. 4). Securitization provides security actors the right to use exceptional means in delivering security and desecuritization can be beneficial to reintroduce an issue into the politicized sphere (Collins, 2016). According to these authors, security is about survival and safety is necessary when an issue is presented as an existential threat to an object (e.g., State, government, society) (Buzan et al., 1998).

The security actors are accountable to securitize issues, and the referent objects are things that threatened and have a legitimate claim to survival (Collins, 2016). In including non-state actors in its definition of security, the Copenhagen School adopted a multi-sectoral approach to security representing a different perspective than the traditional Security Studies focusing primarily on the military sector (Collins, 2016). An essential aspect of the securitization process is that it strongly depends on the power and influence (speech acts) of the securitizing actors to convince a relevant audience that an immediate danger threatens a referent object and that extraordinary measures are required (Collins, 2016). Extraordinary measures may be adopted in response to a threat, and it may vary depending on the circumstances, the context or the environment (Collins, 2016). The danger is subjective and depends on the perception of individuals, and this danger may have a considerable impact on the environment, the sector, the economy or even a state ideology (Collins, 2016). More specifically, it consists of a shared understanding of what constitutes a danger to security in each situation (Collins, 2016).

A Private and Public Partnership Approach to Critical Infrastructure Protection

Bures (2013) argues partnerships do not work since there are too many challenges for both parties. He goes on to discuss this phenomenon in his research by focusing mainly on anti-money laundering issues and terrorist financing. Bossong and Wagner (2017) suggest Bures (2013) remained relatively obscured on how both individual sectors could improve their partnership's information sharing in order to fight terrorism. In her research with Canadians critical infrastructure security professionals, Hoganson (2014) concludes some of the most common barriers to information sharing are a keen lack of awareness of potential threats, inappropriate sharing of information between public and private partners, lack of trust, or disagreement on security priorities. Hoganson (2014) goes on to points out other barriers in the exchange of information, such as the lack of effective communication, competing demands, and limited financial resources to invest in such a partnership (Hoganson, 2014).

In its 2017 report on cybercrime, the World Bank lists several reasons why it is difficult to foster effective cooperation in PPPs (World Bank,

2017). The most common barriers are the lack of prophylactic cooperation (the private sector working with the government when in crisis mode), public perception sensitives of working too closely with the government, the private sector's traditional reactionary posture rather than a proactive stance, a lack of cohesive efforts to integrate individuals from individual sectors in building a resilient society, the government-centric approach focusing primarily on government-owned critical infrastructures as well as the lack of safeguards (World Bank, 2017).

According to the International Center for the Prevention of Crime (2018), some of the most common identified barriers are very much in line with the factors previously articulated by the World Bank (2017). For instance, the Center concludes that stakeholders in PPPs have different cultures and values, divergent interests and expectations, and previous PPPs had limited citizen participation. Other issues related to PPPs are that the roles and responsibilities of stakeholders are not always clear, the level of collaboration, the importance of trusted relationships and the lack of diversity among private sector's participants (The International Centre for the Prevention of Crime, 2018).

Furthermore, Carr (2016) advances the necessity of getting real-time capabilities, having access to actionable cyber-threat and alert information, as well as the possibility of using financial incentives to increase overall participation. The importance of using incentives for the private sector's involvement in cybersecurity was discussed also by Stevens, O'Brien, Overill, Wilkinson, Pildegovics, and Hill (2019). The authors recommend to the UK government to use incentives to implement active cyber defense (ACD) in the private sector as ACD demonstrated great results in the public sector, and that both sectors should rely on active cyber defense strategies to reduce the incidence of cybercrime on government agencies, users, and private organizations (Stevens et al., 2019).

Sarre and Prenzler (2011) identify some best practices to increase the benefits of creating public–private security partnerships. The two authors argue the imperativeness that both sectors must continue to closely collaborate on their mutual interests of reducing crime, identifying individuals with strong leadership skills to effectively manage public–private security teams, continue to foster mutual respect, trust and communication, and to demonstrate a continued willingness to consider ideas brought forward by both public and private partners in policing groups (Sarre & Prenzler, 2011).

Singh, Singh, Park, Lee, and Rao (2009) advocate that the focus of PPPs should revolve around the end-user with the primary goal of near real-time information sharing across key networks to "ensure the right people get the right information at the right time" (p. 3). Information-sharing initiatives should aim to provide information assurance or to the "degree to which information meets the needs of its users" (Singh et al., 2009, p. 5). For these authors, information assurance or quality is about timeliness, security, accessibility, completeness, accuracy, coherence, relevance, validity, and format. Fleming and Goldstein (2012) establish principles to determine the success of information-sharing initiatives; information sharing should be goal-directed, it should only involve actors who can support the achievement of these goals, information-sharing efforts should only be used to achieve these goals, the uncertainty should be minimized while the actors should understand that information sharing cannot eliminate uncertainty (Fleming & Goldstein, 2012).

In their study of international police organizations, Gerspacher and Dupont (2007) claim that the lack of success in implementing security networks between organizations is not because of a lack of awareness, but because of problems related to the execution of the implementation. Change management can be another issue in what they referred to the "redistribution of power" among organizations involved. The creation of security networks can generate resistance from some groups of individuals realizing that such changes will have an impact on their leadership (Gerspacher & Dupont, 2007). Besides, regarding the number of individuals per network, criminal organization networks are relatively small while legitimate security networks can bring together thousands of individuals with different objectives and values (Gerspacher & Dupont, 2007). Moreover, larger networks and its reliance on technology, procedures, and protocols can be a problem to maintain (Gerspacher & Dupont, 2007).

For other academic researchers, led by Greiman (2015), argue a different security model is required to build a viable partnership—specifically a model in which public and private interests are brought together in a shared partnership. The fundamental premise is such a collaborative system would provide greater access to intelligence assistance, as well as greater liability protection for the increased risk assumed by private sector collaboration (Greiman, 2015). This aligns closely with the work of Collier (2018) who suggests the private sector's business-minded perspective would allow the development of new ideas to create more efficient and proactive security networks and/or security assemblages, which are hybrid structures essential for increasing resiliency and to protect the integrity of the financial industry.

In their study, Givens and Busch (2013) analyze many public and private partnerships in different types of U.S. critical infrastructure. They conclude public–private partnerships in information sharing are imperative to effective homeland security operations, however from a theoretical perspective, these partnerships also raise valid questions and challenges. Etzioni (2017) argues the two sectors are characterized with conflicting values, ideological obstacles, divergent interests or values as the public sector is oriented toward the community and the private sector on its self-interests as a private business (International Centre for the Prevention of Crime, 2018).

Manley (2015) argues private companies fear to share information with the government due to essential elements such as trust, contract agreement between parties, legal issues, organizational structure of PPPs as well as the community involvement surrounding public–private entities forming PPPs. Other challenges often cited are privacy concerns, propriety interests, reciprocation and quality control (Sedenberg & Dempsey, 2018). These issues and challenges exist in different pieces of research (Bossong & Wagner, 2017; Carr, 2016; Givens & Busch, 2013; Kumar, 2006; Tropina, 2015; Wanca, 2014). Furthermore, trust between individual actors is critical and the lack of interpersonal relationships between professionals participating in PPPs is often the main challenge reported by various scholars (Boes & Leukfeldt, 2017; Brewer, 2013, 2017; Costantini, 2016; Dunn-Cavelty & Suter, 2009; Dupré, 2014; Garcia, Forscey, & Blute, 2017; Germano, 2014; Hoganson, 2014; Matthew & Cheshire, 2018; Rosemont, 2016; Vroegop, 2017; Wall, 2007; Whelan, 2015; World Bank, 2017) as the degree of trust will also influence the depth and the intensity of the information shared between stakeholders (Mermoud, Keupp, Ghernaouti, & David, 2017; Mermoud, 2019). Brewer (2013) suggests the trust-building relationship between security actors may vary depending on the context as the author explains in his United States versus Australia case study. For Germano (2014), the divergence in values and interests may lead to mistrust and suspicion regarding the other party's ability to take appropriate actions during crisis operations (International Centre for the Prevention of Crime, 2018). The climate of distrust may even exist between members of the same sector or what previous scholars called private to private partnerships or public to public partnerships (International Centre for the Prevention of Crime, 2018; Rosemont, 2016).

Manley (2015) points to the Netherlands where a great Dutch example of private and public partnership can be found demonstrating how to overcome this fear of building a stable relationship based on trust and transparency. In this project, the Netherland's central government created a PPP with Dutch companies by implementing a network system designed for sharing information between organizations (Manley, 2015). This system allowed preventing direct access to the customer's data without the company's consent and intervention (Manley, 2015).

In her research on public–private partnership, Costantini (2016) concludes that private sector professionals tend to have a lower level of trust in its public sector partners than the public sector has in its private sector partners. As the private sector's positive expectations are not being met, trust within the partnership with their public counterparts remains fragile (Costantini, 2016). Costantini (2016) adds that trust is more important between individuals across sectors than that found between sector-level partners. She points out just how essential personal relationships are much more important than a simple calculation of risk and reward as professionals expressed a more profound knowledge-based form of trust (Costantini, 2016).

The concept of trust is often mixed with the idea of loyalty (Barbalet, 2009). Barbalet (2009) suggests that trust can be understood by; "a) the acceptance of dependency in, b) the absence of information about the other's reliability in order to c) create an outcome otherwise unavailable" (Barbalet, 2009, p. 367). Quigley, Bisset, and Mills (2017) suggest there are two tendencies in defining trust; the strategic dimension of trust in an organizational setting and the relational and social dimension of building trust. In the strategic dimension of trust, two elements are vital in understanding the potential of trust in relationships. The first one is that knowledge enables one person to trust another and the second element is the private incentive for the person to honor and fulfill that trust (Quigley et al., 2017). In the relation and social dimension of trust, Kunnel and Quandt (2016) define relational trust as "an essential communicational ingredient that enables interaction and the growth of human relationships through mutual confidence" (p. 1). As for building trust in information sharing between private organizations and the government, Quigley et al. (2017) state that instead of focusing on building a trusted relationship with the private sector, the government should build trust among the population by demonstrating that it can govern and regulate critical infrastructures to protect society. The use of a framework such as the National Institute of Standards and Technology (NIST) is an example of a framework allowing to set standards, procedures, processes as well as methodologies to align policy and private businesses while having a technological approach to address the current issues in cybersecurity and to improve the resiliency of the financial industry (Laughlin, 2016). Other issues found in the literature related to information-sharing partnerships are the lack of cooperation between law enforcement and service providers on the procedures to follow to share and obtain evidence, the lack of legal framework across countries to defend cyberspace, implementing information security practices, third-party liability, reputation risks, and different motivations to engage in PPP's (Wanca, 2014).

According to Bossong and Wagner (2017), ideal and typical PPPs in information-sharing emphasis on the delivery of services, policy implementation to contrast other forms of policy consultation, shared regulation, and interest representation. They also argue PPPs are likely to benefit from agreements that specify the potential benefits or profits as well as a proportionate shared risk associated with the partnership (Bossong & Wagner, 2017). This idea closely aligns to Dupré's (2014) recommendation after conducting his study with Chief Information Security Officers (CISO) and Chief Security Officers (CSO), senior security experts of public and private partnerships in Europe. To achieve results and implement efficient and functioning PPPs in cybersecurity, Dupré (2014) recommends creating agile PPPs to adapt rapidly to changes, to provide human and financial resources incentives support, to define formal rules and governance at the earliest stage of the PPPs project, and to advertise successful results.

PPPs are often perceived as the answer to various challenges facing cybersecurity governance as they are considered a mode of organization allowing to increase flexibility as well as to share risks by including a wide range of actors for both public and private sectors (Christensen & Petersen, 2017). Some critics such as Dunn-Cavelty and Suter (2009) argue PPPs might be perceived as a potential way of transferring responsibility of national security to the private sector (Christensen & Petersen, 2017).

According to Gordon (2018), there are many benefits to share information between organization; (a) it gives participating organizations access to more data and better intelligence, (b) it allows to leverage the knowledge of others as information sharing allows to reduce the "lifespan of the attack product forcing the attackers to spend more resources developing new attacks" (p. 112), (c) it offers a cost-effective solution to intelligence that would not be available without the partnership, and (d) it offers a protection to members as Gordon (2018) argues the network is as strong as its weakest link. Also, Ponemon Institute (2016) researchers conclude that 39% of all cyber incidents against Canadian firms can be prevented by organizations sharing information between each other. Moreover, sharing information allows to identify common indicators of compromise as the main objective of attackers is to breach the network, learn how it works, what types of data are the most important and valuable, and what are the best ways to exfiltrate the information (Gordon, 2018).

While Christensen and Petersen, (2017) agree private and public actors in security might have diverging interests, they believe that previous scholar's observations underestimate the possibilities of PPPs in governing security. Contemporary corporate management is very attentive to the reputational risk the organization might face due to its business activities as well as the consequences it might encounter when an incident becomes public (Christensen & Petersen, 2017). The reputational concerns are "often at odds with this need for knowledge-sharing" (Christensen, 2018, p. 121). For these authors, the corporate security risk function must deal with a wide array of risks such as political risk, operational as well as reputational risk, but also with the corporate social responsibility and the resilience of the organization when it comes to national security interests (Christensen & Petersen, 2017).

Public and private partnerships are much more important than one might think as these networks represent loyalty or what these scholars referred to as the "social glue" keeping both sectors together for leadership and direction (Christensen & Petersen, 2017). For Christensen and Petersen (2017), it is normal that PPPs members are not always in agreement when it comes the time to unify people on the importance of the threat and what should be the priorities going forward. The rationale behind public–private partnerships is to govern the uncertainty or to gather more knowledge about cybersecurity threats from various partners to be able to assist authorities in having a better understanding of the threat landscape as well as to identify and manage these threats (Christensen & Petersen, 2017). Partners might agree that information sharing is essential, but they might also disagree on the strategies to mitigate the risks (Christensen & Petersen, 2017).

Cyber-Threat Environment

While the medium is certainly different, cybercrime is not fundamentally unlike other types of criminality. This particular type of criminal activity requires having an individual, a group of people or even nation-states, who wish to leverage technology using the Internet as the medium in order to exploit vulnerabilities in computer systems or vulnerabilities in individuals. More specifically, there are two categories of cybercrime; (a) technology as a target and (b) technology as an instrument. In the technology as a target category, criminal offenses are targeting computers such as unauthorized access to data contained in computer servers (Royal Canadian Mounted Police, 2014). In the technology as an instrument category, the Internet and information technologies are instrumental as a mean to commit criminal offenses such as fraud, money laundering, drug trafficking, human trafficking, organized crime activities among other types of illegal activities (Royal Canadian Mounted Police, 2014).

As advanced by Johnson (2016), banks are highly lucrative targets. For instance, Johnson (2016) states as an example the Carbanak attack in which cybercriminals sent spear-phishing emails with infected attachments to financial institution's employees to infect banking systems with a malware. Once successfully deployed inside the financial institution's network, the infected files allowed them to do remote surveillance of operational procedures. After the surveillance period, cybercriminals created fraudulent transactions to transfer funds into their accounts (Johnson, 2016). Johnson (2016) also points out this incident resulted in losses per bank from US$2.5 million to US$10 million per attack for a cumulative loss of US$1 billion to banks. Financial institutions must deal with several cyber-threats, and it is essential to understand the differences between them.

Whereas previous cyberattacks were primarily denial of service attacks to bring down an organization's Internet website and data theft, recent attacks include ransomware to prevent a company from operating and attacks that are launched to destroy assets, which demonstrate that the level of severity has increased and the methods and motivations of attackers have considerably evolved over the years (Gordon, 2018). In his research on financial institutions cyberattacks in Poland, Musiał (2019) argues ransomware, credential-harvesting malware, and social engineering are different cyberattacks representing a growing threat in the financial sector to steal online payment information and customer's personal identifiable information to commit fraud. As for Cunningham (2020), he argues that smartphones are the next "big target" due for a cyberattack just like PCs were two decades ago.

Various sources of threat information types may be shared between partners. For example, partners may share indicators (e.g., technical artifacts, observables), tactics, techniques and procedures, security alerts, threat intelligence reports or tool configurations (Johnson, Badger, Waltermire, Snyder, & Skorupka, 2016). Common sources of cybersecurity-related information are network data sources (e.g., timestamps, source and destination of IP address, domain name, port number, packet payload, type of attack), host data sources (e.g., file attribute, hardware information, MAC address, file hash, action taken), and other data sources (e.g., email header content, attachments, URLs, routing information) (Johnson et al., 2016).

Cyberattacks allow the perpetrators to disrupt, disable, destroy or take over the computer system for economic reasons or to bring down a system as political, social or psychological objective (Kenney, 2015). Cyber-risks are not limited to only one physical location as a cyberattack may come from anywhere in the world (Christensen & Petersen, 2017). Hence, cybersecurity incidents may be related to a system failure, an employee of the organization or an attack by a foreign nation (Christensen & Petersen, 2017).

In 2016, Polish banks and clients of more than 200 branches were affected by a malware called GozNym (Musiał, 2019). In 2018, the BackSwap software was used to commit online fraudulent transfers to defraud clients from five Polish Banks (Musiał, 2019). The recent hacking incidents against financial institutions through the use of the SWIFT money transferring system are only some of the examples of cyber-threats banks are now facing (Cimpanu, 2018; Kolini & Janczewski, 2017). As an example, in 2016, a grand jury in the Southern District of New York indicted a group of seven Iranians, working for the Islamic Revolutionary Guard Corps (Iranian government) for the 176 days campaign of distributed denial of service (DDOS) attacks against U.S. critical infrastructures, which included many financial institutions (United States Department of Justice, 2016).

In 2017, the SWIFT Institute published a report describing the increasing number of attacks on bank networks. In this report, Carter (2017) suggests attackers are becoming more sophisticated in using various modus operandi, that law enforcement is struggling to keep up with the pace of innovation of online offenders, and that banks in Asia are currently the top targets. As an example, in the Bangladesh Central Bank Reserve hack case in 2016, stolen funds were transferred to various accounts in the Philippines, and this incident resulted in a US$ 100 million loss (World Bank, 2017).

The United States versus Park Jin Hyok case in 2018 allows understanding better how nation-states may be orchestrating attacks against financial institutions. The members of the Lazarus Group, working on behalf of the government of the Democratic People's Republic of Korea (DPRK or North Korea)—commonly referred to as North Korea—, defrauded the Central Bank of Bangladesh. This case demonstrated how this group gained access to banking systems from financial institutions located in Vietnam, the Philippines, Africa, Asia, Europe, and North America between 2015 and 2018 to commit significant wire frauds (United States District Court for the Central District of California, 2018). The hackers used social engineering techniques and spear-phishing emails to lure banking employees in breaching their employer's network security (United States District Court for the Central District of California, 2018). The evidence in this case shows these hackers were responsible for authoring the malware used in the May 2017 international ransomware cyberattack named "WannaCry 2.0" that infected computers around the world (Greenberg, 2019; United States District Court for the Central District of California, 2018).

In May 2018, two of the largest Canadian banks, Bank of Montreal (BMO) and the Canadian Imperial Bank of Commerce's (CIBC) Simplii Financial were victims of a cyberattack leading to a data breach in which data from 90,000 customers were stolen (Scuffham, 2018). According to the Bank of Montreal, this attack originated from outside of the country and the hackers threatened the banks to release the data publicly (Scuffham, 2018). The hackers requested a CAD$777,000 ransom from each bank to be paid for not releasing the data and this ransom was payable through the cryptocurrency system Ripple's XRP token (Schwartz, 2018). Clients reported their funds were fraudulently stolen from their bank accounts and transferred electronically to another bank

(Alini, 2018). In similar incidents, criminals rely on well-crafted schemes to divert funds through electronic transfers in a short period of time which makes it very difficult for financial institutions to detect and block these transactions. Both BMO and CIBC confirmed they were actively working with law enforcement to investigate this cyberattack (Ligaya, 2018).

In 2018 alone, a total of seven banks were attacked using international money transfer schemes such as SWIFT; the State Bank of Mauritius, Bank Islami in Pakistan, Cosmos Cooperative Bank in India, Banco de Chile, as well as three Mexican banks. In February 2019, the bank of Valletta, located in the Republic of Malta, was the victim of a cyber-heist forcing the bank to temporarily shut down all its operations after it identified the breach (Muncaster, 2019). The bank discovered fraudulent electronic transactions were made by the hackers using international money transfers totaling €13 million (Corfield, 2019).

According to Nish and Naumann (2019), central banks, commercial banks, and financial institutions in developing nations are particularly vulnerable to cyberattacks since they have less mature cybersecurity systems in place, and attackers know they can exploit vulnerabilities in these banks that they are unable to get with top-tier banks in other regions of the world who spend millions of dollars to replace legacy infrastructure and to improve the security of their systems (Nish & Naumann, 2019).

Cyberattackers may attack a bank in South Asia, and minutes later, the same type of attack may happen against another bank in West Africa. One of the bank's systems may be used to send money transfer instructions to wire funds to bank accounts under the control of the attackers. Once the transfers are made, money mules will attempt to withdraw funds as fast as possible once the clearing process of the transactions has been completed by the bank receiving the funds (Nish & Naumann, 2019). Therefore, to prevent these fraudulent transactions, the targeted bank must have the ability to identify fraudulent transactions perpetrated by the attackers and notify the receiving banks to allow them to block the accounts. If the targeted bank is unable to do so, counterparty banks need to be able to identify potential fraudulent messages and raise the alarm to block funds before money mules can withdraw the money (Nish & Naumann, 2019).

Nish and Naumann (2019) argue that three trends emerged since the cyberattacks against banks in 2016; (a) attackers have increased their technical capabilities to attack core banking systems and payment systems, (b) attackers are more aggressive in taking advantage of victim's ability to respond in real-time (e.g., attacks began with distributed denial of service in 2011–2012 escalading to using wiper malware; a self-propagating destructive malware in 2018), and (c) cybercriminals continue to collaborate with criminal organizations located in different countries around the world which makes it very difficult for law enforcement to prosecute these crimes on a global scale (Nish & Naumann, 2019).

In his research on Russian banks, Baulin (2019) claims hackers do target the financial sector on a regular basis. The author argues that 74% of banks were not ready for cyberattacks, and 29% were infected with malware (Baulin, 2019). For Baulin (2019), the most dangerous trends of the past year are what he referred to as the "cross-border domino effect cyberattacks," in which the infected infrastructure of a compromised bank is used to spread the infection further to other banks in the ecosystem. For example, if hackers can compromise the email of a banking employee, emails requesting or confirming wire transfer information will be sent from a legitimate bank, the sender identity is valid, which increases the probability of the recipient to open a malicious attachment (Baulin, 2019). Thus, as Baulin (2019) explains, a chain reaction may be started, and this can lead to multiple financial institutions being compromised from a single incident (Baulin, 2019). In some instances, the stolen funds were withdrawn using payment cards pre-opened in a targeted bank, dummy law firm accounts, payment systems, automatic teller machine (ATM) and SIM cards (Baulin, 2019). By taking control over a bank's systems, hackers aim to withdraw money from a compromised bank, but also to infect as many new victims as possible (Baulin, 2019).

Cyberattacks on banks may create a negative image, leading to reputational damage and in some cases bank's departure from the market as smaller banks may have fewer cybersecurity resources to be able to protect itself against cyberattacks (Baulin, 2019; Musiał, 2019). Ilascu (2019) describes that in some Russian bank attacks, the attacker sent phishing emails to another bank in Kazakhstan to lure employees to click on a malicious email and to infect the bank's system. Then, the cybercriminals ran a phishing campaign using the infrastructure of the Kazakh bank to infect another one in Georgia, making it look like the traffic was legitimate as it was coming from a known bank (Ilascu, 2019).

Operation Icarus is another example of cyberattacks against financial institutions. In this case, the group of hacktivists called Anonymous claimed they would organize 30 days of cyber assault against various stock markets and financial institutions around the world (Murdock, 2016). They managed to bring down the website of the bank of Greece using a distributed denial of service (DDOS) attack as well as the bank of Mexico in the same week (Crosman, 2016; Murdock, 2016). Cyberattacks are problematic as banks are interlinked with the SWIFT network and when one bank is under attack, funds from the victimized bank may be transferred in multiple banks across different jurisdictions (Hämmerli, 2012). As criminals perpetrating cybercrime through the Internet (e.g., phishing banking customers) from a country that is different from the country of the victim (individual or the organization), this situation makes it extremely difficult for law enforcement to collaborate with each other across multiple jurisdictions to arrest the perpetrators and to deter others from committing similar crimes (Cross, 2019). In these incidents, the vulnerabilities are not in the SWIFT message system, but the banks internal processes to identify fraudulent customer's transfer requests as these same customers might have been victims of social engineering or phishing attacks, or the bank's infrastructure might have been compromised through a mistake by a bank employee inadvertently providing his login credentials to the hackers (Bergin & Layne, 2016; Pomerleau & Auger-Perreault, 2020).

Besides, governments and private companies face multiple threats like advanced persistent threats (APT), botnets, code injections, data breaches, data leakage, distributed denial-of-service (DDoS), email viral attachments, logic bomb, identity theft, fraud, man-in-the-middle attack, ransomware, and many others (Akhgar & Brewster, 2016). For instance, business email compromise is a significant problem for financial institutions as employees and customer's emails may be used to commit fraud. Business email compromise is an advanced type of attack that leverages identity deception through phishing schemes to use financial institution's employees or its customers to make fraudulent payment requests (Agari, 2018). For instance, the London Blue is a criminal organization working from Nigeria, the United Kingdom, and the United States that is targeting financial institutions through various fraudulent tactics to get access to legitimate credentials to commit fraud (Agari, 2018). Another type of cyber incidents affecting financial institutions is the hacking of automated teller machines (ATM) using malware or the hacking of financial institutions systems to remove the maximum withdrawal limits or credit or prepaid cards (Pilieci, 2018). According to Volkov (2018), some of the cybercriminals working for gangs were at some point active members of the security community employed by private firms as penetration testers or reverse engineers.

In their study, Paoli, Visschers, and Verstraete (2018) claim there are five types of cybercrime affecting businesses; illegal access to IT systems, cyber espionage, data or system interference, cyber extortion or Internet fraud (Paoli et al., 2018). Domovic (2017) argues that the most significant threats are zero-day attacks, exploits or malware that remain latent in the system for a very long period before being detected and that even when organizations have proper physical and cyber detection systems in place, social engineering tactics can be used against employees and contractors to by-pass the security controls. Closely aligned with Domovic's (2017) findings, the Ponemon Institute's (2018) survey results demonstrated that the mean time for organizations to identify an incident was 197 days and the mean time to contain it appropriately was 69 days.

Ozkaya and Aslaner (2019) claim that in average, it takes 23 days for an organization to recover from a ransomware attack while it takes an average of 50 days to recover from an insider threat incident. A recent example of the impacts of a malicious employee working for a financial institution occurred at Desjardins Group—largest credit union in Canada—when one of their employees stole the information of 2.7 million customers and 173,000 businesses account information leading to potential identity theft victimization in the future (Montpetit, 2019). In November 2019, Desjardins Group confirmed the breach was wider in scope and affecting 4.2 million of its banking customers (Laframboise, 2019). Later in December, the organization announced the breach was even more important than previously mentioned as Desjardins Group confirmed that the same breach also included the data of 1.8 million of its credit card customers (Laframboise, 2019). As written by Christensen (2018), managing the visibilities of cybersecurity incidents requires knowledge about the occurrence of an incident and the detection of these incidents is rarely straightforward due to the complexity of the systems in place.

Most of these cyber-related crimes committed against private companies have been analyzed as well by Smith, Smith, and Smith (2011), and these authors estimate the cost of a four-year period to show a significant increase in losses. The authors also describe the effects of hacking on the company stock price for companies that have been victimized like

Amazon, eBay, JP Morgan Chase, and on its reputation after the incident went public (Smith et al., 2011). They assert there was a significant stock price reduction right after the incident was reported publicly (one company lost 9%) and even though it lasted for a short period (between 0 and 3 days), they conclude this type of crime sets back the reputation of the enterprise, thus creating a negative impact on the shareholder value (Smith et al., 2011).

Kenney (2015) refers to hacktivism when the purpose of the cyberattack is to draw attention to a cause and to get publicity for the disruptions of a selected set of targets and not necessarily for profit-making as cybercrime. For this author, cyber-terrorism is a form of "digital politics" carried by non-state actors for various reasons. Some of these reasons are for political, social, or religious causes (Kenney, 2015). Kenney (2015) goes on to explain that in order to be categorized as cyber-terrorism, the attack needs to cause enough physical harm or violence to instigate fear and intimidation to the general population or more people than the direct victims of the incident (Kenney, 2015). This definition of cyber-terrorism is similar to the one provided by Rudner (2013):

> Cyber-terrorism denotes the use of Web-based information technology to conduct enabling, disruptive, or destructive operations in the digital domain to create and exploit fear through violence or the threat of violence at the behest of a militant belief system. (Rudner, 2013, p. 455)

Cyber warfare is a term used to refer to offensive computer assaults to damage, destroy or deter the enemy's infrastructures and networks (Kenney, 2015). Cyber-terrorism and cyber-warfare differ from cybercrime. For example, cyber-terrorism is done to instigate fear in a population; cyber warfare is when two nations attack each other, and cybercrime is committed to gain an economic advantage on the victims.

However, as Rid (2017) states, even though cyberattacks increased in numbers and some attacks reached new heights, no cyberattacks would qualify as an act of war per its original definition in its use of force. For this author, if an act of war is defined as being a violent, instrumental, and a political act, there is no cyber offense to this date that would meet all three criteria (Rid, 2017).

Johnson (2015) claims there is no universally adopted definition for cyber-incident, cybercrime, and cyberattack. For the author, a cyber-incident is an illegal action enabling a technology used to access proprietary information, system or infrastructure to read, manipulate or extract confidential or sensitive information (Johnson, 2015).

Many scholars focused on the extent to which offenders committing cybercrimes are involved or not in organized crime groups, the nature of the relationship between cybercriminals and the way they collaborate in an online environment. Even if criminal networks engaged in cybercrime demonstrate certain characteristics of organized crime groups, many scholars concluded that cybercrime does not correspond to the actual organized crime or Mafia definition (Lusthaus, 2018). Moreover, according to Dixon (2019), there is not much deterrence for hackers as the chances of being investigated and prosecuted for a cyberattack in the United States is estimated at five percent while for violent crime, the probability is forty-six percent. As explained by Cunningham (2020), the main goal of hackers is not only to gain access to a system, it is to be in a position to dive deeper into a network in order to find areas for future operations in what he referred to "cross-domain maneuverability."

Lusthaus (2018) conducted 238 interviews with law enforcement and private sector professionals, former cybercriminals and subject matter experts from seven countries. The author demonstrates that cybercrime evolved into a sophisticated and profit-oriented industry. However, even if the organized crime may play a role in cybercrime, there was no empirical evidence showing that cybercrime firms exhibited the same characteristics of traditional organized groups since cybercrime groups tend to operate in small groups (Lusthaus, 2018). Cybercriminals are technical, do not use violence, they generally do not steal money from each other, and they don't need any protection from other criminals (Lusthaus, 2018).

Besides, other scholars came to a similar conclusion in confirming that cybercrime is not dominated by organized crime groups (Broadhurst, Grabosky, Alazab, and Chon, (2014), Lavorgna and Sergi (2016), Leukfeldt, Lavorgna, and Kleemans (2017), and Lusthaus (2013). However, Hutchings (2014) claims the results of her study indicates that computer crime offenders are "highly networked" criminals who collaborate to commit online offenses as the online environment facilitates cooffending and organized crime.

As illustrated by Lusthaus (2018), there is a fine line between the definition of cybercrime and what is defined as an organized crime. The data gathered by Lusthaus (2018) shows that cybercrime groups organizational structures are entirely different than traditional organized crime structures. Lusthaus (2018) advances that an important distinction is necessary to explain the difference between structured cybercrime networks and traditional organized crime. The use of technology plays a central role in the commission of cybercrime compared to other forms of crimes as cybercrime requires technical skills. Organized crime structures might use cybercrime experts to commit different types of crime. Despite these differences between cyber-enabled and cyber-dependent crime, Lusthaus (2018) defines cybercrime as "the use of computers or other electronic devices via information systems such as organizational networks or the Internet to facilitate illegal behaviors" (p. 8).

In most of the recent high-profile cyberattacks on private companies and critical government infrastructures, it was difficult to attribute responsibility to a group of criminals or nations to apprehend the perpetrators or to hold countries accountable for their actions (Akhgar & Brewster, 2016). Most organization's cybercrime and cybersecurity intrusion detection systems do not prevent breaches against tactical skills, funding, technological resources, and political wills of cyber adversaries (Akhgar & Brewster, 2016). Mandala (2016) provides an overview of cybercrime and cyberterrorism. The author discusses issues related to the lack of availability of cybercrime data. He focuses on how cybercrime can be prevented and how advanced technology can play a significant role for cybercriminals to disseminate their information. The author concludes that until law enforcement improves their awareness of this crime and has an adequate picture of the reality, it will not be possible to solve this issue (Mandala, 2016). McCreight and Leece (2016) provide a series of recommendations for companies and governments to improve cybersecurity in taking into consideration the convergence of physical and IT risks in managing cyber-related incidents by referring to the ASIS International Information Technology Security Council six recommendations. They conclude that having a distinct network for physical security is now obsolete and organizations need to take into consideration the convergence of risks from physical security and the IT ecosystem (McCreight & Leece, 2016).

There is an international agreement between countries to combat cybercrime. The Budapest Convention includes provisions providing international cooperation for all criminal cases related to computer systems and data (Wanca, 2014). Countries that have signed the Convention are required to have criminalized crimes like child pornography, illegal access, data interference, and other types of criminal activities (Wanca, 2014). Canada signed this Convention and is part of this agreement between Nations.

Gendron and Rudner (2012) conducted a study for the Canadian Security Intelligence Service on the assessment of cyber threats to Canadian infrastructures. The authors held the major threats to Canada against critical infrastructures are international terrorism, state-sponsored espionage or sabotage, and hacktivism (Gendron & Rudner, 2012). Gendron and Rudner (2012) claim that existing defensive measures in place would not be sufficient to maintain the integrity and the availability of Canadian information systems and preventing attacks on the critical infrastructures of the country (Gendron & Rudner, 2012). The country's dependency on digital networks, its reliance on Internet-based communication, advanced industries, strong international relationships, and its open society makes it an attractive target for cyberattacks as a mean to steal its intellectual property as well as for industrial espionage (Gendron & Rudner, 2012). The authors state many cyberattacks had been identified to originate from hackers working for China and Russia's governments (Gendron & Rudner, 2012).

For instance, some of the criminal groups attacking banks are Cobalt, Money Taker, Silence (Russian-speaking hackers) and Lazarus which is a North Korean group (Group-IB, 2018a). In previous attacks orchestrated by the Silence group, the criminal organization had access to nonpublic malware samples, patched Trojans that are usually only available to security experts, which shows that they probably had assistance from individuals working at legitimate security firms (Group-IB, 2018b). If hackers could have access to critical infrastructures computer-controlled operating systems, it would be a significant threat to national security; it could potentially lead to the exposure of confidential government files and the loss of confidence in government, causing social chaos or turmoil to our democratic way of living (Gendron & Rudner, 2012; Leuprecht, 2019; Rogers, 2016).

Recent statistics on losses produced by the Ponemon Institute (2018) show that a single breach incident of 1 million records represents an average cost of US$40 million per organization and that a breach of 50 million records has an average loss of US$350 million for victimized companies. When estimating the impact of cybercrime financial losses, Paoli et al. (2018) came to a different conclusion than the results from consulting firms and nonprofit organizations in their research on Belgium cyber-incidents. Cybercrime may lead to varying harms for private organizations such as reputational risks, but in their study, most of the private organizations that suffered serious cyber incidents did not incur considerable financial losses. Large and medium-size organizations were affected more frequently than small organizations, but the victimized organizations did not generate significant losses (Paoli et al., 2018). For example, for all illegal accesses to the networks of the firms participating in this research (Revenue lost as a result of the cyber incidents suffered), 72.4% reported having no losses, 14.6% reported a loss category between 1 and 9999 euros while 9.8% did not know if they experienced any financial losses (Paoli et al., 2018). These authors claim that approximately 5–10% of the victimized businesses experienced serious or grave harm to the services provided to its customers, the business reputation and the privacy of the information they were accountable to protect (Paoli, Visschers, & Verstraete, 2018). Ganan, Ciere, and Eeten (2017) concluded statistics about cyber-incidents often lead to unreliable results since this data is based on self-reported data or survey with participants that are unable to estimate the direct or indirect cost of cyberattacks accurately.

Financial sector organizations are highly affected by cybercrime, and this industry, like many others, underreports these crimes to law enforcement mainly to avoid reputational risk and potential market share negative impacts (Lagazio, Sherif, & Cushman, 2014). Lagazio et al. (2014) confirm that the cost of cybercrime is not only influenced by the number of incidents experienced by the financial sector; the cost varies depending on the way financial services companies decide to protect their business interests in investing in security to protect their market positions. The potential loss of customer's trust and loyalty are also significant determining factors for financial services companies in determining the trust cost of cybercrime (Lagazio et al., 2014).

Many scholars argue that internal and external human factors are often ignored while analyzing cyber-incidents (Ayereby, 2018; Jaf et al., 2018; Leukfeldt, 2017). The human behavior is directly associated with the role of individuals in the system's attacks and data breaches (Ayereby, 2018; Jaf et al., 2018; Leukfeldt, 2017). Employees are often the "weakest link" (Leukfeldt, 2017) as they may contribute to internal or external data breaches or the compromise of information systems by clicking on a malicious email link, becoming the victims of social engineering ploys, or by making mistakes as part of their employment (Pomerleau & Auger-Perreault, 2020). These actions allow external attackers to exploit human's weaknesses to get access to the internal systems through flaws or by exploiting unknown vulnerabilities in the organization's infrastructure. As mentioned by Ayereby (2018), these incidents represent a significant portion of the vulnerabilities leading to cyberattacks.

References

Agari. (2018). *London Blue: UK-based multinational gang runs BEC scams like a modern corporation*. Retrieved from https://www.agari.com/cyber-intelligence-research/whitepapers/london-blue-report.pdf.

Akhgar, B., & Brewster, B. (2016). *Combatting cybercrime and cyberterrorism: Challenges, trends, and priorities*. Cham, Switzerland: Springer.

Alini, E. (2018). *BMO, Simplii attack: Canadians describe illicit e-transfers out of Simplii accounts*. Retrieved from https://globalnews.ca/news/4236852/bmo-simplii-attack-canadians-describe-illicit-interac-e-transfers-out-of-simplii-accounts/.

Ayereby, M. P. (2018). *Overcoming data breaches and human factors in minimizing threats to cyber-security ecosystems* (Order No. 13425430). Available from ProQuest Dissertations & Theses Global (2164781286). Retrieved from http://search.proquest.com.proxy1.ncu.edu/docview/2164781286?accountid=28180.

Barbalet, J. (2009). A characterization of trust, and its consequences. *Theory and Society, 38*(4), 367–382. Retrieved from https://link.springer.com/article/10.1007/s11186-009-9087-3.

Baulin, V. (2019). *Group-IB: More than 70% of Russian banks are not ready for cyberattacks*. Retrieved from https://www.group-ib.com/media/banks-readiness/.

Bergin, T., & Layne, N. (2016). *Special report: Cyber thieves exploit banks faith in SWIFT transfer network*. Retrieved from https://www.reuters.com/article/us-cyber-heist-swift-specialreport/special-report-cyber-thieves-exploit-banks-faith-in-swift-transfer-network-idUSKCN0YB0DD.

Boes, S., & Leukfeldt, E. R. (2017). Fighting cybercrime: A joint effort. *Cyber-physical security*, 185. Retrieved from https://www.researchgate.net/publication/306035727_Fighting_Cybercrime_A_Joint_Effort.

Borghard, D. E. (2018). *Protecting financial institutions against cyber threats: A national security issue*. Retrieved from https://carnegieendowment.org/files/WP_Borghard_Financial_Cyber_formatted_complete.pdf.

Bossong, R., & Wagner, B. (2017). A typology of cybersecurity and public-private partnerships in the context of the EU. *Crime, Law & Social Change, 67*(3), 265–288. https://doi.org/10.1007/s10611-016-9653-3.

Bouveret, A. (2018). *Cyber risk for the financial sector: A framework for quantitative assessment*. Retrieved from https://www.imf.org/en/Publications/WP/Issues/2018/06/22/Cyber-Risk-for-the-Financial-Sector-A-Framework-for-Quantitative-Assessment-45924.

Brewer, R. (2013). Enhancing crime control partnerships across government: Examining the role of trust and social capital on American and Australian waterfronts. *Police Quarterly, 16*(4), 371–394. Retrieved from http://journals.sagepub.com/doi/abs/10.1177/1098611113488115?journalCode=pqxa.

Brewer, R. (2017). The malleable character of brokerage and crime control: a study of policing, security and network entrepreneurialism on Melbourne's waterfront. *Policing & Society, 27*(7), 712–731. Retrieved from https://www.tandfonline.com/doi/full/10.1080/10439463.2015.1051047?scroll=top&needAccess=true.

Broadhurst, R., Grabosky, P., Alazab, M., & Chon, S. (2014). Organizations and cybercrime: An analysis of the nature of groups engaged in cybercrime. *International Journal of Cyber Criminology, 8*(1), 1. Retrieved from http://proxy1.ncu.edu/login?url=https://search.ebscohost.com/login.aspx?direct=true&db=edo&AN=97333470&site=eds-live.

Bures, O. (2013). Public-private partnerships in the fight against terrorism? *Crime, Law & Social Change, 60*(4), 429–455. https://doi.org/10.1007/s10611-013-9457-7.

Buzan, B., Wawever, O., & De Wilde, J. (1998). *Security: A new framework for analysis*. Retrieved from https://www.amazon.ca/Security-Framework-Analysis-Barry-Buzan/dp/1555877842/ref=sr_1_1?s=books&ie=UTF8&qid=1542036275&sr=1-1&keywords=security+a+new+framework+for+analysis.

Carr, M. (2016). Public-private partnerships in national cyber-security strategies. *International Affairs, 92*(1), 43–62. https://doi.org/10.1111/1468-2346.12504.

Carter, W. (2017). *Forces shaping the cyber threat landscape for financial institutions*. Retrieved from https://papers.ssrn.com/sol3/papers.cfm?abstract_id=3047730.

Choucri, N. (2012). *Cyberpolitics in international relations*. Cambridge: MIT Press.

Christensen, K. K. (2018). *Corporate zones of cyber security* (Doctoral dissertation). Retrieved from https://www.saxo.com/dk/corporate-zones-of-cyber-security_kristoffer-kjaergaard-christensen_pdf_9788772091402.

Christensen, K. K., & Petersen, K. (2017). Public-private partnerships on cyber security: A practice of loyalty. *International Affairs, 93*(6), 1435–1452. https://doi.org/10.1093/ia/iix189.

Cimpanu, C. (2018). *Hackers crashed a bank's computer while attempting a SWIFT hack*. Retrieved from https://www.bleepingcomputer.com/news/security/hackers-crashed-a-bank-s-computers-while-attempting-a-swift-hack/.

Collier, J. (2018). Cybersecurity assemblages: A framework for understanding the dynamic and contested nature of security provision. *Politics & Governance, 6*(2), 13–21. https://doi.org/10.17645/pag.v6i2.1324.

Collins, A. (2016). *Contemporary security studies*. Retrieved from https://www.amazon.com/Contemporary-Security-Studies-Alan-Collins/dp/0198708319/ref=sr_1_1?s=books&ie=UTF8&qid=1542036106&sr=1-1&keywords=contemporary+security+studies.

Communications Security Establishment. (2018). *Canadian centre for cyber security; National cyber threat assessment 2018*. Retrieved from https://cyber.gc.ca/sites/default/files/publications/national-cyber-threat-assessment-2018-e_1.pdf.

Corfield, G. (2019). *Hackers KO Malta's bank of Valletta in attempt to nick €13m*. Retrieved from https://www.theregister.co.uk/2019/02/13/bank_of_valletta_13m_euro_hackers_shutdown/.

Costantini, L. P. (2016). *Perceptions of trust in public-private partnerships for critical infrastructure protection - implications for civil security, leadership, policy, and management* (Order No. 10259626). Available from ProQuest Dissertations & Theses Global (1882247286). Retrieved from http://search.proquest.com.proxy1.ncu.edu/docview/1882247286?accountid=28180.

Crosman, P. (2016). *The real threat Anonymous poses to banks*. Retrieved from https://www.americanbanker.com/news/the-real-threat-anonymous-poses-to-banks.

Cross, C. (2019). 'Oh we can't actually do anything about that': The problematic nature of jurisdiction for online fraud victims. *Criminology & Criminal Justice*. https://doi.org/10.1177/1748895819835910.

Cunningham, C. (2020). *Cyber warfare—Truth, tactics, and strategies*. Retrieved from https://www.amazon.ca/-/fr/Dr-Chase-Cunningham-ebook/dp/B084ZN2HBD/ref=sr_1_1?__mk_fr_CA=%C3%85M%C3%85%C5%BD%C3%95%C3%91&keywords=cyber+warfare+truth+tactics+and+strategies&qid=1586915567&s=books&sr=1-1.

Dixon, W. (2019). *Fighting cybercrime—What happens to the law when the law cannot be enforced?* Retrieved from https://www.weforum.org/agenda/2019/02/fighting-cybercrime-what-happens-to-the-law-when-the-law-cannot-be-enforced/.

Domovic, R. (2017). *Cyber-attacks as a threat to critical infrastructure*. Retrieved from https://www.researchgate.net/publication/321344653_Cyber-attacks_as_a_threat_to_critical_infrastructure.

Dunn-Cavelty, M., & Suter, M. (2009). Public-private partnerships are no silver bullet: An expanded governance model for critical infrastructure protection. *International Journal of Critical Infrastructure Protection, 2,* 179–187. https://doi.org/10.1016/j.ijcip.2009.08.006.

Dupont, B. (2004). Security in the age of networks. *Policing & Society, 14*(1), 76. https://doi.org/10.1080/1043946042000181575.

Dupré, L. (2014). *EP3R 2010-2013: Four years of Pan-European public-private cooperation*. Heraklion, Greece: European Union Agency for Network Information Security. Retrieved from https://www.researchgate.net/publication/270592099_EP3R_2010-2013_-_Four_Years_of_Pan-European_Public_Private_Cooperation.

Etzioni, A. (2017). The fusion of the private and public sectors. *Contemporary Politics, 23*(1), 53–62. https://doi-org.proxy1.ncu.edu/10.1080/13569775.2016.1213074.

Fleming, H. M., & Goldstein, E. (2012). *Metrics for measuring the efficacy of critical-infrastructure-centric cybersecurity information sharing efforts*. Retrieved from https://www.researchgate.net/publication/251348625_Metrics_for_Measuring_the_Efficacy_of_Critical-Infrastructure-Centric_Cybersecurity_Information_Sharing_Efforts.

Ganan, H. C., Ciere, M., & Eeten, V. M. (2017). *Beyond the pretty penny; The economic impact of cybercrime*. Retrieved from https://dl.acm.org/citation.cfm?id=3171535.

Garcia, M., Forscey, D., & Blute, T. (2017). Beyond the network: A holistic perspective on state cybersecurity governance. *Nebraska Law Review, 96*(2), 252. Retrieved from https://digitalcommons.unl.edu/cgi/viewcontent.cgi?article=3116&context=nlr.

Gendron, A., & Rudner, M. (2012). *Assessing cyber threats to Canadian infrastructures*. Report prepared for the Canadian Security Intelligence Service. Retrieved from https://www.csis.gc.ca/pblctns/ccsnlpprs/20121001_ccsnlpprs-en.php.

Germano, H. J. (2014). *Cybersecurity partnerships: A new era of public-private collaboration*. New York, NY: The Center on Law and Security, New York University School of Law. Retrieved from https://www.lawandsecurity.org/wp-content/uploads/2016/08/Cybersecurity.Partnerships-1.pdf.

Gerspacher, N., & Dupont, B. (2007). The nodal structure of international police cooperation: An exploration of transnational security networks. *Global Governance, 13*(3), 347–364. Retrieved from https://www.researchgate.net/publication/261776013_The_Nodal_Structure_of_International_Police_Cooperation_An_Exploration_of_Transnational_Security_Networks.

Givens, D. A., & Busch, E. N. (2013). Realizing the promise of public-private partnerships in U.S. critical infrastructure protection. *International Journal of Critical Infrastructure Protection*, *6*, 39–650. https://doi.org/10.1016/j.ijcip.2013.02.002.

Gordon, W. R. (2018). Information sharing and collaboration. In A. K. Sood (Ed.), *Canadian cybersecurity 2018: An anthology of CIO/CISO enterprise-level perspectives* (pp. 107–128). Retrieved from https://issuu.com/clxforum/docs/canadian-cybersecurity_2018.

Greenberg, A. (2019). *Sandworm: A new era of cyberwar and the hunt for the Kremlin's most dangerous hackers*. Retrieved from https://www.amazon.com/Sandworm-Cyberwar-Kremlins-Dangerous-Hackers/dp/B07RGRTZM6/ref=sr_1_1?dchild=1&keywords=Sandworm%3B+A+new+era+of+cyberwar+and+the+hunt+for+the+Kremlin%E2%80%99s+most+dangerous+hackers&qid=1586827484&s=books&sr=1-1.

Greiman, V. (2015). *Public-private partnerships in cyberspace: Building a sustainable collaboration*. Paper presented at the Proceedings of the 10th International Conference on Cyber Warfare and Security, ICCWS 2015. Retrieved from https://www.jinfowar.com/journal/volume-14-issue-3/publicprivate-partnerships-cyberspace-building-sustainable.

Group-IB. (2018a). *Hi-tech crime trends 2018*. Retrieved from https://www.group-ib.com/resources/threat-research.html.

Group-IB. (2018b). *Silence: Moving into the darkside*. Retrieved from https://www.group-ib.com/resources/threat-research.html.

Hämmerli, B. (2012). Financial service industry. In J. Lopez, R. Setola, & S. D, Wolthusen (Eds.), *Critical infrastructure protection: Information infrastructure models, analysis, and defense* (pp. 301–329). Retrieved from https://link.springer.com/chapter/10.1007/978-3-642-28920-0_13.

Heldeweg, A. M., & Sanders, T. P. M. (2014). Towards a design framework for legitimate public-private partnerships: A general approach applied to innovative renewable energy infrastructures. *European Procurement & Public Private Partnership Law Review*, *9*(3), 187–201. Retrieved from https://pdfs.semanticscholar.org/a29e/150c4635493cf5a40345501c94be86b4e7f7.pdf.

Hoganson, C. (2014). *Bridging the gaps: Voices from the private sector on counter-terrorism*. The Conference Board of Canada, Ottawa. Retrieved from https://conferenceboard.ca/(X(1)S(afa5xtbs5ztfbgbzchvx0hbn))/e-library/abstract.aspx?did=6112.

Holt, J. T. (2018). Regulating cybercrime through law enforcement and industry mechanisms. *Annals of the American Academy of Political and Social Science*, *679*(1), 140–157. https://doi-org.proxy1.ncu.edu/10.1177/0002716218783679.

Hutchings, A. (2014). Crime from the keyboard: Organized cybercrime, co-offending, initiation and knowledge transmission. *Crime and Law and Social Change, 62*(1), 1–20. https://doi.org/10.1007/s10611-014-9520-z.

Ilascu, I. (2019). *Hackers use compromised banks as starting points for phishing attacks*. Retrieved from https://www.bleepingcomputer.com/news/security/hackers-use-compromised-banks-as-starting-points-for-phishing-attacks/.

International Centre for the Prevention of Crime. (2018). *6th International Report on Crime Prevention and Community Safety: Preventing Cybercrime*. Retrieved from http://www.crime-prevention-intl.org/en/publications/report/report/article/6th-international-report-on-crime-prevention-and-community-safety-preventing-cybercrime.html.

Jaf, S., Ghafir, I., Prenosil, V., Saleem, J., Hammoudeh, M., Faour, H., & Baker, T. (2018). Security threats to critical infrastructure: The human factor. *Journal of Supercomputing, 74*(10), 4986–5002. https://doi-org.proxy1.ncu.edu/10.1007/s11227-018-2337-2.

Johnson, N. K. (2015). Cyber risks: Emerging risk management concerns for financial institutions. *Georgia Law Review, 50*(1), 131–211. Retrieved from https://papers.ssrn.com/sol3/papers.cfm?abstract_id=2847191.

Johnson, A. L. (2016). Cybersecurity for financial institutions: The integral role of information sharing in cyber-attack mitigation. *North Carolina Banking Institute, 20*, 277. Retrieved from http://scholarship.law.unc.edu/cgi/viewcontent.cgi?article=1400&context=ncbi.

Johnson, C., Badger, L., Waltermire, D., Snyder, J., & Skorupka, C. (2016). *NIST special publication 800-150; Guide to cyber threat information sharing*. Retrieved from http://dx.doi.org/10.6028/NIST.SP.800-150.

Kaijankoski, A. E. (2015). *Cybersecurity information sharing between public-private sector agencies*. (Master thesis). Retrieved from https://apps.dtic.mil/dtic/tr/fulltext/u2/a620766.pdf.

Kenney, M. (2015). Cyber-terrorism in a post-Stuxnet world. *Orbis, 59*, 111–128. https://doi.org/10.1016/j.orbis.2014.11.009.

Kolini, F., & Janczewski, L. (2017). *Two heads are better than one: A theoretical model for cybersecurity intelligence sharing (CIS) between organisations*. Retrieved from https://www.acis2017.org/wp-content/uploads/2017/11/ACIS2017_paper_199_RIP.pdf.

Kumar, A. (2006). *The development of homeland security partnerships: A comparative analysis from the financial security arena* (Order No. 3243932). Available from ProQuest Dissertations & Theses Global (305353348). Retrieved from http://search.proquest.com.proxy1.ncu.edu/docview/305353348?accountid=28180.

Kunnel, A., & Quandt, T. (2016). Relational trust and distrust: Ingredients of face-to-face and media-based communication. In B. Blöbaum (Ed.), *Trust and communication in a digitized world: Models and concepts of trust*

research (pp. 27–49). Cham: Springer. https://doi-org.proxy1.ncu.edu/10.1007/978-3-319-28059-2pass:[_]2.
Laframboise, K. (2019). *Desjardins credit card holders also affected by massive data breach*. Retrieved from https://globalnews.ca/news/6278790/desjardins-data-breach-credit-cards/.
Lagazio, M., Sherif, N., & Cushman, M. (2014). A multi-level approach to understanding the impact of cybercrime on the financial sector. *Computers & Security, 45*, 58–74. https://doi.org/10.1016/j.cose.2014.05.006.
Laughlin, C. (2016). Cybersecurity in critical infrastructure sectors: A proactive approach to ensure inevitable laws and regulations are effective. *Colorado Technology Journal, 2*, 345. Retrieved from https://ctlj.colorado.edu/wp-content/uploads/2016/06/v3.final-Laughlin-4.26.16-JRD.pdf.
Lavorgna, A., & Sergi, A. (2016). Serious, therefore organised? A critique of the emerging "Cyber-Organised Crime" rhetoric in the United Kingdom. *International Journal of Cyber Criminology, 10*(2), 170–187. https://doi-org.proxy1.ncu.edu/10.5281/zenodo.163400.
Leukfeldt, R. (2017). *Research agenda: The human factor in cybercrime and cybersecurity*. Retrieved from https://www.amazon.com/Research-Agenda-Factor-Cybercrime-Cybersecurity/dp/9462367531.
Leukfeldt, E., Lavorgna, A., & Kleemans, E. (2017). Organised cybercrime or cybercrime that is organised? An assessment of the conceptualisation of financial cybercrime as organised crime. *European Journal on Criminal Policy & Research, 23*(3), 287. https://doi.org/10.1007/s10610-016-9332-z.
Leuprecht, C. (2019). *Mitigating cyber risk across the financial sector*. Retrieved from https://www.cigionline.org/articles/mitigating-cyber-risk-across-financial-sector.
Ligaya, A. (2018). *CIBC's Simplii and BMO investigating hacks that may have leaked customer data*. Retrieved from https://toronto.citynews.ca/2018/05/28/hack-cibc-simplii-financial-hack/.
Lusthaus, J. (2013). How organized is organized cybercrime? *Global Crime, 14*(1), 52. Retrieved from https://www.tandfonline.com/doi/abs/10.1080/17440572.2012.759508.
Lusthaus, J. (2018). *Industry of anonymity*. Retrieved from https://www.amazon.ca/Industry-Anonymity-Inside-BusinessCybercrime/dp/0674979419/ref=sr_1_1?s=books&ie=UTF8&qid=1540945343&sr=1-1&keywords=industry+of+anonymity.
Maimon, D., Alper, M., Sobesto, B., & Cukier, M. (2014). Restrictive deterrent effects of a warning banner in an attacked computer system. *Criminology, 52*(1), 33. https://doi.org/10.1111/1745-9125.12028.
Maimon, D., Testa, A., Sobesto, B., Cukier, M., & Wuling, R. (2019). Predictably deterrable? The case of system trespassers. In G. Wang, J. Feng,

M. Bhuiyan, & R. Lu (Eds.), *Security, privacy, and anonymity in computation, communication, and storage*. Cham: Springer.

Mandala, M. (2016). Policing cybercrime and cyberterror. *Security Journal, 29*(3), e13–e15. https://doi-org.proxy1.ncu.edu/10.1057/sj.2015.47.

Manley, M. (2015). Cyberspace's dynamic duo: Forging a cybersecurity public-private partnership. *Journal of Strategic Security, 8*, 85–98. https://doi.org/10.5038/1944-0472.8.3S.1478.

Matthew, J. A., & Cheshire, C. (2018). *A fragmented whole: Cooperation and learning in the practice of information security*. Retrieved from https://www.pch.net/resources/Papers/A_Fragmented_Whole/AFragmentedWhole.pdf.

McCarthy, R. D. (2018). *Privatizing political authority: Cybersecurity, public-private partnerships, and the reproduction of liberal political order*. Retrieved from https://www.cogitatiopress.com/politicsandgovernance/article/viewFile/1335/1335.

McCreight, T., & Leece, D. (2016). Physical security and IT convergence: Managing the cyber-related risks. *Journal of Business Continuity & Emergency Planning, 10*(1), 18–30. Retrieved from https://www.ncbi.nlm.nih.gov/pubmed/27729098.

Mermoud, A. (2019). *Three articles on the behavioral economics of security information sharing: A theoretical framework, an empirical test, and policy recommendations* (Doctoral dissertation). Retrieved from https://serval.unil.ch/search.

Mermoud, A., Keupp, M. M., Ghernaouti, S., & David, P. D. (2017). *Using incentives to foster security information sharing and cooperation: A general theory and application to critical infrastructure protection*. Retrieved from https://link.springer.com/chapter/10.1007/978-3-319-71368-7_13.

Merriam, S. B., & Tisdell, E. J. (2016). *Qualitative research: A guide to design and implementation*. San Francisco, CA: Jossey-Bass.

Mezher, T., El Khatib, S., & Sooriyaarachchi, T. M. (2015). Cyber-attacks on critical infrastructure and potential sustainable development impacts. *International Journal of Cyber Warfare & Terrorism, 5*(3), 1. https://doi.org/10.4018/IJCWT.2015070101.

Montpetit, J. (2019). *Personal data of 2.7 million people leaked from Desjardins*. Retrieved from https://www.cbc.ca/news/canada/montreal/desjardins-data-breach-1.5183297.

Moustakas, C. (1994). *Phenomenological research methods*. Thousand Oaks, CA: Sage.

Muncaster, P. (2019). *Hackers target Maltese bank in €13 m cyber heist*. Retrieved from https://www.infosecurity-magazine.com/news/hackers-target-maltese-bank-in-15m/.

Murdock, J. (2016). *Operation Icarus: Anonymous to attack stock markets and world banks in 30-day cyber assaults*. Retrieved from https://www.ibtimes.co.

uk/operation-icarus-anonymous-attack-stock-markets-world-banks-30-day-cyber-assault-1558196.

Musiał, N. (2019). Cyber risk in financial institutions: A Polish case. In P. Linsley, P. Shrives, & M. Wieczorek-Kosmala (Eds.), *Multiple perspectives in risk and risk management*. Springer Proceedings in Business and Economics. Cham: Springer.

Nish, A., & Naumann, S. (2019). *The cyber threat landscape: Confronting challenges to the financial system*. Retrieved from https://carnegieendowment.org/2019/03/25/cyber-threat-landscape-confronting-challenges-to-financial-system-pub-78506.

O'Donnell, B., & Nesbitt, R. (2016). *Cyber risk and security in Canada*. Retrieved from https://globalriskinstitute.org/publications/cyber-risk-security-canada/.

Ozkaya, E., & Aslaner, M. (2019). *Hands-on cybersecurity for finance*. Retrieved from https://www.packtpub.com/networking-and-servers/hands-cybersecurity-finance.

Paoli, L., Visschers, J., & Verstraete, C. (2018). The impact of cybercrime on businesses: a novel conceptual framework and its application to Belgium. *Crime, Law & Social Change, 70*(4), 397–420. https://doi-org.proxy1.ncu.edu/10.1007/s10611-018-9774-y.

Pilieci, V. (2018). *FBI warns banks about looming cyber-attacks*. Retrieved from https://ottawacitizen.com/news/local-news/fbi-warns-banks-about-looming-cyber-attacks.

Pomerleau, P. L., & Auger-Perreault M. (2020). Fraud risk management: Using fraud analytics to combat external and insider threats. In L. Shapiro & M. H. Maras (Eds.), *Encyclopedia of security and emergency management*. Cham: Springer. Retrieved from https://link.springer.com/referenceworkentry/10.1007/978-3-319-69891-5_296-1.

Ponemon Institute. (2016). Flipping the economics of attacks. Retrieved from https://www.ponemon.org/news-2/70.

Ponemon Institute. (2018). *2018 cost of a data breach study: Global overview*. Retrieved from https://www.ibm.com/security/data-breach.

Public Safety Canada. (2018). *New cybersecurity strategy bolsters cyber safety, innovation, and prosperity*. Retrieved from https://www.canada.ca/en/public-safety-canada/news/2018/06/new-cyber-security-strategy-bolsters-cyber-safety-innovation-and-prosperity.html.

Quigley, K., Bisset, B., & Mills, B. (2017). *Too critical to fail: How Canada manages threats to critical infrastructure*. Retrieved from https://www.amazon.ca/Too-Critical-Fail-Manages-Infrastructure/dp/0773551611/ref=sr_1_1?s=books&ie=UTF8&qid=1548361193&sr=1-1&keywords=too+critical+to+fail.

Rid, T. (2017). *Cyber war will not take place*. Retrieved from https://www.amazon.ca/Cyber-War-Will-Take-Place/dp/0190660716/ref=sr_1_1?s=books&ie=UTF8&qid=1540427356&sr=1-1&keywords=cyberwar+will+not+take+place.

Rightmier, E. J. (2017). *The effect of state-sponsored attacks on the private sector* (Order No. 10273922). Available from ProQuest Dissertations & Theses Global (1894220723). Retrieved from http://search.proquest.com.proxy1.ncu.edu/docview/1894220723?accountid=28180.

Rogers, J. (2016). *Public-private partnerships: A tool for enhancing cybersecurity* (Doctoral dissertation). Retrieved from https://jscholarship.library.jhu.edu/handle/1774.2/40245.

Rosemont, H. (2016). *Public-private security cooperation: From cyber to financial crime*. Retrieved from https://rusi.org/publication/occasional-papers/public%E2%80%93private-security-cooperation-cyber-financial-crime.

Royal Canadian Mounted Police. (2014). *Cybercrime: An overview of incidents and issues in Canada*. Retrieved from http://www.rcmp-grc.gc.ca/en/cybercrime-an-overview-incidents-and-issues-canada.

Rudner, M. (2013). Cyber-threats to critical national infrastructure: An intelligence challenge. *International Journal of Intelligence & Counterintelligence, 26*(3), 453–481. https://doi.org/10.1080/08850607.2013.780552.

Sarre, R., & Prenzler, T. (2011). *Private security and public interest: Exploring private security trends and directions for reform in the new era of plural policing*. Brisbane: Australian Security Industry Association Ltd. Retrieved from http://www.asial.com.au/documents/item/12.

Schwartz, J. M. (2018). *Hackers demand $770, 000 ransom from Canadian banks*. Retrieved from https://www.bankinfosecurity.com/hackers-demand-770000-ransom-from-canadian-banks-a-11050.

Scuffham, M. (2018). *Cyber crook claim to hit two Canadian banks*. Retrieved from https://ca.reuters.com/article/technologyNews/idCAKCN1IT1PQ-OCATC.

Sedenberg, M. E., & Dempsey, X. J. (2018). *Cybersecurity information sharing governance structures: An ecosystem of diversity, trust, and tradeoffs*. Retrieved from https://arxiv.org/abs/1805.12266.

Shackelford, S. J. (2013). Toward cyberpeace: Managing cyberattacks through polycentric governance. *American University Law Review 62*(5), 1273–1364. Retrieved from https://papers.ssrn.com/sol3/papers.cfm?abstract_id=2132526.

Singh, P., Singh, P., Park, I., Lee, J., & Rao, H. R. (2009). *Information sharing: A study of information attributes and their relative significance during catastrophic events*. Retrieved from https://www.researchgate.net/publication/228689425_Information_sharing_A_study_of_information_attributes_and_their_relative_significance_during_catastrophic_events.

Smith, K. T., Smith, L. M., & Smith, J. L. (2011). Case studies of cybercrime and their impact on marketing activity and shareholder value. *Academy of Marketing Studies Journal, 15*(2), 67–81. Retrieved from https://www.abacademies.org/journals/academy-of-marketing-studies-journal-home.html.

Stevens, T. (2016). *Cyber security and the politics of time*. Retrieved from https://www.amazon.ca/Cyber-Security-Politics-Time-Stevens/dp/1107109426.

Stevens, T. (2018). Global cybersecurity: New directions in theory and methods. *Politics and Governance, 6*(2), 1–4. https://doi-org.proxy1.ncu.edu/10.17645/pag.v6i2.1569.

Stevens, T., O'Brien, K., Overill, R., Wilkinson, B., Pildegovics, T., & Hill, S. (2019). *Active cyber defence: A public good for the private sector*. Retrieved from https://www.kcl.ac.uk/sspp/policy-institute/publications/uk-active-cyber-defence.pdf.

Taplin, R. (2016). *Managing cyber risk in the financial sector: lessons from Asia, Europe, and the USA*. London: Routledge.

Testa, A., Maimon, D., Sobesto, B., & Cukier, M. (2017). Illegal roaming and file manipulation on target computers: Assessing the effect of sanction threats on system trespassers' online behaviors. *Criminology and Public Policy, 16*(3), 687–726. https://doi.org/10.1111/1745-9133.12312.

Tropina, T. (2015). Public-private collaboration: Cybercrime, cybersecurity, and national security. In T. Tropina, & C. Callanan (Eds.), *Self & co-regulation in cybercrime, cybersecurity & national security* (1–36). Cham, Switzerland: Springer.

United States Department of Justice. (2016). *Seven Iranians working for Islamic Revolutionary Guard Corps-affiliated entities charged for conducting coordinated campaign of cyber attacks against U.S. financial sector.* Retrieved from https://www.justice.gov/opa/pr/seven-iranians-working-islamic-revolutionary-guard-corps-affiliated-entities-charged.

United States District Court for the Central District of California. (2018). *United States v. Park Jin HYOK, also known as ("aka") "Jin Hyok Park", aka "Pak Jin Hek"*. Retrieved from https://www.justice.gov/usao-cdca/press-release/file/1091951/download.

Vagle, M. D. (2018). *Crafting phenomenological research.* Retrieved from https://www.amazon.com/Crafting-Phenomenological-Research-Mark-Vagle/dp/1138042668/ref=pd_lpo_sbs_14_t_0?_encoding=UTF8&psc=1&refRID=HBVBCCNKWD3CPVWG8946.

Van Manen, M. (2014). *Phenomenology of practice: Meaning-giving methods in phenomenological research and writing*. Walnut Creek, CA: Left Coast Press.

Volkov, D. (2018). *Silence: Moving into the darkside*. Retrieved from https://www.group-ib.com/resources/threat-research/silence.html.

Vroegop, R. (2017). *The state of information and intelligence sharing in Canada*. The Conference Board of Canada. Retrieved from http://www.conferenceboard.ca/e-library/abstract.aspx?did=8487.

Wæver, O. (1995). Securitization and desecuritization. In R. D. Lipschutz (Ed.), *On security* (pp. 46–87). New York: Columbia University Press. Retrieved from https://www.amazon.com/Security-Ronnie-Lipschutz/dp/0231102712.

Wall, D. S. (2007). Policing cybercrimes: Situating the public police in networks of security within cyberspace. *Police Practice & Research, 8*(2), 183–205. https://doi-org.proxy1.ncu.edu/10.1080/15614260701377729.

Wanca, I. (2014). *Structuring public-private partnership for reducing cyber risk to critical infrastructure*. Kindle Edition. Retrieved from https://www.amazon.ca/dp/B00JARC3EU.

Whelan, C. (2015). Managing dynamic public-sector networks: Effectiveness, performance, and a methodological framework in the field of national security. *International Public Management Journal, 18*(4), 536–567. https://doi.org/10.1080/10967494.2015.1030484.

Whelan, C., & Dupont, B. (2017). Taking stock of networks across the security field: A review, typology and research agenda. *Policing & Society, 27*(6), 671–687. Retrieved from https://www.tandfonline.com/doi/full/10.1080/10439463.2017.1356297?scroll=top&needAccess=true.

Wilson, T., Maimon, D., Sobesto, B., & Cukier, M. (2015). The effect of a surveillance banner in an attacked computer system: Additional evidence for the relevance of restrictive deterrence in cyberspace. *Journal of Research in Crime and Delinquency, 52*(6), 829–855. Retrieved from https://journals.sagepub.com/doi/abs/10.1177/0022427815587761.

World Bank. (2017). *Combatting cybercrime: Tools and capacity building for emerging economies*. Retrieved from https://openknowledge.worldbank.org/handle/10986/30306?locale-attribute=fr.

CHAPTER 5

Major Themes in the Literature of Cybersecurity and Public–Private Partnerships; A Focus on Financial Institutions

Critical Infrastructure Protection

Public Safety Canada (2018a) defines critical infrastructures as the "processes, systems, facilities, technologies, networks, assets and services essential to the health, security and economic well-being of Canadians" (p. 2). Canada's National Strategy for Critical Infrastructures has ten critical sectors while the United States has sixteen, the United Kingdom thirteen, and Australia has eight (Quigley, Bisset, & Mills, 2017). In Canada, the ten interconnected sectors are: energy and utilities, information and communication technology, finance, food, water, transportation, safety, government, and manufacturing (Quigley et al., 2017). To share information with the private sector and critical infrastructure in Canada, the Royal Canadian Mounted Police (RCMP) developed a system call the Suspicious Incident Reporting (SIR) which is a system that organizations may use to report suspicious activity and threat indicators with the RCMP (National Critical Infrastructure Intelligence Team, 2015). Also, this online system allows the RCMP to share information with stakeholders, notifications and to offer a library of information and intelligence products (National Critical Infrastructure Intelligence Team, 2015).

In 2015, the U.S. intelligence agencies confirmed cyberattacks orchestrated by foreign governments and criminal organizations as one of the significant security threats to the country and as the responsibility of both public and private partners (Etzioni, 2017). According to the Center

P.-L. Pomerleau and D. L. Lowery, *Countering Cyber Threats to Financial Institutions*,
https://doi.org/10.1007/978-3-030-54054-8_5

for Strategic and International Studies (2019), there is a considerable increase of cyber incidents toward government agencies, defense, and high-tech companies over the years. In their analysis, the center focused on economic crimes with losses of more than US$1M. The results showed that cyber-incidents increased 377% in the last five years as the number of cyber incidents of more than US$1M in 2018 was of $N = 83$ incidents while this number was of $N = 22$ in 2014 (Center for Strategic & International Studies, 2019). Besides, the number of events increased every year during this five-year period (Center for Strategic & International Studies, 2019).

Carr (2016) argues there are several reasons why cybersecurity PPPs in a critical infrastructure protection context have been perceived as a potential strategy for a collaborative project by the public and private sectors to protect critical infrastructures. The first reason is that the state is viewed as being responsible and accountable for the response and the provision of national security (Carr, 2016; Christensen & Petersen, 2017; Etzioni, 2017; World Bank, 2017). It means the protection of critical infrastructure, assets, and systems necessary to preserve national security are recognized as being fundamental to ensure the safety of the state (Carr, 2016). However, as argued by Quigley et al. (2017), as critical infrastructures have been privatized, government entities lack the knowledge, skills, and flexibility to properly monitor critical infrastructure owners in managing cyber-risks.

As mentioned by McCarthy (2018), from a national security perspective, cybersecurity appears to have a character of a public good. Both the government and the private sector have an interest in the provision of cybersecurity, but public–private partnerships do not work as they have too many challenges (Bures, 2013; Carr, 2016). The provision of security is a function of the state while most of the cybersecurity of critical infrastructures is maintained by the private sector (McCarthy, 2018). Thus, in the event of a significant cyberattack on critical infrastructure, it would be natural for the government to request having authority and responsibility for the matter (Carr, 2016). However, due to the fragmentation in the provision of security, the state is unable to take a traditional standing as a primary security provider when it comes to cybersecurity matters related to critical infrastructures (Collier, 2018).

In protecting critical infrastructure, the responsibility to identify goals and objectives is under government accountability, but the implementation and the mitigation of vulnerabilities are primarily under the private sector responsibility which owns most of the corporate assets (Auerswald, Branscomb, Laporte, & Michel-Kerjan, 2005). The criticality of the risk versus the probability of occurrence needs to be evaluated in any business decision to know if it would be profitable or cost-effective to invest in risk management solutions. Most of the risk management tools have been proven inadequate in dealing with high-impacts and low-probability events like terrorism (Auerswald et al., 2005). Private organizations invest in minimizing risks of major operational failures while accepting some level of risk (Quigley et al., 2017). Unfortunately, in the event these organizations need to take their systems offline due to an unexpected issue, the market will punish them, and these companies might notice a decline in the value of their stock (Quigley et al., 2017).

Regarding low-probability events, Quigley et al. (2017) use the *black swan* metaphor developed by Taleb (2007) to explain that an unlikely event may occur and generate significant consequences while this same incident will be rationalized and deemed as inevitable. Auerswald et al. (2005), state that risks associated with critical infrastructures are becoming interdependent and the threat from terrorism has influenced the creation of a new relationship between the private sector and national security teams. Because these critical infrastructures are interdependent assets, the fact that some organizations are underspending on risk management might affect other organizations in the industry as well as the government while responding to a crisis (Quigley et al., 2017).

Rudner (2013) examines the intentions, strategies, objectives, and capabilities of the different groups that have threatened critical national infrastructures globally in the past few years. The author argues that Al-Qaeda and fellow jihadists have the necessary skills and capabilities to prepare a cyberattack targeting critical infrastructures of the West as well as Canada (Rudner, 2013). At the early stage of a cyberattack, it is almost impossible to know who the perpetrator behind the attack is as well as his motivation. In forensic investigations, it may be complicated to attribute the responsibility for the offense to one individual or a specific group of cybercriminals. In some instances, the investigation of a cyberattack may be a lengthy process, and it might not be possible to identify who committed the attack (Rudner, 2013). Cyberattacks are relatively cheap to commit comparing some physical attacks, and they can generate significant collateral damages (Rudner, 2013). Additionally, Rudner (2013) points out critical infrastructures are susceptible targets for cyberattacks because of the value they represent, their inherent vulnerabilities and the harm they can inflict on a given country. The author claims that from the various critical infrastructures of a country, financial services represent a specific cyber-terrorism target (Rudner, 2013).

An important reason for the collaboration of both sectors is to maintain confidence in organizations, the market, and the financial industry. In other words, the unavailability of products and services could have significant societal and commercial consequences impacting other sectors of the industry, other jurisdictions as well as provincial and federal entities (Gendron & Rudner, 2012). Also, the Internet of things (IoT) and the dependence on new technologies will bring new challenges in critical infrastructure protection in the coming years. Actions taken by organizations will affect others in the ecosystem and private sector executives, as well as policymakers, will have to deal with greater uncertainties than ever before in the face of new dynamic threats (Auerswald et al., 2005).

Wanca (2014) argues that principles and standard practices are needed in any PPPs in information sharing to protect critical infrastructure. The protection of infrastructure is never done in a silo, and it requires shared responsibility for the actions and the coordination of government, private companies as well as citizens to succeed. Trust in information sharing is vital and partners lacking communications skills could have an adverse influence on the project and the willingness to share (Wanca, 2014). Moreover, partners in critical infrastructure protection should agree on deliverables; they should commit to executing plans and recommendations as well as to provide the appropriate resources and staff for the security of the critical infrastructure (Wanca, 2014).

Wilson (2014) points out many different technological vulnerabilities could affect critical infrastructures. The author maintains that critical infrastructures are high-valued targets for a cyberattack, and it would be relatively easy to protect them if most software updates were done on older systems, patches, and proper investments were made to avoid leaving critical systems unsecured (Wilson, 2014). Even if no cyberattack on critical infrastructure has been attributed to terrorist groups or extremists as of today, the technical skills of some of the cyber terrorists are growing rapidly, they have access to more sophisticated tools, and they could even decide to hire experts in the field to fulfill their requests (Wilson, 2014).

In his research between Australia's public and private partnerships to protect critical infrastructure, Grant (2018) suggests the solutions for cybersecurity would come from the private sectors as this sector can adapt and respond more rapidly to incidents. However, this author argues that a significant ethical adjustment would be necessary, and the private sector should not be solely responsible for protecting critical infrastructures as it focuses primarily on profit-making (Grant, 2018). Grant (2018) claims that four elements are essential in creating effective PPPs to defend critical infrastructures. This author states that partnerships should focus on collaboration and sharing best practices, facilitate commercial incentives to increase the private sector's involvement, new regulations ensuring cybersecurity standards (not impacting profit-making) should be developed, and finally, a clear understanding of when and how leadership responsibility will change between actors when an incident occurs (Grant, 2018).

In Canada, there is a need for the federal government and private owners of the nation's critical infrastructure to share cyber threat information to protect critical assets. The consequences of cyberattacks on critical infrastructure can have economic, social and environmental impacts that are not limited to the boundaries of a country (Mezher, El Khatib, & Sooriyaarachchi, 2015). Critical infrastructures have complex networks, processes, supervisory control systems and data acquisition (SCADA) in place, and a single incident could cause physical, technological and human harm (Mezher et al., 2015). Both the public and private sectors can promote information sharing to protect essential assets like financial institutions from cyberattacks. The financial sector is the "backbone" of the Canadian national economy as it provides essential services such as depositing funds, making payments, providing credit and liquidity to customers, allowing to invest funds in the stock exchanges as well as providing currencies, bonds, shares, derivatives, equity, and loans (Hämmerli, 2012). Significant disruptive or destructive attacks against the financial industry or a single bank could have catastrophic effects on the economy and could considerably threaten the financial stability of the country (Borghard, 2018). Thus, a single cyberattack on a financial institution could create a systemic risk in the financial industry since the victimized organization could be unable to meet its payments and settlements, and this situation could have repercussions on other participants by not allowing them to proceed with their obligations (Crovini, Ossola, & Marchini, 2017; Gallagher, Mcmahon, & Morrow, 2014; Gordon, 2018; Nish & Naumann, 2019). As written by Quigley et al. (2017), "one often doesn't realize the extent of interdependence of a system until a failure occurs" (p. 11). Crovini et al. (2017) advance the cybersecurity response should rely on a systemic approach instead of building on each firm's activities to protect their critical assets.

Gorniak et al. (2011) argue that financial institutions are particularly vulnerable to the cascading effects of technical, human, or natural disasters. If cyberattacks would be successful against one or many financial institutions in a short period, a series of potential events could occur in the market since citizens would have difficulty getting access to their account, to withdraw cash, to use their credit cards and trading floors would not be able to make any transactions on the markets. According to Quigley et al. (2017) as well as the findings of the cybercrime research conducted by the World Bank (2017), if such an incident would occur, blame management would be noticeable and the public would hold the government responsible for the critical infrastructure failure even though most of the critical infrastructures are owned by the private sector. A similar incident would also generate considerable media coverage and considerably impact to the reputation of the government as well as the private organization under attack.

Many interdependencies exist between financial institutions to move funds and providing services to customers, governments, and enterprises. On a global scale, financial institutions deal with correspondent banking partners, direct customers, companies, investment-banking dealers, third-party companies, and suppliers among many others. It is the reason why the interruption of services for the financial industry is critical in avoiding the population to doubting the resilience of the financial system. Thus, to be efficient in dealing with various threats against critical infrastructures, the government must engage and collaborate with the private sector (Auerswald et al., 2005; Spencer, 2017). As Nish and Naumann (2019) explain, the increasing connectivity and interdependence of financial institutions through online channels, the complexity of networks and system interfaces increasing the challenge of network defense, and the expansion of offensive cyber capabilities of attackers will be key challenges for financial institutions to overcome. Thus, Nish and Naumann (2019) recommend (a) to enhance collaboration between institutions in focusing on areas such as machine-readable intelligence, (b) in trying to simplify security in making sure executives understand what security is and is not, and (c) in improving response capabilities against attackers in finding creative ways for law enforcement, banks and member of communities to work together to disrupt and deter threat groups of attacking financial institutions (Nish & Naumann, 2019).

According to Quigley et al. (2017), a proactive risk management mindset is necessary to protect critical infrastructure. However, in a market where the private sector owns most of the critical infrastructures, corporate executives may be reluctant to spend money on risk management when it is not possible to quantify future benefits or to explain shrinking margins to shareholders (Quigley et al., 2017). These authors argue the Canadian government effort to establish an information-sharing methodology to share sensitive information with critical infrastructure owners is limited due to markets competition, legal, and logistic issues as well as institutional problems (Quigley et al., 2017). Financial institutions increasingly rely on digital infrastructure, various financial technologies, interconnected systems, and automated processes that are attractive targets for motivated threat actors which are highly capable of disrupting the economy (Borghard, 2018). Since these institutions are interconnected through various technologies, they become more vulnerable to cyber exploitation (Leuprecht, 2019).

In the interest of brand protection and competitive interests, the financial industry should be able to depend on government intelligence to prevent intrusions and to bring both civil and criminal actions against the intruders. In the latest key findings from their Global State of Information Security survey with 9500 executives from 122 countries conducted by PricewaterhouseCoopers (PWC), "40 percent of the participants confirmed the disruption of operations as the biggest potential consequences of cyberattacks, 39 percent mentioned the compromise of sensitive data, 32 percent harm to the product quality, 29 percent damage to physical property and 22 percent cited harm to human life" (PWC, 2017, p. 4). Thus, the Federal government and private owners of the nation's critical infrastructure must find new methods to share cyber threat information to protect critical assets.

Legal and Organizational Barriers to Information Sharing

Dealing with different levels of legal frameworks in cybercrime investigations can be a daunting task for private companies, law enforcement, and government agencies. Since the terrorist attacks of 9/11 in the United States, the Canadian government relied on legislation to increase its capacities in gathering intelligence through various information-sharing initiatives with critical infrastructure owners and the private sector

(Quigley et al., 2017). However, this information is being shared from the critical infrastructures and the private sector to the government, but there is not much reciprocity. In other words, the information is not shared both ways (public to private and private to public) as the government does not share sensitive information with the private sector. For Quigley et al. (2017), information sharing should be a "two-way street" as critical infrastructures and the private sector should share vulnerabilities with government and the public sector should intelligence with private organizations.

Private sector enterprises tend to believe that they can deal with cybercrime by themselves and that they don't need to share intelligence, data, or information with the public sector. For their part, public sector organizations might fear exchanging information with private companies because some of its members don't have proper security clearances. It is a challenge that has been discussed by Dupont (2015) when he states that anti-terrorist networks are faced with multiple problems preventing professionals to do their work correctly and share information as they should. This issue is also highlighted by Vroegop (2017) when he claims survey participants in his study indicated that security clearances and potential reputational damages were common obstacles in information sharing. The difficulty in sharing confidential information was also a vital issue in PPPs studied by Dupré (2014) and intelligence sharing challenges discussed by Maras (2017).

Also, the culture of the organization regarding the importance of information sharing is of critical importance. If the organization does not believe in information sharing and does not have any legal obligation to share the information, it is possible that essential pieces of data will not be shared with the appropriate party. In some instances, members of the same organization do not have equal privileged access to the information since there is a different level of security clearances, and some security networks are dealing with many organizational pathologies as well as an inability to analyze an enormous quantity of data (Dupont, 2015). Laughlin (2016) argues the gap between government and private sector's motivations require additional laws and regulations to improve cybersecurity practices as a voluntary approach to work together will not work.

Shore and Schafer (2015) conclude federal agencies have different objectives, organizational structures, cultural constraints, and these agencies have incentive structures that are not inclined to transmit information

(Quigley et al., 2017). This lack of information-sharing issue was also found between federal agencies, which demonstrates that the lack of information sharing is not only between government and the private sector, but also within government (Quigley et al., 2017). The same study provided many recommendations to improve the state of information sharing in Canada. Shore and Schafer (2015) argue to prevent terrorism and enhance national security, information sharing is essential, and new procedures to share information are needed among various levels of governments and agencies. Additionally, formal organizational rules and procedures for information sharing should be clear and documented, and the federal government should provide a clear direction on the importance of balancing privacy rights and security aspects. Furthermore, Shore and Schafer (2015) state "the appropriate balance should be struck between sharing information to enhance national security and protecting the privacy of Canadians" (Shore & Schafer, 2015, p. 2).

In their study with private security professionals in the United States, Willis, Lester, and Treverton (2009) indicate participants confirmed they did not feel they needed more classified information to do their work. This situation may be explained by the fact that classified information might be critical in some instances and not relevant in other conditions as it does not mean that classified information is necessarily essential for private organizations (Quigley et al., 2017). Context, goals, priorities and the type of emergency should be taken into consideration as well when sharing information. Quigley et al. (2017) contend senior business executives seldom have security clearances, which is an issue to share information with their internal security professionals holding a security clearance. Because of this, security professionals often cannot share key information with executives as they do not have a security clearance.

Quigley (2013) maintains Canadian private sector professionals participating in a critical infrastructure study stated that classified briefings are vague, and these briefings often do not provide actionable information for them. Even for private security professionals holding a security clearance, Quigley et al. (2017) add there is a misunderstanding between the intelligence community and the private sector regarding how to use intelligence reports. Private security professionals holding a security clearance expect to get a detailed security threat briefing from the government, but these professionals are often disappointed (Quigley et al., 2017).

Besides, the situation is further complicated as intelligence agencies, law enforcement, and private security professionals do not have the same objectives (Quigley et al., 2017). Intelligence agencies want to gather information to build intelligence, law enforcement wants to use the information to prosecute criminals (Quigley et al., 2017), and private security professionals want to use the information to protect their organization's critical assets.

Other legal challenges for security networks are associated with the obligation of achieving results mixed with an obligation of means as defined by the Canadian Charter of Rights and Freedoms in protecting privacy (Dupont, 2015). The public sector may also believe that sensitive information might be released publicly. As mentioned by Willis et al. (2009), the fact the proprietary information might be released publicly is a significant concern for the private sector. It is a common challenge for the private sector as some organizations might decide to keep the knowledge of a cyberattack inside "its four walls" since they want to preserve their reputation and maintain the confidence of their customers. These situations allow criminals to commit their crimes without impunity and consequences.

Wanca (2014) advances that numerous legal challenges have an impact on the effectiveness of PPPs. The main difficulties among others are jurisdictional variations on data retention and data sharing of the evidence gathered in the investigation. The European Union Directive on Network and Information Security allowed the Member States to create and to identify a national authority responsible and accountable to manage information security risks and incidents (Wanca, 2014). These directives did impose obligations for companies to notify authorities when they experience a cybersecurity incident (Wanca, 2014). Some countries like the United States are currently adopting voluntary disclosure in the PPP model, and other countries in the EU are pushing for mandatory disclosure requirements or a top-down approach as an information-sharing model (Wanca, 2014).

Prosecuting illegal content that crossed multiple jurisdictions and perpetrated by cybercriminals located in a foreign jurisdiction is an excellent example of legal issues and challenges that cybercrimes generate (Akhgar & Brewster, 2016; Cross, 2019; Holt, 2018). In their study, Sullivan and Burger (2017) address the issue of sharing IP addresses of bad actors and the privacy implications for organizations. They contend that in the European Union (EU), the automated business to business information sharing of IP address, potentially associated with bad actors, can be done in the public interest under Article 6(1)(f) of the

General Data Protection Regulation (GDPR) as well as the 1995 Directive (Sullivan & Burger, 2017). This key finding was astutely corroborated as well by Borden, Mooney, Taylor, and Sharkey (2018) when they analyzed the lawful activity of threat information sharing by the Financial Services Information Sharing and Analysis Center (FS-ISAC) under the umbrella of the General Data Protection Regulation (GDPR).

Johnson (2016) argues the industry should start implementing solutions to mitigate and prevent cyberattacks by using a collaborative and proactive approach and by creating and enabling the proper environment to share information between the government and the private sector. Johnson (2016) proposes that financial institutions should build new initiatives to prevent cyber threats in the industry like the Financial Services Information Sharing and Analysis Center (FS-ISAC) which is an initiative to gather, to share, to monitor, and to evaluate the information from both sectors to prevent cyber and physical threat incidents in the financial industry. Over the years, two additional sector-led bodies were created to facilitate PPPs to address cyber challenges primarily in the areas of information sharing, policy coordination, and threat analytics; in 2003, the Financial Services Sector Coordinating Council (FSSCC) was created, and the Financial Systemic Analysis and Resilience Center (FSARC) was created in 2016 (San Juan Menacho & Martin, 2018). FS-ISAC focus primarily on tactical information sharing between members (Real-time information sharing). The FSSCC is a smaller group and its mission is to advocate for the private sector in collaborating with the U.S. federal government to strengthen the resilience of the financial sector (Policy coordination), while the FSARC's mission is to coordinate and mitigate systemic risks to the U.S. financial system (Resilience and systemic risks) (San Juan Menacho & Martin, 2018). Johnson (2016) concludes that by sharing data and trends with the government, it allows both the public and the private sector to have a comprehensive view of this issue and to be in a better position to defend themselves against cyberattacks.

Many legal issues remain to share information between private and public partners. In terms of national security, the Security of Canada Information Sharing Act defines how Government of Canada institutions can share threat information between each other to protect the country against activities that could undermine the sovereignty, territorial integrity, or the lives or security of Canadians (Government of Canada, 2015). However, the same type of legislation does not explicitly exist between private entities (critical infrastructures) and public institutions, thus creating a critical gap in intelligence.

The Canadian Section 7 (3) (d.1) of the PIPEDA Act stipulates that it is possible for an organization to disclose personal information without the knowledge or the consent of the individual when it is for investigating a breach of an agreement of a contravention to the laws of Canada "that is being or about to be committed" (Office of the Privacy Commissioner of Canada, 2017). The reform of the PIPEDA Act in 2015 with the Digital Privacy Act through Bill S-4 restrained how financial institutions can share information regarding criminal activities under the new Section 7 (3) (d.2) (Office of the Privacy Commissioner of Canada, 2017). Prior to the reform, banks used to be able to share information about any type of criminal activities to prevent crime as the Canadian Bankers Association (CBA) Bank Crime Prevention and Investigation Office (BCPIO) was recognized as one of many "investigation bodies" under the law. Under the new regime and the new Section 7 (3) (d.2), the CBA BCPIO is no longer recognized as an investigation body and has been replaced by the Bank Crime Prevention and Investigation Framework's (BCPIF). Under this framework, participants may use personal information "to facilitate the investigation of criminal and dishonest activity including contraventions of the laws of Canada for fraud prevention only, when it is provided that the fraud is likely to be committed" (Office of the Privacy Commissioner of Canada, 2017).

The Canadian Criminal Code article 462 also has a section explaining what and when it is possible to share information to prevent crime (Government of Canada, 2017). Also, to manage emergency and share information between government and critical infrastructures, Quigley et al. (2017) argue the Canadian government could facilitate the exchange of sensitive information through the Emergency Management Act (EMA). The EMA allows sharing information with critical infrastructure owners to enhance emergency management (Government of Canada, 2019). Challenges in understanding these different legal remedies to share information between the public and the private sector to prevent cybercrime and to protect critical infrastructure while maintaining privacy rights remain problematic. Hence, the lack of information exchange between various public and private actors could significantly reduce the possibility of preventing cyberattacks on critical infrastructure such as financial institutions. As an example, to reduce legal challenges in information sharing in Europe, the EU introduced e-evidence legislation that will significantly aid with sharing data "at speed for investigators to use in case work" (Dixon, 2019).

To be efficient in combatting cybercrimes, government and law enforcement (from local, regional to international levels) must have a proper legal framework to work together in investigating these matters, to share information and to be able to assist the private sector in reducing the impact of these crimes on society. As Borghard (2018) attests, it is imperative for the financial industry and the government to have defined thresholds that may trigger the sharing of threat information. Both sectors would benefit from having access to contextual information and intelligence to be able to defend the country's critical infrastructure networks against nation-state adversaries, to focus on relevant intelligence collection efforts and for both sectors to have a better understanding of the threat environment (Borghard, 2018).

Public Safety's Role in Cybercrime and Cybersecurity Incidents

In Canada, Public Safety Canada is responsible for implementing Canada's cybersecurity strategy, to assure the safety of government systems and networks as well as to work with other partners to secure the systems outside of government to protect Canadians (Gallagher et al., 2014; Government of Canada, 2010). In the 2009 National Strategy for critical infrastructure report, Public Safety Canada announced the three main objectives were to build relationships, to implement an all-hazards risk management approach and to advance timely sharing and protection of information with partners (Quigley et al., 2017). These objectives would be achieved by developing a consistent approach between critical infrastructure's sectors to share information through new tools and information-sharing mechanisms such as secure websites (Quigley et al., 2017).

Different membership networks for each critical infrastructure's sector would be created with key members from both public and private; participation would be voluntary and self-funded and individual stakeholders would be responsible for implementing the risk management approach they believe appropriate for their situation (Quigley et al., 2017). Even though the Canadian government wrote in its National Strategy for critical infrastructure reports that information sharing and trust building with the private sector is essential since 2009 (Public Safety Canada,

2009), these information-sharing concepts and how sensitive information is shared between both sectors remain ambiguous (Quigley et al., 2017). In the latest Canadian cybersecurity strategy, the focus is primarily on increasing cyber resilience which consists of preventing, mitigating, and responding to cyberattacks that are targeting Canadian systems and institutions (Public Safety Canada, 2017). This strategy will be implemented by assisting businesses to get a recognized cybersecurity standard, working with private sector's executives and board members to increase their cybersecurity posture and to build cyber awareness to educate the population of Canada about cyber threats as well as how to protect themselves (Public Safety Canada, 2017).

Before 2018, private businesses had to communicate with different government agencies to get assistance in hardening their IT networks to improve their cybersecurity posture. In October 2018, the Canadian government created the Canadian Centre for Cyber Security to regroup different teams. A total of 750 employees from Public Safety Canada (Cyber Incident Response Center (CCCIR) and the Get Cyber Safe public awareness campaign), Shared Services Canada, and the Communications Security Establishment (CSE) were consolidated under one center to have a unified approach to cybersecurity issues (Government of Canada, 2018a). This new center is now under the responsibility of the CSE, and it will become the primary voice and resources for senior leadership in government on cybersecurity matters, incident management, situational awareness, technical advice, guidance, communication, and to educate Canadians about cybersecurity issues (Government of Canada, 2018a). This new center will also collaborate with the RCMP for cybercrime investigations (Government of Canada, 2018a). The RCMP will create the National Cybercrime Coordination Unit as the federal police will act as the cybercrime hub for the country, a resource for local and provincial police forces, and become the single place for citizens to report cybercrime (Solomon, 2018). One of the objectives of this new center will be to focus on the prevention of cybercrime instead of solely rely on the reactive phase which is associated with the investigation of an incident (Solomon, 2018). In focusing on prevention, this center will be closely working with the private sector, critical infrastructures, and international partners.

For national security matters, intelligence sharing with Five Eyes Partners (Australia, Britain, Canada, New Zealand, the United States) the investigation of suspected activities constituting threats to the security of Canada is under the responsibility of the Canadian Security Intelligence Service (CSIS) (Barkin, 2018; CBC, 2016; Government of Canada, 2018b). Through its powers to disrupt in the Bill C-51 and the Anti-Terrorism Act of 2015, CSIS is the intelligence agency responsible for preventing attacks from non-state actors or terrorism-related matters on Canadian critical infrastructure such as financial institutions (CBC, 2016; Government of Canada, 2018b). As for state actors cyberattacks against Canada, the Communications Security Establishment Act (Bill C-59) will allow the Communications Security Establishment (CSE) to conduct offensive and defensive cyber operations to neutralize and mitigate the risks against Canadian critical infrastructure (Leuprecht & Maclellan, 2018). Wright (2017) defines state actors as agencies and authorized personnel seeking intelligence or social control in an attempt to engage in espionage or cyber-warfare. An important challenge is that state actors tend to rely on non-state actors to achieve anonymity in committing cyberattacks, which make it very difficult for law enforcement and intelligence agencies to provide attribution of malicious cyberattacks (Leuprecht & Maclellan, 2018; Rid & Buchanan, 2015). Moreover, state and non-state actors have considerably increased their cyber capabilities and they are mainly driven by geopolitical goals (Leuprecht, Szeman, & Skillicorn, 2019).

Since cyberattacks could have devastating consequences for the state, Gallagher et al. (2014) argue that effective collaboration between financial market infrastructures (FMI's), financial institutions, and the federal government is essential. The Canadian government must work with the private sector to fulfill its responsibilities. Most countries are in the process of developing and implementing their cybersecurity strategies and setting the focus for years to come (Levin & Goodrick, 2013). Different states around the world are coordinating their policies with international partners, and there is a shift from combating cybercrime from a law enforcement perspective to one of strategic cybersecurity (Levin & Goodrick, 2013). Gallagher et al. (2014), as well as Levin and Goodrick (2013), focus on the role and responsibilities of the Canadian federal government in protecting critical infrastructure. Gallagher et al. (2014) describe how financial institutions, FMIs, and States are interacting with each other to protect the financial industry's market against cyberattacks while Levin and Goodrick (2013) elaborate on the global policy shift on cybercrime, cyberwar, and what it means for the Canadian government.

Public Sector (Law Enforcement) and Government Roles and Responsibilities

The law enforcement role in public–private partnership in information sharing is regularly associated with the deterrence of crime, the disruption of organized crime rings and the application of the law. Under the Criminal Code, law enforcement in Canada is mandated to investigate any types of criminal activities which may be committed online through the Internet or in the physical world (Public Safety Canada, 2017). The role of the government is to foster cybersecurity initiatives to explore innovative ways of making businesses and Canadians cyber secure (Public Safety Canada, 2018b).

According to the International Centre for the Prevention of Crime (2018), the primary motivations of the public sector in establishing private and public partnerships is to facilitate the implementation of a national cybersecurity strategy, to allow the private sector to participate in cybersecurity as well as providing a range of resources that are not available to the public sector. As Cesteros (2017) argues, funds available for public security are not enough to be able to fight cybercrimes. This situation leads to the private sector having to drive most initiatives and investigations affecting a private person or a private company (Cesteros, 2017).

The functioning and culture of the public sector differ in various ways, and the concept of threat and incident do not hold the same meaning for both sectors (International Centre for the Prevention of Crime, 2018). Maras (2017) states the intelligence community follows a bureaucratic model of operations structured with strict rules and procedures. Besides, contrary to the private sector, public authorities must inform the public which may be problematic for the private sector to maintain its reputation and customer's trust when a private organization is victim of a cyberattack (International Centre for the Prevention of Crime, 2018). Due to these differences, the issues of dealing with cybercrime are perceived differently by the actors (Germano, 2014; International Centre for the Prevention of Crime, 2018).

Gendron and Rudner's (2012) study focuses specifically on Canada, and they provide many recommendations to the government on how to improve the protection of critical infrastructures through a proactive intelligence approach. From a public sector's landscape, the authors believe the major threats to Canadian critical infrastructures are international terrorism, state-sponsored espionage or sabotage, and hacktivism (Gendron & Rudner, 2012). They claim the existing defensive measures in place would not be enough to maintain the integrity and the availability of Canadian information systems and preventing attacks on the critical infrastructures (Gendron & Rudner, 2012).

International Public and Private Partnership Initiatives

Governments also have the responsibility to stimulate the development of partnerships with the private sector to combat cyber-threats. Public and private partnerships offer two types of outputs; (a) knowledge and insight sharing to support strategic analysis allowing to develop typologies and best practices and (b) tactical information-sharing facilitating sensitive and relevant sharing of information between governmental entities such as law enforcement or intelligence agencies and regulated entities (Maxwell, 2019). Several PPPs projects are currently functionals around the world, and according to Akhgar and Brewster (2016), organizations need to adapt rapidly to protect their assets, systems, and networks. Also, they need to learn how to cooperate in fighting cybercrime adequately with organizations operating in other countries (Akhgar & Brewster, 2016). Some of these projects have been put forward by creating integrated teams of lawyers, private security experts, regional, state or national law enforcement agents and international police organization like Interpol. Interpol is the international policing agency responsible for dealing with cyber terrorism on the international scale, the International Telecommunication Union (ITU) is responsible for the cybersecurity at the global level, and the United Nations is the lead with international criminal activities (Mezher et al., 2015).

Bossong and Wagner (2017) describe the role of Europol and its European Cybercrime Center (EC3), as well as the role of the European Union Agency for Network and Information Security (ENISA) in PPPs to improve the technical reliability and resilience of cyberspace and critical information infrastructure (Bossong & Wagner, 2017). ENISA is an organization owned by the private sector (Bossong & Wagner, 2017). The European Center Crime Centre (EC3) is an integrated unit in charge of operational exchanges with IT security companies to address cybercrime and sophisticated threats, such as botnets, malware, and viruses in a proactive and preventative manner (Bossong & Wagner, 2017). Memorandum of Understanding (MoU) has been signed between EC3 and financial institutions, antivirus companies and private security firms to share information legally (Bossong & Wagner, 2017). Avina (2011) and Dixon (2019) also describe operational partnerships in Europe such as the Microsoft's Digital Crime Unit, Europol, and the UK's National Cybersecurity Centre's work with telecommunications providers. Avina (2011) focuses primarily on the IT industry to understand how companies such as McAffee and Microsoft partnered with governmental and intergovernmental agencies like Interpol and the United Nations Office on Drugs and Crime (UNODC) using "Corporate Social Responsibility" (CSR) type of investments to combat different crimes such as cybercrime.

In the UK, the creating of the Joint Money Laundering Intelligence Taskforce (JMLIT) in 2015, a PPP to tackle financial crime and the creation of the Cyber-security Information Sharing Partnership (CISP) in 2013 under the responsibility of the CERT-UK are two leading and highly effective examples of mechanism to enhance information sharing between the private and the public sector (Rosemont, 2016). These PPPs are now centralized under the UK National Cyber Security Center (NCSC) created in 2016 to regroup various agencies and initiatives (Rosemont, 2016; Maxwell, 2019). As Rosemont's (2016) describes, the CISP is a social networking platform hosted on the Internet allowing members from across sectors to exchange cyber threat in real-time, in a secure environment protecting the confidentiality of shared information. The primary objective of the CISP was to:

> Give the government and industry far richer, more immediate intelligence picture of the cyber threat. For the first time a new secure, virtual collaborative environment will allow government, including the Security Service, GCHQ, and the National Crime Agency, and industry partners to exchange information on threats and vulnerabilities as they're identified. (Rosemont, 2016, p. 19)

Maxwell (2019) describes at length public and private information-sharing partnerships to combat terrorist financing and money laundering. These partnerships are the UK Joint Money Laundering Intelligence Taskforce (JMLIT), the Australian Fintel Alliance launched in March 2017, the Singapore Anti-Money Laundering and Counter-Terrorist Financing Industry Partnership (ACIP) launched in April 2017, the Hong

Kong Fraud and Money Laundering Intelligence Taskforce (FMLIT) launched in May 2017, the Netherland Terrorist Financing Taskforce (TF Taskforce) launched as a pilot in July 2017, the U.S. Financial Crimes Enforcement Network (FINCEN) Network launched in December 2017, the Europol Financial Intelligence Public–Private Partnership (EFIPPP) launched in December 2017, and the Canadian Major Reporters Forum Initiatives including Project Protect to combat human trafficking launched in 2016 (Maxwell, 2019).

From these PPPs projects, Maxwell (2019) states that JMLIT in the United Kingdom benefited from a wide legislative gateway to sharing information between partners, the Fintel Alliance in Australia did not benefit from a new legislation but from a legal authority to rely on a secondment model to include private sector analysts into the Australian Transaction Reports and Analysis Center (AUSTRAC) investigation team (Chadderton & Norton, 2019; Maxwell, 2019). In the United States, the Financial Crimes Enforcement Center (FINCEN) has a unique legislative provision in place under the 2001 Patriot Act 314(a) to share information but only formalized a partnership model in 2017 (Maxwell, 2019).

After analyzing these PPPs initiatives, Rosemont (2016) proposes three recommendations to decision-makers wanting to create new PPPs in order for these initiatives to work: (a) the importance of establishing appropriate metrics, (b) making sure to drive more effective coordination, and (c) to define and develop a better understanding of what constitutes a "partnership" for stakeholders (Rosemont, 2016).

In the United States, the U.S. Patriot Act of 2001 includes provisions allowing the U.S. Secret Services to stand up a specialized crime task force, a unit created for electronic crime investigations and to protect the nation against potential attacks on the financial industry or critical infrastructure, to do its work (Wanca, 2014). This multidisciplinary task force includes law enforcement agents, lawyers, academics, and representatives from the private sector (Wanca, 2014). In the United States, the equivalent of EC3 is the Internet Crime Complaint Center (IC3), acting as a central hub and partnering with the private sector, Local, State, Federal and international agencies to prevent cybercrime (Federal Bureau of Investigation Internet Crime Complaint Center, 2017).

Over the past two decades, the number of PPPs increased in the United States and currently has more than 100 formal security partnerships with the Department of Homeland Security (DHS) or the Federal Bureau of Investigation (FBI) (Christensen & Petersen, 2017). Wanca

(2014) and Kaijankoski (2015) explain the role of the National Cyber-Forensic and Training Alliance (NCFTA) which is a joint project between the FBI, the US Postal Inspection, and the private sector in the United States, focusing on identifying, mitigating, and neutralizing cybercrime threats. Borghard (2018) describes the Project Indigo that began in 2017 illustrating how the Financial Systemic Analysis and Resilience Center (FSARC) played an integral role in sharing information such as nation-state threat actors between financial institutions and the newly established U.S. Cyber Command. Cleary (2019) describes four other active PPPs in the United States These partnerships are the National Cybersecurity and Communications Integration Center (NCCIC—Central hub for cyber threat indicator between public and private sectors) established to share malicious cyber activities, the Cyber Information Sharing and Collaboration Program (CISCP) under DHS to share threats, incidents and vulnerabilities, and the Enhanced Cybersecurity Services (ECS) which is an intrusion detection and prevention capability available to both sectors to partner against unauthorized access, exploitation, and data exfiltration. The Automated Indicator Sharing (AIS) is a PPP initiative allowing private and public partners to share cyber threat information in real-time (Cleary, 2019).

In Canada, O'Donnell and Nesbitt (2016) discuss the Canadian Cyber Threat Exchange (CCTX) initiative. CCTX is a not-for-profit organization created in 2015 to assist Canadian businesses and customers in protecting themselves against cyber threats (Gordon, 2018). This organization was founded by nine private companies to provide a neutral platform for participants to share actionable cyber threat data, to be able to share best practices with cyber professionals from various companies and to adapt to the cybersecurity landscape (Gordon, 2018). Also, the CCTX promotes the sharing of information about cyber threats and vulnerabilities between private companies, government, and academia (Canadian Cyber Threat Exchange, 2015). The information is gathered from three sources; members, the Canadian Federal Government (e.g., Canadian Center for Cyber Security), and the other source of data is from private vendors providing commercial threat services (Gordon, 2018). As of today, CCTX is now represented by more than thirty organizations such as telecommunications companies, financial institutions, insurance and transport companies (Gordon, 2018). Unstructured data or structured format can be submitted by members through a web portal

(Gordon, 2018). Then, the organization relies on STIX and TAXII protocols to characterize the data and to transfer it electronically between members to reduce human intervention (Gordon, 2018). A critical aspect of data sharing between CCTX members is that the data is anonymized which means that an organization receiving the information will not be able to identify the organization providing it to the consortium (Gordon, 2018).

Gallagher et al. (2014) explain the list of initiatives brought forward to test cybersecurity in the financial industry. The Joint Operational Resilience Management (JORM), a Bank of Canada initiative, conducted tabletop exercises with potential crisis scenarios to measure how the private and public sectors would react to a crisis (Gallagher et al., 2014). Also, the Public Safety Canada's Canadian Cyber Incident Response Center (CCIRC) is a government information-sharing initiative of intelligence of data related to cyberattacks reported by participants across different industries as well as government and law enforcement agencies (Gallagher et al., 2014). The Canadian Bankers Association has a cyber-incident committee, and the organization is also working in PPPs with FMI's, and other partners in having a coordinated framework to manage incidents that could impact more than one financial institution (Gallagher et al., 2014).

A recent public–private partnership launched in Canada is an initiative called CanCyber, which is a not-for-profit company created by the Government of Canada. The primary objective of CanCyber is to offer a cyber threat intelligence automated tool for public and private companies to engage in countering threats such as advanced persistent threats and interference from hostile foreign nations. Laughlin (2016) states that advanced persistent threats represent approximately 15% of all cyberattacks threat vector against critical infrastructures. Various private companies can participate in sharing information through the CanCyber initiative, but the primary focus is on companies managing critical infrastructures. CanCyber offers real-time indicators sharing tools allowing members to turn threat indicators into action (CanCyber, 2019). This is possible using free open source software such as the Malware Information Sharing Platform (MISP), Yara rules allowing to identify and classify malware-based string or binary patterns and Zeek which is a free platform allowing to analyze complex and high throughput networks (Ahl & Lyer, 2018; CanCyber, 2019; Kerravala, 2018; Sedenberg & Dempsey, 2018). Leuprecht and Maclellan (2018) astutely point out these organizations remain untested and how these public and private initiatives may assist in responding to a crisis remains to be seen. For these authors, private organizations participating in an Information Sharing and Analysis Center's (ISAC) initiatives may come from the standard of care expected from companies that are under the scrutiny of regulators after being compromised in a cyberattack (Leuprecht & Maclellan, 2018). An ISAC is a cybersecurity public–private partnership involved in sharing experiences and information to mitigate risks.

Another excellent example of a country launching public–private partnership initiatives is Israel, who created different public–private partnerships to include other stakeholders such as the Israeli Defense Forces in researching how to develop and implement cyber-defenses in their ecosystem (O'Donnell & Nesbitt, 2016). Israel established the Advanced Technology Park at Ben Gurion University to promote cyber research centers and created two new agencies for cybersecurity; (a) the National Cyber Security Authority, which is a governmental agency and (b) the Israeli Defense Forces Cyber force, a new unit in the Israel National Defenses Forces (O'Donnell & Nestbitt, 2016).

Boes and Leukfeldt (2017) explain how the Dutch National Cyber Security Centre (NCSC) built from a previous governmental organization charged with cybersecurity and incidence response to create a new entity focusing primarily on improving resilience by increasing monitoring capabilities, exchanging knowledge, and by enhancing prevention through different campaigns and incident handling processes. The NCSC works closely with members from academia, the industry and government as these actors are permanent stakeholders within the new NSCS organization (Boes & Leukfeldt, 2017). For each critical sector, an ISAC was established. In this case, the Dutch financial sector ISAC's involved the NCSC, the High-Tech Crime unit from the Dutch National police, and the General Intelligence and Security Service (Boes & Leukfeldt, 2017). As mentioned by these authors, two of the limitations of this PPP was the bottom-up approach model in which the government influences parties to work together instead of directing them, and the differences in culture and responsibility toward cybersecurity between law enforcement, intelligence services, and industry partners (Boes & Leukfeldt, 2017).

Private Sector

In private organizations identified as critical infrastructure, decisions are made within a business model based on profit margins, the customer's experience, and shareholder's interests (Carr, 2016). Cybersecurity risks are inevitable for private businesses, and these risks need to be evaluated based on the risk appetite of each organization (Christensen & Petersen, 2017). The tolerance to risks is unique to each organization, and risk is an integral part of doing business (Christensen & Petersen, 2017). As a fiduciary for its clients, the private sector has obligations to protect their personal information, and the government can directly benefit from private sector innovation assuming the right governance structures are in place. As explained by Petersen (2014), private organizations have moral and civic duties to citizens and customers which is associated with the concept of Corporate Social Responsibility (CSR). Hence, private companies such as financial institutions are not only accountable to their shareholders, but also their employees, customers, society, and the environment (Petersen, 2014). In the private sector's responsibility toward society, the private organization's role of contributing to national security is vital. As argued by Petersen (2014), companies can evaluate for themselves if they should take an active stance as well as investing in national security should they perceive that national security is a corporate benefit as it is a public good.

The role and responsibilities of the private sector, more specifically the Canadian financial institutions security professional's role in cybersecurity incident management regarding information sharing with the public sector to improve national security, is not always clear. As mentioned by Petersen (2014), many academics still do not fully understand the role of the private sector in the management of national security. The private sector generally wants to respond rapidly when a cyber incident occurs to protect its customer information, its reputation and to reduce its losses. Financial institutions are regrouping different teams together to create synergies and some organizations are regrouping data analytics and machine learning functions in a single group that is often called a fusion center (Cowley, 2018).

As described by Bright and Whelan (2018), the fusion center concept refers to intelligence collection and sharing information, but also to the facility at which intelligence can be shared between members of the fusion center. The main objective of fusion centers is to analyze the information collected from various sources to improve information sharing and the validity of the actionable intelligence that will be produced for its members (Bright & Whelan, 2018). According to these authors, there are currently over 70 recognized fusion centers within the United States under either the Department of Homeland Security or the Federal Bureau of Investigation organizational purviews, but technically these fusions are often joint task forces under the responsibility of their respective local jurisdictions (Bright & Whelan, 2018). Bright and Whelan (2018) explain there are very few fusion centers and most of them are focused primarily of national security and law enforcement.

The private sector motivations to participate in public and private partnerships are to be able to exercise its influence over the regulatory framework regarding legislation and public policy (International Centre for the Prevention of Crime, 2018). This allows for the overcoming of key limitations, to advance its private interests, to access resources, to share the risks and costs, to improve coordination in adapting to the changing nature of threats, to reduce its vulnerabilities, and to demonstrate that cybersecurity is a priority on the collective agenda (International Centre for the Prevention of Crime, 2018). However, information-sharing procedures and protocols have not been documented as of today, and there is no regulation in place nor an obligation to implement a cybersecurity framework (e.g., National Institute of Standards and Technology framework) in Canada. Many pieces of research on the public and private relationship in information sharing were conducted in other countries than Canada. The European Union Agency for Network and Information Security (ENISA) in Europe is an organization that various authors relied upon as an example in their analysis of previous private and public partnerships (International Centre for the Prevention of Crime, 2018). The private sector has commitments to its customers, and the government can directly benefit from the private sector innovation assuming the right governance structures are in place.

As Parker and Taylor (2010) advocate, there is now an emergence of what they refer to a "new security paradigm" in which financial borders and parameters are understood as "complex assemblage" in which financial institutions are capable and authorized to make security decisions themselves without the necessity to wait for approval by the public sector or other parties. According to Gallagher et al. (2014), Canadian financial institutions demonstrate a proactive behavior in building defense capabilities against cyberattacks; they are collaborating well between each other to fight the attacks as well as with the federal government. Unlike these researchers, Levi and Williams (2013) suggest the private's sector perception of the public sector is that it does not know enough about cybercrime and is not effective in managing it due to a lack of regulations.

The Corporate and Private Security Domain

The corporate or private security domain differs from the public police, the private security "contract" companies, or the loss prevention aspect of security (Walby & Lippert, 2014). As argued by Walby and Lippert (2014), corporate security is proprietary to a private organization or publicly traded firm. Its private security professionals are not contracted as they are full-time employees and these professionals must deal with complex situations to protect multiple assets of the organization (Walby & Lippert, 2014). Private sector professionals do not analyze security risks the same way public sector professionals do (Christensen & Petersen, 2017). In their study of Danish cybersecurity PPPs and interviews with CISO's, Christensen and Peterson (2017) demonstrate that public and private actors disagree over three aspects of cybersecurity which are the cybersecurity knowledge (actor versus vulnerabilities), the scope of partnerships (national versus global) and the nature of the expertise required (general information about trends versus technical details). The private security approach to cybersecurity risks is "vulnerability-focused" as they are less interested than the public sector in knowing if the issue at hand should correspond to a crime or a national security matter since the consequences for the business might be the same (Christensen & Petersen, 2017). When a security incident occurs, the private sector's primary focus is on maintaining the operations of the company, mitigating risk, and on improving the procedures, methods or processes to avoid a similar incident in the future (Christensen & Petersen, 2017). For the public sector, focus centers on the actor, potential motives, and technical methods, which is the reason why it does not always correspond to the perspective of the private sector and it becomes an obstacle to share information between public and private partners (Christensen & Petersen, 2017). Additionally, the private sector organizations must interact with a myriad of actors such as other private companies, citizens, or other groups with private interests not necessarily organized around the government (Christensen & Petersen, 2017). Private sector networks may be characterized as what Der Derian (2009) refers to as "heteropolarity" which is the "emergence of actors who are different in power and kind (state, corporate, group, individual) and connected globally through networks rather than hierarchically through state" (Christensen & Petersen, 2017, p. 1447).

As previously mentioned by Christensen and Petersen (2017) the actual state of information sharing between public and private partners relies on annual meetings consisting of sharing general information and trends. However, the private sector seeks to mobilize a continuous sharing of indicators of compromise and concrete technical information related to incidents to be able to scan their networks to mitigate risks and to manage internal security operations (Christensen & Petersen, 2017). For Christensen and Petersen (2017), partnerships are more than a set of procedures between organizations. Partnerships constitute a set of commitment and shared moral principles based on loyalty (Christensen & Petersen, 2017). A complete alignment between participants is not possible neither recommended as partnerships must balance two essential concerns; the need for community and national security through leadership and the need for pluralism and debate between its members (Christensen & Petersen, 2017). To avoid partnerships having "carte blanche" in sharing any information in the name of security, Christensen and Petersen, (2017) advocate that ***partnering through dissent***, encouraging divergence and contestation, is essential to embrace differences that are critical to the effectiveness and the democratic accountability of partnerships, continuous innovation as well as to enhance the democratic legitimacy of these information-sharing partnerships (Christensen, 2018).

The Importance of Technology

As mentioned by Kolini and Janczewski (2017), it is not possible to share timely information and complex data sets without the use of technology. Organizations use different systems to prevent, detect and respond to threats and cyber incidents. For example, financial institutions may use a security information and event management (SIEM) system and various technological tools to analyze logs and create alerts or events that investigative analysts will review for early detection of anomalies (Pomerleau & Auger-Perreault, 2020). To verify, analyze, and correlate the information, firewalls, intrusion detection and prevention systems (IDS and IPS), data integrity systems, access management tools, antivirus and system logs are standard tools for public and private organizations (Kolini & Janczewski, 2017).

Also, computer systems, network pieces of equipment and computer hardware's are essential for processing a large quantity of data in a secure manner between two or more organizations. Using the proper level of encryption is also key to protect, transfer and store confidential information. Dixon (2019) states new tools and platforms using technology such as homomorphic encryption is needed. Such tools will allow to protect victim's data as well as to enable global investigations, while also respecting the right to privacy.

Intelligence and information systems with technical standards such as MITRE'S (Mitre Corporation) or OASIS Cyber Threat Intelligence (CTI), standardized language such as the Structured Threat Information eXpression (STIX), or standardized exchange mechanisms such as the Trusted Automated eXchange of Indicator Information (TAXII) or the Cyber Observable eXpression (CybOX) normalized schema for communication events in system and network operations are used by various organizations to share information (Kolini & Janczewski, 2017; Skopik, Settanni, & Fiedler, 2016; United States Computer Emergency Readiness Team, n.d.). Also, to share information using technological systems, different data exchange protocols like Organization SOC (OSOC) or National SOC (NSOC) are necessary to collect data, and the Real-Time Inter-Network Defense (RID) protocol is a standard transport protocol various organization use to securely share information between each other (Settanni et al., 2017).

Summary

Many conclusions can be drawn from the literature on the topic of PPPs in information sharing to prevent cybercrime. There is a consensus that governments are ill-equipped to fight cybercrime without the involvement of the private sector, its resources, and its skills (Dixon, 2019; International Centre for the Prevention of Crime, 2018). Within this literature review, several themes have emerged. As articulated by Dunn-Cavelty and Suter (2009), public–private partnerships are no silver bullet, and there is a need to implement a new security framework for critical infrastructure protection. Private and public partnerships are not working as they should in sharing information to prevent cyberattacks on financial institutions. Also, private businesses require adequate incentives to participate in PPPs (Carr, 2016; Dixon, 2019; Mermoud, 2019). The information and the intelligence need to be shared in both ways to encourage reciprocity. Besides, the trust between members is critical to strengthening interorganizational relationships in fostering information sharing. Carr's (2016) conclusions resume what other scholars mentioned in the literature on this topic; the lack of trust, the absence of a legal framework in these partnership projects, and the importance of the personal relationship between the professionals of both sectors lead to PPPs that are not as efficient as they should be (Carr, 2016).

There are still significant disagreements about how to proceed to increase collaboration and to develop information-sharing policies, but everyone agrees that both public and private sectors need to share intelligence about attacks (Kaplan, Bailey, O'Halloran, Marcus, & Rezek, 2015). Some security professionals argue that governments will have to implement a legal framework to facilitate information sharing for better protection of critical infrastructures and find creative ways to remove legal challenges and barriers (Kaplan et al., 2015).

References

Ahl, I., & Lyer, R. (2018). *Detect and block email threats with customer YARA rules*. Retrieved from https://www.fireeye.com/blog/products-and-services/2018/12/detect-and-block-email-threats-with-custom-yara-rules.html.

Akhgar, B., & Brewster, B. (2016). *Combatting cybercrime and cyberterrorism: Challenges, trends, and priorities*. Cham, Switzerland: Springer.

Auerswald, P., Branscomb, L. M., La Porte, T. M., & Michel-Kerjan, E. (2005). The challenge of protecting critical infrastructure. *Issues in Science & Technology, 22*(1), 77–83. Retrieved from http://proxy1.ncu.edu/login?url=https://search.ebscohost.com/login.aspx?direct=true&db=edswss&AN=000232232900031&site=eds-live.

Avina, J. (2011). Public-private partnerships in the fight against crime: An emerging frontier in corporate social responsibility. *Journal of Financial Crime, 18*(3), 282.

Barkin, N. (2018). *Exclusive: Five eyes intelligence alliance builds coalition to counter China*. Retrieved from https://www.reuters.com/article/us-china-fiveeyes/exclusive-five-eyes-intelligence-alliance-builds-coalition-to-counter-china-idUSKCN1MM0GH.

Boes, S., & Leukfeldt, E. R. (2017). Fighting cybercrime: A joint effort. *Cyber-Physical Security*, 185. Retrieved from https://www.researchgate.net/publication/306035727_Fighting_Cybercrime_A_Joint_Effort.

Borden, M. R., Mooney, A. J., Taylor, M., & Sharkey, M. (2018). *Threat information sharing and GDPR: A lawful activity that protects personal data*. Retrieved from https://www.fsisac.com/sites/default/files/news/Threat%20Information%20Sharing%20and%20GDPR_TLP%20WHITE.pdf.

Borghard, D. E. (2018). *Protecting financial institutions against cyber threats: A national security issue*. Retrieved from https://carnegieendowment.org/files/WP_Borghard_Financial_Cyber_formatted_complete.pdf.

Bossong, R., & Wagner, B. (2017). A typology of cybersecurity and public-private partnerships in the context of the EU. *Crime, Law & Social Change, 67*(3), 265–288. https://doi.org/10.1007/s10611-016-9653-3.

Bright, D., & Whelan, C. (2018). On the relationship between goals, membership and network design in multi-agency "fusion" centres. *Policing: An International Journal of Police Strategies & Management*. https://doi.org/10.1108/PIJPSM-05-2018-0070.

Bures, O. (2013). Public-private partnerships in the fight against terrorism? *Crime, Law & Social Change, 60*(4), 429–455. https://doi.org/10.1007/s10611-013-9457-7.

Canadian Cyber Threat Exchange. (2015). *About CCTX*. Retrieved from https://cctx.ca/aboutcctx/.

CanCyber. (2019). *CanCyber cyber threat intelligence*. Retrieved from https://www.cancyber.org/?lang=en.

Carr, M. (2016). Public-private partnerships in national cyber-security strategies. *International Affairs, 92*(1), 43–62. https://doi.org/10.1111/1468-2346.12504.

CBC. (2016). *CSIS using new powers to disrupt terrorists since Bill C-51 became law*. Retrieved from https://www.cbc.ca/news/politics/c51-law-disrupt-power-1.3460613.

Center for Strategic & International Studies. (2019). *Significant cyber incidents*. Retrieved from https://www.csis.org/programs/cybersecurity-and-governance/technology-policy-program/other-projects-cybersecurity.

Cesteros, J. F. (2017). Collaboration of private investigation with public institutions within the Spanish cybersecurity strategy. How private investigation gathers proof on cyber delinquency. In J. Ramírez & L. García-Segura (Eds.), *Cyberspace; Risks and benefits for society, security, and development* (pp. 165–180). Cham, Switzerland: Springer. Retrieved from https://link.springer.com/chapter/10.1007%2F978-3-319-54975-0_10.

Chadderton, P., & Norton, S. (2019). *Public-private partnerships to disrupt financial crime: An exploratory study of Australia's Fintel alliance*. Retrieved from https://www.researchgate.net/publication/333619510_PUBLIC-PRI

VATE_PARTNERSHIPS_TO_DISRUPT_FINANCIAL_CRIME_AN_EXPLORATORY_STUDY_OF_AUSTRALIA'S_FINTEL_ALLIANCE.

Christensen, K. K. (2018). *Corporate zones of cyber security* (Doctoral dissertation). Retrieved from https://www.saxo.com/dk/corporate-zones-of-cyber-security_kristoffer-kjaergaard-christensen_pdf_9788772091402.

Christensen, K. K., & Petersen, K. (2017). Public-private partnerships on cyber security: A practice of loyalty. *International Affairs, 93*(6), 1435–1452. https://doi.org/10.1093/ia/iix189.

Cleary, C. (2019). Public-private partnerships: Security organizations. In L. Shapiro & M. H. Maras (Eds.), *Encyclopedia of security and emergency management*. Cham: Springer.

Cowley, S. (2018). *Banks adopt military-style tactics to fight cybercrime*. Retrieved from https://www.nytimes.com/2018/05/20/business/banks-cyber-security-military.html.

Collier, J. (2018). Cybersecurity assemblages: A framework for understanding the dynamic and contested nature of security provision. *Politics & Governance, 6*(2), 13–21. https://doi.org/10.17645/pag.v6i2.1324.

Cross, C. (2019). 'Oh we can't actually do anything about that': The problematic nature of jurisdiction for online fraud victims. *Criminology & Criminal Justice*. https://doi.org/10.1177/1748895819835910.

Crovini, C., Ossola, G., & Marchini, L. P. (2017). *Cyber risk: The new enemy for risk management in the age of globalization*. Retrieved from https://www.francoangeli.it/riviste/Scheda_Rivista.aspx?IDArticolo=61391&Tipo=Articolo%20PDF&idRivista=166.

Der Derian, J. (2009). *Virtuous war: Mapping the military-industrial-media-entertainment network*. Retrieved from https://www.amazon.ca/Virtuous-War-Military-Industrial-Media-Entertainment-Network-24-Feb-2009-Paperback/dp/B013ROXXS6/ref=tmm_pap_swatch_0?_encoding=UTF8&qid=1548154190&sr=1-1.

Dixon, W. (2019). *Fighting cybercrime—What happens to the law when the law cannot be enforced?* Retrieved from https://www.weforum.org/agenda/2019/02/fighting-cybercrime-what-happens-to-the-law-when-the-law-cannot-be-enforced/.

Dunn-Cavelty, M., & Suter, M. (2009). Public-private partnerships are no silver bullet: An expanded governance model for critical infrastructure protection. *International Journal of Critical Infrastructure Protection, 2*, 179–187. https://doi.org/10.1016/j.ijcip.2009.08.006.

Dupont, B. (2015). Security networks and counter-terrorism: A reflection on the limits of adversarial isomorphism. In M. Bouchard (Ed.), *Social networks, terrorism, and counter-terrorism* (pp. 155–174). New York, NY: Routledge. Retrieved from https://www.researchgate.net/publication/279561796_Sec

urity_networks_and_counter-terrorism_a_reflection_on_the_limits_of_adversarial_isomorphism.

Dupré, L. (2014). *EP3R 2010–2013: Four years of Pan-European public-private cooperation*. Heraklion, Greece: European Union Agency for Network Information Security. Retrieved from https://www.researchgate.net/publication/270592099_EP3R_2010-2013_-_Four_Years_of_Pan-European_Public_Private_Cooperation.

Etzioni, A. (2017). The fusion of the private and public sectors. *Contemporary Politics*, *23*(1), 53–62. https://doi-org.proxy1.ncu.edu/10.1080/13569775.2016.1213074.

Federal Bureau of Investigation Internet Crime Complaint Center. (2017). *Internet crime report*. Retrieved from https://pdf.ic3.gov/2017_IC3Report.pdf.

Gallagher, H., McMahon, W., & Morrow, R. (2014). Reports: Cybersecurity: Protecting the resilience of Canada's financial system. *Financial System Review*, 47–53. Retrieved from https://www.bankofcanada.ca/wp-content/uploads/2014/12/fsr-december14-morrow.pdf.

Germano, H. J. (2014). *Cybersecurity partnerships: A new era of public-private collaboration*. New York, NY: The Center on Law and Security, New York University School of Law. Retrieved from https://www.lawandsecurity.org/wp-content/uploads/2016/08/Cybersecurity.Partnerships-1.pdf.

Gendron, A., & Rudner, M. (2012). *Assessing cyber threats to Canadian infrastructures*. Report prepared for the Canadian Security Intelligence Service. Retrieved from https://www.csis.gc.ca/pblctns/ccsnlpprs/20121001_ccsnlpprs-en.php.

Gordon, W. R. (2018). Information sharing and collaboration. In A. K. Sood (Ed.), *Canadian cybersecurity 2018; An anthology of CIO/CISO enterprise-level perspectives* (pp. 107–128). Retrieved from https://issuu.com/clxforum/docs/canadian-cybersecurity_2018.

Gorniak, S., Tirtea, R., Ikonomou, D., Cadzow, S., Gierszal, H., Sutton, D., ..., Vishik, C. (2011). *Enabling and management end-to-end resilience*. Retrieved from https://www.enisa.europa.eu/publications/end-to-end-resilience.

Government of Canada. (2010). *Canada's cybersecurity strategy; For a stronger and more prosperous Canada*. Retrieved from https://www.publicsafety.gc.ca/cnt/rsrcs/pblctns/archive-cbr-scrt-strtgy/archive-cbr-scrt-strtgy-eng.pdf.

Government of Canada. (2015). *Security of Canadian Information Sharing Act: Public framework*. Retrieved from https://www.publicsafety.gc.ca/cnt/ntnl-scrt/cntr-trrrsm/shrng-frmwrk-en.aspx.

Government of Canada. (2017). *Disclosure provisions*. Retrieved from http://laws-lois.justice.gc.ca/eng/acts/C-46/page-100.html#h-140.

Government of Canada. (2018a). *The Canadian center for cyber security was established on October 1st, 2018*. Retrieved from https://www.cse-cst.gc.ca/en/backgrounder-fiche-information.

Government of Canada. (2018b). *Canadian Security Intelligence Service*. Retrieved from https://www.canada.ca/en/security-intelligence-service.html.

Government of Canada. (2019). *Emergency management act*. Retrieved from https://laws-lois.justice.gc.ca/eng/acts/E-4.56/page-1.html#h-2.

Grant, V. (2018). Critical infrastructure public-private partnerships: When is the responsibility for leadership exchanged? *Security Challenges, 14*(1), 40–52. Retrieved from https://www.regionalsecurity.org.au/resources/Documents/Grant.pdf.

Hämmerli, B. (2012). Financial service industry. In J. Lopez, R. Setola, & S. D. Wolthusen (Eds.), *Critical infrastructure protection; Information infrastructure models, analysis, and defense* (pp. 301–329). Retrieved from https://link.springer.com/chapter/10.1007/978-3-642-28920-0_13.

Holt, J. T. (2018). Regulating cybercrime through law enforcement and industry mechanisms. *Annals of the American Academy of Political and Social Science, 679*(1), 140–157. https://doi-org.proxy1.ncu.edu/10.1177/0002716218783679.

International Centre for the Prevention of Crime. (2018). *6th international report on crime prevention and community safety: Preventing cybercrime*. Retrieved from http://www.crime-prevention-intl.org/en/publications/report/report/article/6th-international-report-on-crime-prevention-and-community-safety-preventing-cybercrime.html.

Johnson, A. L. (2016). Cybersecurity for financial institutions: The integral role of information sharing in cyber-attack mitigation. *North Carolina Banking Institute, 20*, 277. Retrieved from http://scholarship.law.unc.edu/cgi/viewcontent.cgi?article=1400&context=ncbi.

Kaijankoski, A. E. (2015). *Cybersecurity information sharing between public-private sector agencies* (Master thesis). Retrieved from https://apps.dtic.mil/dtic/tr/fulltext/u2/a620766.pdf.

Kaplan, M. J., Bailey, T., O'Halloran, D., Marcus, A., & Rezek, C. (2015). *Beyond cybersecurity*. Retrieved from https://www.amazon.ca/Beyond-Cybersecurity-Protecting-Digital-Business/dp/1119026849/ref=sr_1_1?s=books&ie=UTF8&qid=1530879571&sr=1-1&keywords=beyond+cybersecurity.

Kerravala, Z. (2018). *Zeek: A free, powerful way to monitor networks, detect threats*. Retrieved from https://www.csoonline.com/article/3313050/security/zeek-a-free-powerful-way-to-monitor-networks-detect-threats.html.

Kolini, F., & Janczewski, L. (2017). *Two heads are better than one: A theoretical model for cybersecurity intelligence sharing (CIS) between organisations*. Retrieved from https://www.acis2017.org/wp-content/uploads/2017/11/ACIS2017_paper_199_RIP.pdf.

Laughlin, C. (2016). Cybersecurity in critical infrastructure sectors: A proactive approach to ensure inevitable laws and regulations are effective. *Colorado Technology Journal, 2,* 345. Retrieved from https://ctlj.colorado.edu/wp-content/uploads/2016/06/v3.final-Laughlin-4.26.16-JRD.pdf.

Leuprecht, C. (2019). *Mitigating cyber risk across the financial sector.* Retrieved from https://www.cigionline.org/articles/mitigating-cyber-risk-across-financial-sector.

Leuprecht, C., & Maclellan, S. (2018). *Governing cyber security in Canada, Australia, and the United States.* Retrieved from https://www.cigionline.org/sites/default/files/documents/SERENE-RISCweb.pdf.

Leuprecht, C., Szeman, J., & Skillicorn, D. B. (2019). The Damoclean sword of offensive cyber: Policy uncertainty and collective insecurity. *Contemporary Security Policy, 40*(3), 382–407. https://doi.org/10.1080/13523260.2019.1590960.

Levin, A., & Goodrick, P. (2013). From cybercrime to cyberwar? The international policy shift and its implications for Canada? *Canadian Foreign Policy (CFP), 19*(2), 127–143. https://doi.org/10.1080/11926422.2013.805150.

Levi, M., & Williams, L. M. (2013). Multi-agency partnerships in cybercrime reduction; Mapping the UK information assurance network cooperation space. *Information Management & Computer Security, 21*(5), 420. https://doi.org/10.1108/IMCS-04-2013-0027.

Maras, H. M. (2017). Overcoming the intelligence-sharing paradox: Improving information sharing through change in organizational culture. *Comparative Strategy, 36*(3), 187–197. https://doi-org.proxy1.ncu.edu/10.1080/01495933.2017.1338477.

Maxwell, J. N. (2019). *Expanding the capability of financial information-sharing partnerships.* Retrieved from https://rusi.org/publication/occasional-papers/expanding-capability-financial-information-sharing-partnerships.

McCarthy, R. D. (2018). *Privatizing political authority: Cybersecurity, public-private partnerships, and the reproduction of liberal political order.* Retrieved from https://www.cogitatiopress.com/politicsandgovernance/article/viewFile/1335/1335.

Mermoud, A. (2019). *Three articles on the behavioral economics of security information sharing: A theoretical framework, an empirical test, and policy recommendations* (Doctoral dissertation). Retrieved from https://serval.unil.ch/search.

Mezher, T., El Khatib, S., & Sooriyaarachchi, T. M. (2015). Cyber-attacks on critical infrastructure and potential sustainable development impacts. *International Journal of Cyber Warfare & Terrorism, 5*(3), 1. https://doi.org/10.4018/IJCWT.2015070101.

National Critical Infrastructure Intelligence Team. (2015). *Modernization of the RCMP's suspicious incident reporting system.* Retrieved from https://carleton.

ca/irrg/wp-content/uploads/Vol-1-Issue-4-IRRG-Journal-FINAL-FINAL.pdf.
Nish, A., & Naumann, S. (2019). *The cyber threat landscape: Confronting challenges to the financial system*. Retrieved from https://carnegieendowment.org/2019/03/25/cyber-threat-landscape-confronting-challenges-to-financial-system-pub-78506.
O'Donnell, B., & Nesbitt, R. (2016). *Cyber risk and security in Canada*. Retrieved from https://globalriskinstitute.org/publications/cyber-risk-security-canada/.
Office of the Privacy Commissioner of Canada. (2017). *Applying paragraphs 7 (3) (d.1) and 7 (3) (d.2) of PIPEDA*. Retrieved from https://www.priv.gc.ca/en/privacy-topics/privacy-laws-in-canada/the-personal-information-protection-and-electronic-documents-act-pipeda/pipeda-compliance-help/gd_d1-d2_201703/.
Parker, M., & Taylor, M. (2010). Financial intelligence: A price worth paying? *Studies in Conflict & Terrorism, 33*(11), 949–959. https://doi.org/10.1080/1057610X.2010.514574.
Petersen, L. K. (2014). The politics of corporate security and the translation of national security. In K. Walby & R. Lippert (Eds.), *Corporate security in the 21st century: Theory and practice in international perspective* (pp. 78–94). Retrieved from https://link.springer.com/chapter/10.1057/9781137346070_5.
Pomerleau, P. L., & Auger-Perreault, M. (2020). Fraud risk management: Using fraud analytics to combat external and insider threats. In L. Shapiro & M. H. Maras (Eds.), *Encyclopedia of security and emergency management*. Cham: Springer. Retrieved from https://link.springer.com/referenceworkentry/10.1007/978-3-319-69891-5_296-1.
Public Safety Canada. (2009). *National strategy for critical infrastructure*. Retrieved from https://www.publicsafety.gc.ca/cnt/rsrcs/pblctns/srtg-crtcl-nfrstrctr/srtg-crtcl-nfrstrctr-eng.pdf.
Public Safety Canada. (2017). *Cyber review consultations papers*. Retrieved from https://www.publicsafety.gc.ca/cnt/rsrcs/pblctns/2017-cybr-rvw-cnslttns-rprt/index-en.aspx.
Public Safety Canada. (2018a). *Critical infrastructure*. Retrieved from https://www.publicsafety.gc.ca/cnt/ntnl-scrt/crtcl-nfrstrctr/index-en.aspx.
Public Safety Canada. (2018b). *National cybersecurity strategy*. Retrieved from https://www.publicsafety.gc.ca/cnt/rsrcs/pblctns/ntnl-cbr-scrt-strtg/index-en.aspx?wbdisable=true.
PWC. (2017). *Strengthening digital society against cyber shocks; Key findings for the Global State of Information Security survey 2018*. Retrieved from https://www.pwc.com/us/en/cybersecurity/assets/pwc-2018-gsiss-strengthening-digital-society-against-cyber-shocks.pdf.

Quigley, K. (2013). "Man plans, god laughs": Canada's national strategy for protecting critical infrastructure. *Canadian Public Administration, 56*(1), 142–164. https://doi-org.proxy1.ncu.edu/10.1111/capa.12007.
Quigley, K., Bisset, B., & Mills, B. (2017). *Too critical to fail: How Canada manages threats to critical infrastructure*. Retrieved from https://www.amazon.ca/Too-Critical-Fail-Manages-Infrastructure/dp/0773551611/ref=sr_1_1?s=books&ie=UTF8&qid=1548361193&sr=1-1&keywords=too+critical+to+fail.
Rid, T., & Buchanan, B. (2015). Attributing cyber-attacks. *Journal of Strategic Studies, 38*(1–2), 4–37. https://doi-org.proxy1.ncu.edu/10.1080/01402390.2014.977382.
Rosemont, H. (2016). *Public-private security cooperation: From cyber to financial crime*. Retrieved from https://rusi.org/publication/occasional-papers/public%E2%80%93private-security-cooperation-cyber-financial-crime.
Rudner, M. (2013). Cyber-threats to critical national infrastructure: An intelligence challenge. *International Journal of Intelligence & Counterintelligence, 26*(3), 453–481. https://doi.org/10.1080/08850607.2013.780552.
San Juan Menacho, V., & Martin, A. (2018). *Cyber governance and the financial services sector: The role of public-private partnerships*. Retrieved from https://osf.io/preprints/socarxiv/ybqgm/.
Sedenberg, M. E., & Dempsey, X. J. (2018). *Cybersecurity information sharing governance structures: An ecosystem of diversity, trust, and tradeoffs*. Retrieved from https://arxiv.org/abs/1805.12266.
Settanni, G., Skopik, F., Shovgenya, Y., Fiedler, R., Carolan, M., Conroy, D., & Olli, P. (2017). A collaborative cyber incident management system for European interconnected critical infrastructures. *Journal of Information Security and Applications, 34*(Part 2), 166–182. https://doi-org.proxy1.ncu.edu/10.1016/j.jisa.2016.05.005.
Shore, M. J. J., & Schafer, C. (2015). *Review of commissions of inquiry with respect to findings of Major, O'connor, Iacobucci concerning information sharing that affects critical infrastructure protection*. Critical information protection—Information sharing protocol project, CSSP-2013-CP-1026. Retrieved from http://cradpdf.drdc-rddc.gc.ca/PDFS/unc199/p801815_A1b.pdf.
Skopik, F., Settanni, G., & Fiedler, R. (2016). A problem shared is a problem halved: A survey on the dimensions of collective cyber defense through security information sharing. *Computers & Security, 60*, 154–176. https://doi-org.proxy1.ncu.edu/10.1016/j.cose.2016.04.003.
Solomon, H. (2018). *Federal budget: RCMP, CSE to get new cybercrime fighting centres*. Retrieved from https://www.itworldcanada.com/article/federal-budget-rcmp-cse-to-get-new-cyber-crime-fighting-centres/402264.

Spencer, M. F. (2017). *Public-private partnerships (PPPs) for cybersecurity infrastructures*. Retrieved from https://www.researchgate.net/publication/332182533_Public-Private_Partnerships_PPPs_for_Cybersecurity_Infrastructures.
Sullivan, C., & Burger, E. (2017). "In the public interest": The privacy implications of international business-to-business sharing of cyber-threat intelligence. *Computer Law & Security Review: The International Journal of Technology Law and Practice*. https://doi.org/10.1016/j.clsr.2016.11.015.
Taleb, N. N. (2007). *The black swan: The impact of the highly improbable*. Retrieved from https://www.amazon.ca/Black-Swan-Impact-Highly-Improbable/dp/1400063515/ref=sr_1_1?s=books&ie=UTF8&qid=1548379708&sr=1-1&keywords=the+black+swan+the+impact+of+highly+improbable.
United States Computer Emergency Readiness Team. (n.d.). *Information sharing specifications for cybersecurity*. Retrieved from https://www.us-cert.gov/Information-Sharing-Specifications-Cybersecurity.
Vroegop, R. (2017). *The state of information and intelligence sharing in Canada*. The Conference Board of Canada. Retrieved from http://www.conferenceboard.ca/e-library/abstract.aspx?did=8487.
Walby, K., & Lippert, R. (2014). *Corporate security in the 21st century: Theory and practice in international perspective*. Retrieved from https://www.amazon.ca/Corporate-Security-21st-Century-International/dp/1349466816/ref=sr_1_1?s=books&ie=UTF8&qid=1548066995&sr=1-1&keywords=Corporate+security+in+the+21st+century%3A+Theory+and+practice+in+international+perspective.
Wanca, I. (2014). *Structuring public-private partnership for reducing cyber risk to critical infrastructure*. Kindle Edition. Retrieved from https://www.amazon.ca/dp/B00JARC3EU.
Willis, H. H., Lester, G., & Treverton, F, G. (2009). Information sharing for infrastructure risk management: Barriers and solutions. *Intelligence & National Security, 24*(3), 339–365. Retrieved from https://doi-org.proxy1.ncu.edu/10.1080/02684520903036925.
Wilson, C. (2014). Cyber threats to critical information infrastructure. In L. J. Thomas & N. Chen, *Cyberterrorism: Understanding, Assessment, and Response* (pp. 123–136). London: Springer-Swansea University. Retrieved from https://www.researchgate.net/publication/264541687_Cyber_Threats_to_Critical_Information_Infrastructure.
World Bank. (2017). *Combatting cybercrime: Tools and capacity building for emerging economies*. Retrieved from https://openknowledge.worldbank.org/handle/10986/30306?locale-attribute=fr.
Wright, S. (2017). Mythology of cyber-crime – insecurity & governance in cyberspace: Some critical perspective. In: J. Ramírez & L. García-Segura (Eds.), *Cyberspace; Risks and benefits for society, security, and development* (pp. 211-227). Cham, Switzerland: Springer. Retrieved from https://link.springer.com/chapter/10.1007/978-3-319-54975-0_13.

CHAPTER 6

Research Findings; Contemporary Perceptions of Canadian Security Professionals Regarding the Challenges in Sharing Information with the Public Sector

The purpose of this qualitative study was to conduct interviews with corporate security professionals (corporate and information security) representing Canada's national-level financial institutions. The primary research focus was (a) to obtain information to understand better the challenges these private security professionals face in sharing information aimed at preventing cybersecurity incidents with the public sector and (b) to provide recommendations for national banking key decision-makers on how best to robust their existing cybersecurity protections. Additionally, this study sought to determine if the Network Security Governance Framework approach first proposed by Dupont (2004) and later adapted by Whelan and Dupont (2017), facilitates a better understanding this phenomenon or aids in identifying best practices for collective information sharing. This study sought to address the central problem of why private and public partnership relationships have been ineffective in monitoring, detecting, and reacting to cybersecurity incidents—all while attempting to share information and intelligence.

P.-L. Pomerleau and D. L. Lowery, *Countering Cyber Threats to Financial Institutions*,
https://doi.org/10.1007/978-3-030-54054-8_6

Results

The resulting data of this qualitative study include various direct quotes from the interviews with private security professionals working for Canadian financial institutions. This analysis illustrated the perceptions of these security professionals regarding the phenomenon under study. Also, this study provided more information about why information sharing between PPPs actors is not optimal. This analysis allowed to propose recommendations to decision-makers about what should be done to improve information sharing between public and private actors in Canada and to reduce the impacts of cyber-threats on financial institutions in the future.

Demographic Data

A total of 44 security professionals ($N = 17$ CSO & $N = 27$ CISO) or direct deputies—members of the Financial Crime Investigation and Response Specialists Group (FCIRSG) or and the Cyber Security Specialists (CSSG) groups—working for 24 separate major Canadian financial institutions received the email invitation from the Canadian Bankers Association (CBA) to participate in this study. The final sample consisted of 10 survey respondents, which represented approximately 23% of the security professionals (or their direct deputies) who received the original Canadian Bankers Association email invitation. From these ten survey respondents, nine security professionals (90%) accepted to participate in the June 2019 research interviews. Unfortunately, one of the 10 willing survey participants was unable to schedule an interview during the two weeks interview timeframe in June 2019, due to scheduling conflicts. For the survey, five participants were CSOs (50%), four participants were CSO's deputies (40%), and the last participant was a CISO's deputy (10%). A total of seven participants (70%) worked in Toronto, and the other three participants (30%) were working in Montreal.

For the interviews, four participants were CSOs (44.44%), four participants were CSO's deputies (44.44%), and the last participant was a CISO's deputy (11.11%). As for banking representation, six participants (60%) were working for a major "Schedule 1" banks with five of these six participants working directly for one of the six largest banking institutions in Canada that are members of the Canadian Banking Association. More specifically, the six participants working for Schedule 1 banks represented 19% of all domestic schedule 1 banks across Canada (Table 6.1).

Table 6.1 Study participants by bank

Schedule 1	*Schedule 2*	*Others*
$N = 6$ (60%)	$N = 2$ (20%)	$N = 2$ (20%)

Note Schedule 1 are domestic banks, Schedule 2; foreign banks subsidiaries, Others includes Schedule 3 banks and credit unions. There are 67 federally regulated financial institutions which represent 31 domestic banks, 15 foreign bank subsidiaries, and 21 foreign bank branches that are members of the Canadian Bankers Association (CBA) (Canadian Bankers Association, 2019)

A total of six interviews—four in-person and two by phone—were conducted from the CBA office in Toronto (one participant interviewed in-person in Toronto even though he works full-time in Montreal). The other three interviews were conducted at the participant's respective office (one in Toronto and two in Montreal) since site permission was provided to the researcher by email. All participants were legal residents and working professionals in Canada. All participants were responsible for corporate security or cybersecurity operations at the national level. Thus, seven interviews were conducted in Toronto, five in-person, and two by phone, while the remaining two interviews were conducted in-person in Montreal.

As we can see from Table 6.2, all the study participants were males (90%) except for one female (10%). A total of five participants (50%) were between 48 and 57 years of age. Four participants had a bachelor's degree (40%), one had a master's degree (10%), and six participants confirmed holding a professional certification (60%). The most common professional certification among participant was the Certified Fraud Examiner (CFE) since four participants (40%) hold this certification title.

In terms of professional experiences, four participants (40%) previously worked in the law enforcement arena—both at the provincial and federal levels—and two other participants (20%) worked for an intelligence agency before joining their respective financial institution. Four participants (40%) confirmed having more than ten years of experience in the banking sector. All participants attested having participated in a public–private partnership within their current employment. Four participants confirmed (40%) having participated in one or more public–private partnerships for three to five years' duration, and two participants (20%) confirmed participating in some form of public–private partnerships for seven years or more.

Table 6.2 Demographical information of participants

Characteristics	N
Gender	
Male	9
Female	1
Age	
18–27	
28–37	2
38–47	2
48–57	5
58–67	1
68 and older	
Education	
High school	1
College or Cégep (Quebec)	3
Associate	
Bachelor	4
Master	2
Doctorate	
Professional certifications	
Yes	6
No	4
Previous career experience	
Law enforcement	4
Intelligence agencies	2
Financial industry only	2
Other industry	2
Years of experience in banking sector	
1–3	3
3–5	
5–7	1
7–10	2
More than 10	4
Previous experience in PPP	
Yes	10
No	

For both survey and interview samples, each participant was assigned a professional descriptor; Chief Security Officers were identified as CSO, Chief Security Officers deputies as CSO-Deputy. Chief Information Security Officers were identified as CISO and Chief Information Security Officers deputies as CISO-Deputy.

Table 6.3 Emergent themes from interviews

Number	*Emergent themes*
Theme 1	Receiving Timely Information Sharing for Prevention Purposes
Theme 2	Joint-Ventures—Integrated Public–Private Fusion Centers
Theme 3	Mechanisms to Share Information
Theme 4	Lack of Legal Framework for Crime Prevention
Theme 5	Conflicting Organizational Missions & Objectives
Theme 6	Interpersonal Trust Relationships
Theme 7	Unclear Roles, Responsibilities, and Processes in Critical Infrastructure Protection
Theme 8	CyberAttacks on Banks; A Potential Domino Effect
Theme 9	Cross-Sector Critical Infrastructure Information Sharing
Theme 10	Necessity to Increase Cyber-Threat Information Sharing
Theme 11	Governance Model to Share Information; The BCPIF Framework
Theme 12	Various Types of Security Networks Are Necessary

A total of 12 core themes emerged from the data collection and analysis of the interviews conducted with security professionals working for Canadian financial institutions. The themes presented in Table 6.3 stemmed from the analysis of the four research questions in this study. Each of these themes is addressed in greater detail in the following discussion.

Theme 1: Receiving Timely Information Sharing for Prevention Purposes

Participants in this study mentioned that to be able to deal with cyber-threats, it is critical for banking security professionals to receive information and intelligence promptly. To prevent incidents, financial institutions security professionals want to receive information or actionable intelligence, and they would like to receive in near real-time or as frequent as possible. This intelligence may come from both sectors. By receiving the information in a matter of minutes, hours, or days, they will be in a better position to prevent an incident of occurring, or they will be able to respond in a timely manner to mitigate losses or the impacts to their organization and its stakeholders. Four participants mentioned the importance of receiving timely information for prevention purposes:

CSO #1: "I think, particularly with cyber, we've got to be very quick in our response. So, we can't sit there and go, ah, you know, I've got a meeting in a month maybe we can discuss it then. Cyber works very, very quickly so we've got to have a network in place that we can either communicate quickly with the members to say, heads up, we've got an issue here, this is what's happened, it's just happened and be able to get that information very quickly. So hopefully, the banks that have been impacted can put processes in place to prevent them from being and becoming a victim. So, I think it is the speed of everything."

By sharing information between banks or by receiving intelligence from the public sector, one financial institution being victimized may assist the others in preventing the same incident of being perpetrated a second time. For study participants, the same logic also applies to threat actors. CSO #2 referred to the importance of receiving critical information in real-time or near real-time when it comes to cyber-fraud attempts against his organization as fraud incidents may lead to significant monetary losses. CSO #3 also mentioned that in his perspective, timely information sharing should be perceived as a best practice and that while sharing sensitive information, it is possible to avoid sharing classified, proprietary, or confidential information:

CSO #3: "Best practices. Obviously timely sharing, very similar to what we need to do in relation to reporting irregularities, within twenty-four, forty-eight or seventy-two hours maximum, I think is gravely important so that it's done in a timely basis. I think it needs to be full, fair, and frank disclosure similar to wiretap law. It has to be that. Don't hold anything back."

Hackers and cybercriminals do exchange information with each other regularly. These bad actors share vulnerabilities of potential victims they can attack. By sharing timely information about threats, banks can reduce their vulnerabilities to make it harder for criminals to attack them.

Standard Operating Procedures (SOPs) to Share Data

Several participants mentioned that it would be essential for PPPs partners to have common definitions of the types of data that is being shared as the definitions and classifications of data sets for each organization might defer, thus significantly impacting the quality of the information transferred between partners. Each organization and banking security professionals might define a cyber-related or fraud incident differently. Data quality is critical for members of a PPP to enable knowledgeable business decisions or for law enforcement to make sure they identify the right individuals within a group of hackers, fraudsters, or organized crime ring. For instance, the definition of a fraud types such as an account takeover (Fraudulently changing the information on a client's account, e.g., address) or a true name fraud application (fraudulent applications for a bank loan with the full identify of another individual) might not be the same for each security professionals or their respective financial institution employees. Additionally, participants recognized the importance of using common procedures to share critical information allowing organizations to better analyze the root cause of the incidents or the individuals responsible for criminal activities at multiple financial institutions and to learn from previous incidents as mentioned by CSO #4:

> *CSO #4*: "You know, what could be discussed is also the standardization of definitions amongst the private sector and also amongst the public sector."

Theme 2: Joint-Ventures—Integrated Public–Private Fusion Centers

Another best practice described by five participants was the importance of having law enforcement and private sector banking security professionals working together "side by side" in a fusion center type of operational team. CSO-Deputy #2 explained that many banks are currently creating their fusion center within their organization, but he added that a similar fusion center should be created between banks and law enforcement to combat cyber-threats and financial crime as this kind of centralized team does not exist today:

> *CSO-Deputy #2*: "I think a joint venture in that way, in that regard, would go a long way in improving resiliency and response, being more quickly and effective."

Study participants explained that it would be important to have a virtual fusion center as people from both public and private sectors do not necessarily need to be physically sitting in the same location to share information between each other. Technology now allows sharing information through virtual platforms. CSO #3 described that to become effective, a fusion center is necessary to gather different information and intelligence feeds holistically in a centralized operational team. He provides an example he witnessed in a bank with operations in the United States:

CSO #3: "So, I've been exposed to that where I've seen that down in the United States with [Bank] where there was social media information being picked up, there was newsfeed that was being picked up, there was world events being picked up. All of those things to see and then, of course, then there is the entire network system that's being monitored in relation to attacks, right, and where it's coming from."

Collective Defense for a Holistic View of the Threats

Participants argued PPPs are necessary to get a holistic view of the threats both sectors are facing. The private sector has a large data set that may allow law enforcement or intelligence agencies to identify common suspects and cyber threat actors. The public sector often has strategic intelligence that is perceived as the "needle" the private sector needs to be able to identify bad actors in the "haystack" of each financial institution's holdings. Seven interviewees felt that both sectors should work together to implement a continuous intelligence-sharing cycle. By sharing information about crimes such as cyber-fraud, both sectors would be in a better position to counter organized crime or to prepare for state actors attacks against the financial industry. Overall, a collective defense and collaboration against common threats toward the public and private sectors should be possible through information sharing between financial institutions among themselves (Private to private) as well as from the private sector to the government and law enforcement to the private sector and vice versa (Public to private and private to the public sectors).

Each sector has data that could be beneficial for the other sector in identifying threats or common data sets they do not know about by looking at it individually. By combining these various types of data sets and information and removing silos, it would allow identifying relationships, new patterns, to identify more actors, and to understand better who is behind these criminal activities:

CSO-Deputy #2: "Well, I think it's important that, you know, we don't work in silo anymore. I think … or we shouldn't be because the nature of the threat is that it's a, and I think you will agree with me that it's multi-dimensional and it comes from different vectors."

Theme 3: Mechanisms to Share Information

Study participants explained that various mechanisms exist to communicate with the public sector. Even if meeting each other in-person, verbal communications over the phone, and exchanging secure emails are still commonly used between public and private partners; virtual private platforms are the most appropriate communication mechanism to exchange information securely.

The Canadian Financial Intelligence Initiative (CFII) is an initiative brought forward with the financial institutions to be able to share information with each other. This virtual platform facilitates secure communications. CSO #2 explained the CFII initiative:

> *CSO #2*: "I know that we're in the process right now of using something [CFII - Intralinks] that we have built as an industry to exchange information, but it's something that we built, right. So, it's a communication vehicle; it's a platform for data sharing, it's encrypted and has all the honorability in governance we want so we can tell who looked at it, what they took etcetera. That is envisioned as a private-to-private sharing mechanism that can be utilized to exchange information with law enforcement."

CSO #2 added that the CFII initiative could be enhanced in the future:

> *CSO #2*: "And what you really could do if you want to go far enough and it was something that we've examined under what we call the CFII, the Canadian Financial Intelligence Sharing Initiative, we had that, but we stopped short of it. There is a sort of peer to peer intelligence sharing, where the data resides on everybody's respective machines, kind of like Napster, I guess, right, but this is legal Napster."

Participants mentioned CFII is still rudimentary, but it is the best communication tool they have to share information. Also, participants mentioned they had access to some virtual platforms to share information with law enforcement or intelligence agencies (e.g., SIR).

> *CSO-Deputy #3*: "I know of SIR [Suspicious Incident Reporting] through the RCMP. I know that there is a secure platform through the service."

According to the participants, improvements were made over the years by the Canadian Security Intelligence Service to improve the threat indicators sharing to assist financial institutions in identifying potential risks. As mentioned by CSO #4, the **agency** considerably improved how information is being shared between public and private actors or vice versa to prevent potential incidents that may have significant impacts on the financial industry and the security of the country. One of the ways the agency improved information sharing with financial institutions is by using a new two-way secure information exchange system:

> *CSO #4*: "If you look at the CSIS and the [Redacted] program [Canadian Security Intelligence Service Secured online platform] you know, the process used to be very archaic and old school and inefficient and sometimes even insecure. And so [Redacted] is basically a security electronics communication portal that the private sector has with the Canadian Intelligence Security Service basically to have a two-way method of communicating in either by sharing documents or even having a chat platform to send messages which enables for a quick and secure sharing of information."

Encrypted communications through a secure virtual platform allow to share threat indicators in a very short timeframe and to automate this information within the banking systems:

> *CISO-Deputy #1*: "STIX TAXII is great because the point of it is that you don't need a person in the middle. The IOCs come in, they automatically get into the system, and the system looks for all the vulnerabilities. It's, it's like a security, and it's a cybersecurity blanket."

Theme 4: Lack of Legal Framework for Crime Prevention

All nine participants in this study were unequivocal and unanimous in emphasizing the actual legal framework as a critical challenge in sharing information with the public sector to be efficient in preventing crime against the financial institutions. Under this lack of a legal information-sharing framework, participants also mentioned privacy issues associated with getting the consent from victims, customers, or the individuals under investigation to share information as well as the potential reputational risks associated with sharing information in these circumstances.

There is currently a framework in place between banks (e.g., bank to bank) which is the Bank Crime Prevention and Investigation Framework (BCPIF) that enables the sharing of information with the intention of preventing crime, but such a framework does not exist to share information with the public sector. Moreover, there is no legal framework to share information between financial institutions and other private organizations (e.g., telecommunications companies to a bank) to help prevent cyber-related attacks.

For criminal matters such as threats to life and extenuating circumstances, private security professionals may provide information to law enforcement without consent of the individual via an exception provided in Canadian privacy legislation (PIPEDA). However, these situations do not apply to cyber-threats and financial crimes against financial institutions. The culture of information sharing, the reason to share, and the need to share information are not the same between public sector executives and private security professionals. As mentioned, some exceptions in the current legislation allow both public and private actors to share information while responding to an emergency, threats to life or terrorism-related matters, but as mentioned by CSO #4, there are not enough legal remedies to share information to prevent and detect incidents:

> *CSO #4*: "So, we'll see how things go but before, for things to effectively change, to have an effective PPP framework in place with any private sector, if we're looking at critical infrastructure in Canada, there needs to be a drastic change of mentality and the ability to influence government to change legislation to enable that."

Participants compared the current legal framework in Canada to similar legal frameworks in the United Kingdom and the United States. Security professionals referred primarily to the obligation to share information versus having a voluntary approach. Some participants were under the impression that the public sector professionals misunderstand the type of information financial institutions would like or need to receive. Financial institutions security professionals do not want to receive information about the bad actors under investigation, but they would like to get specific and detailed threat indicators to be able to manage the risks they are facing in having similar bad actors targeting their organization:

> *CSO #2*: "So, on the public side there's a perception of a legislative blockage. So, in some cases, there is a strong belief that there is a

regulatory prohibition against sharing. And while that's true, it protects certain elements of information but not all elements, right. So, for example, they may not be able to share specifics about individuals, but they can share general threat factors as an example."

Other amendments in Bill S-4 in 2015 eliminated the notion of investigative bodies under the law, and these changes created uncertainty among banking security professionals who were attempting to suppress crimes while adding the limitation to banks to share information for no other crimes than fraud (Canadian Bankers Association, 2015). CSO #2 explained his perspective:

CSO #2: "Back in 2001, we had PIPEDA [The Personal Information Protection and Electronic Act] had the right to share information between banks for pretty much any type of crime under the umbrella of, like a body of investigation, that was CBA [Canadian Bankers Association]. Since then, in 2016 or 2017 the Bill S4 removed the body of investigation of CBA from being a body of investigation and to share mostly information for fraud-related matters, instead of like other crimes."

Even though banks have a framework (BCPIF) to share information among themselves for fraud prevention purposes, such a framework is not in place to share information with the public sector. Private security professionals may share information on a voluntary basis with the public sector or vice versa, but participants argued that the current legal framework is not robust enough to influence people to share. Interviewees mentioned they do share information in emergency situations, but the public sector professionals do not have clear protections under the law to share information for crime prevention purposes as reported by CSO #4:

CSO #4: "So, I would say the biggest problem is with the public sector, the lack of clear and find a legal framework that allows them to share not just in case of emergencies but is in more of a preventative way."

Participants explained that in their experience, there are different perspectives among lawyers regarding the possibility to share information with the public sector when it comes to crime prevention. Some would say that you can share information for fraud prevention only while others might conclude that you can share for fraud prevention as well as for contraventions of the laws of Canada which makes it difficult for security professionals to know when they can share information to prevent crime and when they cannot share information to prevent crime.

Privacy and Consent to Disclose

When it comes to managing the investigation of a data breach and share information with law enforcement, seven participants mentioned they had difficulty to understand how they could get the consent of all the clients potentially victimized in the breach to share the information with law enforcement. CSO-Deputy #3 explained how she is experiencing it:

> *CSO-Deputy #3*: "Yes. Consent 100%. Especially when you have, like with relation to cyber, it usually relates to multiple accounts. So, you have to go and try to get consent from all, from the actual customer in order to release that information to law enforcement that is a big, big thing. The governance in which information is exchanged is always fundamental."

For study participants, there is a blurred line in terms of national security and privacy laws. Security professionals are trying to understand what is considered private and when does privacy become less important than national security:

> *CISO-Deputy #1*: "Maybe it needs to be improving Canada's laws around what is considered private and when does privacy become less important than national security. But that's a very slippery slope."
>
> "I think that there's room for improvement in the legislation because these laws are typically, like 50 years old. They don't even consider a digital aspect to it."

This participant continued to explain what other participants mentioned and he explained that what the private sector needs is not necessarily personally identifiable information (PII), but indicators that they can use in their prevention and detection systems:

> *CISO-Deputy #1*: "Although the data contains privacy information there's not often any desire to find anything related to the privacy aspect of it. At the end of the process, what we want is an indicator that can say this bad thing happened right here. That's from a cybersecurity point of view."

Reputational Risks

Reputation risks to the organization also need to be considered when sharing information with the government or with law enforcement. In some instances, the perceptions of study participants are that some security professionals might not want to share information as it may expose a vulnerability within the organization, and if they share that information, it may become public and affect the company's reputation. Also, if there is an erroneous data that is provided such as the misidentification of a potential suspect, the impact of sharing that information may have significant reputation repercussions for the organization sharing it:

> *CSO #2*: "Some may have concerns about risk specifically reputational risk if they're seeing something and they don't necessarily want others to know because it exposes some weakness perhaps in their own organization, so that does happen."

Theme 5: Conflicting Organizational Missions & Objectives

When it comes to crime prevention, most of the participants expressed the public and the private sector have different missions and organization objectives, which significantly reduce the efficiency of current PPPs. Law enforcement and intelligence agencies want to protect the public, to arrest, and deter criminals while the private sector focuses its efforts on crime prevention, on reducing potential losses, and protecting their customers. Study participants explained that cyberattacks on financial institutions may originate from outside of the country, and it may be difficult to get law enforcement involved in investigating these files since these types of incidents might not be a priority for law enforcement:

> *CSO-Deputy #1*: "And that could be a national criminal organization. It could be somebody hitting us from outside the country. And that's another thing, as you're aware, the cyber-attacks that are coming from other countries into our banks."
>
> *CSO-Deputy #1*: "And when we have something, you know, they say sorry, we're not taking that. And we're sitting there with, well, we can't, you know, we can't send a message we can't."

CSO #2 and CSO-Deputy #1 explained the difference in priorities of both sectors. They resumed the perspective of the private sector as three critical pillars; (a) prevent (b) detect, and (c) respond to criminal activities. According to CSO #2, law enforcement solely focuses on the response (c) pillar while banks want to prevent (a) and detect incidents (b):

> *CSO #2*: "You know, when I do an investigation it's, you know, stop the bleeding, right, fix the problem and then we report it to the police, right? It's the third element. The third element, you know, reporting to the public sector, if I felt that there was a significant amount of benefit either to stop the bleeding or fix the problem, then it would move up into first or second place. But at this point given, again, it would be unrealistic, right. I mean, you know the banks and the private sector have to really do a lot of this stuff to protect themselves."

Security Clearances and Intelligence Classification Levels

When it comes to holding a security clearance, study participants mentioned that maintaining a security clearance is often required from the public sector to share information with the private sector. However, study participants confirmed that holding such a security clearance does not affect the frequency, the quality, and the type of intelligence they are receiving from the public sector:

> *CSO-Deputy #2*: "And all of the engagements that I've had with government ever since that legislate required a secret clearance to attend. You know, after attending those sessions there was very little or anything that was shared that would be considered classified information. It's just refined open-source intelligence, and you know what, we have very excellent people in the private sector that does that already. So, the value, the current value of my experience to date of how, of requiring a top-secret or a secret clearance, I have seen very little value from the government in that vein."

Many private security professionals had a secret and top secret clearances over the years. From their perspective, they feel the information they are receiving is dated, and it does not allow the private sector in being effective in its primary objective of being proactive. Most of the time, security professionals confirmed the same information from public sources, and they compared security clearance as a "background check vetting process" allowing to reduce the risk for the public sector to share information with private security professionals:

CSO #4: "I think it's still hard for certain agencies to relinquish that information and provide it to a cleared individual even though they do have the clearance, it's just a question that it goes back to the silo effect that I mentioned before. Even though they have the capacity to share it because of the clearance, it still hasn't been done effectively."

Security clearances did not allow private security professionals to get strategic or "secret" information for them to be able to act upon it. Clearances are perceived by the private sector security professionals as an unnecessary formality to participate in some public sector activities:

CSO #4: "So, it allows you to participate in certain activities and to be part of a sort of circle of trust, but I can't say that I've received anything that has been strategic or allowed me to proceed with any actionable Intel to do anything preventatively, so."

Study participants believed that security clearances are not necessary for having an effective PPP in information sharing as argued by CSO #4:

CSO #4: "You know, to have an effective private-public partnership you don't need clearances."

CISO-Deputy #1 resumed what was mentioned by other participants. There is a misunderstanding regarding the necessity of holding a security clearance between public and private stakeholders. The private sector does not want to know how the intelligence was gathered; the private sector wants to receive indicators to protect itself:

CISO-Deputy #1: "And at the end of the day, I don't think a lot of the top-secret information is what's required by financial institutions. The top-secret portion of the information is mainly around how it was obtained and the techniques and tactics that are used to attain the information. The value of the information is not in that. The value is in what's the indicator and how do I apply it in my space to prevent or mitigate attacks against me."

Theme 6: Interpersonal Trust Relationships

Trust: Private to Private Relationships

Study participants demonstrated they have trust in their private security colleagues to exchange information to assist them in preventing crime against their respective organization. Between private security professionals, trust and reciprocity have increased over the years, and the human element played a role in building that trust level in the banking sector.

Interviewer: "So, if I understand properly, you believe that the private-to-private information sharing is at a better level than the private to public information sharing, why?"

CSO-Deputy #4: "Definitely. Because their, I think the trust is there ... the ... there's a minimum of a framework in place for information sharing. And the benefits that I've been seeing times and times again of sharing information, most of the players know each other, they know of the importance of it, and most of the players are agreeing not to, well, to act into the common good for that specific information."

As described by CSO-Deputy #4, trust within the private sector was built from the process of sharing information with another private entity and being able to see the benefits they got by sharing the information. According to participants, when both partners can see the benefits, it motivates them to continue sharing information. When asked about private to private information sharing between financial institutions, CSO #4 confirmed the private to private information-sharing process is not perfect, but he believed it is more mature than what he experienced with the public sector. He argued that in a trusted relationship, strategic information allows focusing on prevention and detection:

CSO #4: "If I limit myself to the financial institutions, I think that the framework that we have and the ... our circle of trust enables us to actually share quite fluently. We are, or we have the ability to share, and we do share on a regular basis a lot of information that is actually strategic, that is valuable in terms of prevention, detection."

CSO-Deputy #1 added that in a trusted relationship, members need to have confidence that the information they provide will not be shared to individuals outside the trusted group. This participant noted that a new member might be included in a trusted relationship network even if he does not personally know every other member. A trusted group will include new members that are contributing to the group:

> *CISO-Deputy* #1: "But also, you can't possibly know every single person that you need to know. So, it sorts of becomes a trust in the group and a trust in the group's ability to sort of select the right members that could be the right model, it could be the wrong model, but I see that kind of thing happening now."

Trust: Private to Public Relationships

Participants cited trust as being a challenge in having efficient information sharing with public sector stakeholders. Study participants demonstrated a certain level of trust in the public sector, but lower than the level of trust they currently have with private security professionals working in the financial industry.

As claimed by CSO-Deputy #4, reciprocity in sharing information was key to build trust for participants. If you share information with other partners, the information needs to be shared both ways so that both partners may benefit from sharing it:

> *CSO-Deputy #4*: "On that front, the biggest problem would be the two-way communication. We send information; we have no idea what's happening with that information, so that's a bit of an issue. It's hard for us to pinpoint exactly which information would be really useful if we don't know how it's used."

As explained by participants, reciprocal sharing also reduces the risk for both individuals since they each played a role in the information-sharing "transaction." For study participants, having a trusted relationship also means the information that participants share with the public sector will not be attributed back to them and tarnish their organization's reputation as CSO #4 explained:

> *CSO #4*: "And it's both ways, you know, just showing, knowing that if we share information with the public sector that it's not going to come back and burn us after, right?"

Theme 7: Unclear Roles, Responsibilities, and Processes in Critical Infrastructures Protection

As private entities such as financial institutions own most of the financial sector's risk, the specific role that the private sector and the public sector hold in relation to the protection of financial institutions assets is unclear. Each bank ensures its own security, but the government must protect the industry. Participants were critical about the fact that they must deal with different agencies when dealing with potential national security matters. Depending of the threat (e.g., physical threat, terrorism, terrorist financing, cyber-threat, money laundering), a financial institution might have to report or share the same information with a federal law enforcement agency such as the RCMP, an intelligence agency like CSIS or CSE [Communications Security Establishment of Canada], and various other governmental agencies such as FINTRAC [Financial Transactions and Report Analysis Centre of Canada] and CBSA [Canadian Border Services Agency]. In some instances, these financial institutions might need to report criminal matters to provincial law enforcement depending on the crime. For study participants, each agency has its responsibility under the national security umbrella. National security roles and responsibilities are not always clear for private security professionals as described by CSO-Deputy #2:

> *CSO-Deputy #2*: "Well, I think the, I want to ... you know, when it comes from a Federal Government's national security point of view, I think the power structure is extremely fragmented. I mean, we ... you have multiple agencies with multiple mandates that they don't talk to each other all the time."

In terms of national security, one of the Canadian government's responsibility is to work with the private sector's partners to increase resilience and protect assets such as the financial industry sector (Public Safety Canada, 2015). Study participants agree and understand that it's the public sector's responsibility to protect the financial industry as a whole.

However, when managing the individual security posture of their respective financial institutions, private security professionals are also accountable for the security of a portion of the country's critical infrastructure; the financial industry. Study participants indicated they clearly understand that national security accountability is under the public sector, but they believe they have the resources and expertise to deal with most cyber and financial crime threats against financial institutions. The private sector owns most of the critical infrastructure of the country, and the financial industry is essential for the Canadian economy. In addition, survey results demonstrated as well that 70% of the study participants strongly agree, and 20% agree that security is viewed as a shared responsibility between the public–private partnership.

Depending on the threat, roles and responsibilities are unclear in terms of national security. When it comes to managing cyber-threat from nation-states, participants confirmed only the public sector could assist in defending against rogue nations:

> *CSO #2*: "But when you get into cyber, you know, cyber-enabled crime or cybercrime that is state-sponsored, we're talking a completely different ... like it's a game-changer. So that's why I think when the banks start talking about, you know, we can protect our individual perimeter but there's a larger perimeter that's more national security perspective that the only entity that can possibly do that is the public sector. I mean, that's really, they're the only ones that determine if someone is trying to do something, right?"

To explain the power structure between the public and private sector's relationship to manage national security, another participant mentioned that the private sector might hold a **piece** of information that would help the public sector to confirm the intelligence they gathered in a national security investigation:

> *CSO #4* "So, we might have insight on certain things that proxies are doing that the government doesn't know about, but if we did share the information, we'd give them a better view of what's going on and vice versa."

Theme 8: CyberAttacks on Banks; A Potential Domino Effect

During the interviews, participants were asked the following additional question:

Interviewer: "If a financial institution or multiple financial institutions would be the victims of a cyber-attack in a short period, do you believe it could have an impact on other financial institutions? Why and how?"

Most participants agreed that simultaneous attacks on banks could have significant negative impacts on investors, the customer's confidence in the financial system, the reputation of organizations under attack as well as on the stock markets. One participant said:

CSO-Deputy #2: "Because we all know that the banks are a critical part of the infrastructure. The banks afford the government the ability to operate, and without that level of confidence it's just, it's going to have a domino effect not just, you know, on the markets and stocks, stock prices, everything, right?"

CSO #2 added the "tipping point" would be if banks under attack would not be in a position to make a payment settlement between each other:

CSO #2: "The problem will be when the payment systems go down between banks to banks. I think that can happen for a very short period of time. I can't tell you what the tipping point would be, I don't know it could be hours, it could be days."

Another participant explained his perspective of this hypothetical scenario:

CSO #4: "So that's where sharing information is quite valuable because it's not necessarily going to be organized crime that's going to attack. If you're going to have a systemic attack against the financial industry in Canada, most likely it will be a nation-state."

CISO-Deputy #1 provided his perspective of such a critical event such as a ransomware attack:

CISO-Deputy #1: "And this is why it is so critical to the sector to have a higher bar when it comes to security because the second one or two banks get attacked in a ransomware scenario is a really good example. There's going to be a total lack of trust for those institutions, and you might see a few clients, maybe a few thousand clients switch, but they would be switching because they don't understand that this could happen to any bank."

Theme 9: Cross-Sector Critical Infrastructure Information Sharing

Study participants confirmed the financial industry should share information with other Canadian critical infrastructures since some of them are highly interconnected and might be dependent on each other as claimed by CISO-Deputy #1:

> *CISO-Deputy #1*: "So, when you look at it across the board, they're all interdependent, and they're all related to each other. So how are we supposed to run a bank without any power? And how can we have consumers continue to live their life without a bank because they can't get access to their money because like everything is on your card now."

Telecommunication Companies and Internet Service Providers

Among all Canadian critical infrastructures, most participants confirmed the banking industry is closely interconnected with the telecommunication sector when evaluating which other sectors financial institutions should share information to prevent cyber and financial crime threats. This sector includes telecommunication and internet provider companies. CSO #3 stated:

> *CSO #3*: "So, when you think of today's way of life then those Telco's are key, right, because everything is working through internet, mobile etcetera."

Because of the nature of the threats financial institutions must face daily, and since banking is now done through mobile phones and the use of the Internet, synergies are more important with the telecommunication industry than with other critical infrastructure's sectors in Canada. The importance of sharing information with telecommunication companies is also influenced by the types of products financial institutions and telecommunications have in common as customers use mobile phones and internet banking to make financial transactions:

CSO #4: "And being an FI, you know, we ... especially when it comes to second factor identification nowadays where the Telco's hold that side of the stick where a lack of security on the Telco's side has an impact on the financial industry because of sim-swapping, of even ISP [Internet service provider], held email accounts being compromised to get second factor authentication or even confirmation messages from the FIs."

Theme 10: Necessity to Increase Cyber-Threat Information Sharing

A total of eight participants agreed it is essential to continue to enhance information-sharing capabilities between public and private partners. For most of them, they felt it would be imperative to share more information than they share now. As mentioned by CSO-Deputy #1, sharing more information about threats is perceived as a way to increase success in mitigating cyber-threats:

CSO-Deputy #1: "So, I think that goes without saying, I mean, you know in order to be successful in this day and age I think sharing out any information involving threats against the industry is critical for success."

CSO #4 argued they should share more information with the public sector if there is a legal framework in place to do so:

CSO #4: "I think there shouldn't be an extent. I think all information should be shared. That being said, we don't necessarily have the frameworks in place to or the legal framework in place to do so. Cyber threats impact everyone, and regardless if you're public or private, you're still a potential target."

CSO-Deputy #4 confirmed as well both sectors should share more information, and the public sector should know the private sector has critical information to assist them in better protecting the country against threats:

CSO-Deputy #4: "Well, I strongly believe that we sit on a gold mine of information and most, if not all, of the important data, is like somewhere in our server or on the financial industry's servers. So, I believe that we should share as much information as possible if that was allowed and to make sure that we are as efficient as possible to create a safe environment, not only for the industry but for Canada itself."

CISO-Deputy #1 was also of the opinion that private and public sectors should share more information as criminals do share vulnerabilities learned from previous attacks, and if an attack does not work against one financial institution; they will attempt the same type of attack against others. He claimed that information sharing would allow increasing resilience among the private sector:

CISO-Deputy #1: "I think honestly, from my point of view, sharing information is one of the most important things that anybody can do to sort of prevent and in some cases mitigate attacks. And the reason I think it's so important is typically these actors that they don't have just one target in mind; they have multiple targets in mind. And they'll start with the easiest target and move progressively to the more complex targets."

Theme ii: Governance Model to Share Information

The Bank Crime Prevention and Investigation Framework (BCPIO)

The BCPIF framework is perceived as the governance model in place for financial institutions to share information with other BCPIF members, and study participants do agree this framework is the best tool they have to share information. This framework clearly defines when, how, and what information banks can share among themselves. CSO #4 explained how the BCPIF works:

CSO #4: "It leverages existing laws, exceptions, in current privacy laws to enable banks to share information amongst each other. So, I think that it's a great example of how you can have a legal framework as well as an operational framework to show how the exchange of information can be done."

CSO-Deputy #2 added that the issue is BCPIF allows to share information between banks, but such a framework does not exist to prevent crime by sharing information with the public sector:

CSO-Deputy #2: "So, I think that the current CBA model is fairly good, but it only involves the private sector, right."

Under this BCPIF framework, banks can also centralize the information at the Canadian Bankers Association (CBA) in which the CBA will coordinate with law enforcement for all the participants as mentioned by CSO #1:

> *CSO #1*: "Well, I think that, well, one of the examples that I will use is that we've been involved in projects where for example in the CBA has, has been a conduit or they'll take the information from all the banks."

The Low Maturity Level of Canadian PPPs

Participants were asked the following question: "Are there any PPP in Canada that you believe that was successful, that we should try to learn from and try to replicate in the future?" Most of this study participants confirmed some PPPs projects were attempted over the years, but most of them failed. As described by CSO #2, there was a significant PPP initiative started by the federal government a couple of years ago, but according to him, it did not work because it was managed by the government:

> *CSO #2*: "But then what they tried to build I think was just too big, like they didn't understand it. I think they tried to build something that was inappropriate and then again, that was being run by the government, right. So, I think it's better when it's run by us, right, with the government involved, just because I think it will be a little bit more resilient and also a little bit more nimble in how we achieve things."

Two participants mentioned one PPP project with law enforcement as the only example of a successful PPP project over the years. According to them, the primary reason this project was successful is that it was a secondment PPP project in which financial institutions assumed to costs associated with one financial institution's analyst to work with law enforcement.

> *CSO #4*: "It wasn't a project that was run by the federal government but actually with the provincial government the majority of the time. So, Project [Redacted] had to do with credit card fraud where we actually had a member of one of the FI's actually directly in the provincial police officers working the file."

CSO-Deputy #4 referred to the same project as CSO #4 as the most efficient PPP that he participated in his career so far:

CSO-Deputy #4: "I think it's one of the good examples because it's one example where the goal was shared. People, both the public and private sectors were going against the same people, the same bad actors. The information sharing was way more direct. So, we had people from the private sector embedded in a public sector team, I don't think that's been seen before."

This project was successful in terms of the number of arrests made but the project was too long as the secondment project within this PPP lasted for a couple of years:

CSO-Deputy #4: "And basically, they allowed us to start a project, share information, act on that information, and then arrest the bad actors. It was not done in a timely fashion, but I think it's something that could be used as an example to people in time."

Partnerships in the UK and the USA

Participants acknowledged there are some great PPP ongoing initiatives in Australia, and the Netherlands, but they have been focusing primarily on information-sharing partnership initiatives in the United Kingdom and in the United States when referring to countries that implemented PPPs they believe to be leading examples in this field.

The United Kingdom

Participants cited the UK Joint Money Laundering Intelligence Taskforce (JMLIT) project as a leading example of PPP. The JMLIT project is structured around three teams; (a) an operational group, (b) a strategic group, and (c) an alerts service (Joint Money Laundering Intelligence Taskforce, n.d.). CSO-Deputy #1 explained it in his own words:

CSO-Deputy #1: "I think the UK is light years ahead of everybody, that's just me, but they've been doing it longer, and they had lots of growing pains. And they had … but they worked through it. Now, they … what they did, they did instant reviews of all the information intelligence sharing that they did where they ran into issues, and they put gaps and they put controls in place to make sure that they were able to fix that. They had all the appropriate stakeholders at the table."

CSO-Deputy #2 also mentioned JMLIT as an example:

> *CSO-Deputy #2*: "Yes. So, I think that, there's something … I know that they do have INSETs [Integrated National Security Enforcement Teams], you know, spread out around the country. There's A INSET, B INSET, but integrated security enforcement teams."

The United States

FS-ISAC was mentioned by two participants as a very successful PPP example:

> *CSO-Deputy #2*: "I think they [FS-ISAC-The Financial Services Information Sharing and Analysis Center] are good models or good examples for Canada to follow that are out there."

The National Cyber-Forensic and Training Alliance (NCFTA) which is a public–private co-location model located in Pittsburgh was another second example of a U.S. PPP mentioned by five participants:

> *CSO #2*: "But it's interesting because NCFTA actually has elements of academia because it's part of Carnegie Mellon. You've got the public sector in that, you've got all the three-letter agencies that are located there, and then you've got elements of the private sector. And not only do you have elements from the banking perspective, you have elements from other areas of technology and such."

CSO-Deputy #4 added about the NCFTA:

> *CSO-Deputy #4*: "The NCFTA is one of the best examples out there about how we can all work together on sharing the right information at the right time and acting on that information."

The last example that was brought forward as a great example of U.S. PPP was the National Cybersecurity and Communications Integration Center (NCCIC) described by CISO-Deputy #1:

> *CISO-Deputy #1*: "But what they do is they have an analyst from their organization embedded in the SOCS [Security Operation Centers] of various organizations, which is a very different model. And they can do

the opposite as well where somebody from an institution can come and sit on their floor."

Theme 12: Various Types of Security Networks Are Necessary

All participants confirmed information-sharing PPPs between financial institutions and its public sector stakeholders should be categorized as security networks as per Dupont's (2004) definition. They also argued that each level is essential, but the model of security networks they have been a part of would-be categorized as "private" institutional networks operating at the national level. When discussing ongoing PPP projects that are undertaken at the federal level, CSO #4 believed the type of networks would be a virtual operating network at the national level.

CSO #4: "But I mean what we're looking at with the government is a national private-public partnership. So, it would be a national network, and nowadays it's probably going to be virtual."

The researcher asked the following question to all participants: "If so, what type (s) of security networks your organization is currently part of (based on the typology definition provided by Whelan and Dupont [2017]; the information exchange networks, knowledge generation networks, problem-solving networks, and the coordination networks)"? The majority of study participants confirmed that each type of network within the typology created by Whelan and Dupont (2017) should exist and these networks are mutually exclusive.

From Whelan and Dupont (2017) typology types of network, participants confirmed the type of PPP security network they used in the past, and they still use today is the information exchange network as stated by CSO-Deputy #4:

CSO-Deputy #4: "I would say that the current system that we are using is closer to probably information exchange network because we're exchanging more and more information, but we don't necessarily know what the results are. I know for a fact that a lot of that information is just not acted on at all or even analyzed properly. So, we are not yet in the knowledge generation network or even further ahead from the problem-solving networks. We're trying to head there."

Future Security Networks

The following question to participants was: "In the future, what type (s) of security networks your organization should be part of to prevent cyber-related attacks on your organization or the Canadian financial industry"? In responding to this question, participants explained how some of the banks are now expanding internationally, the international aspect of the threats they face and the assistance they will need to get from international partners in the future. As stated by CSO-Deputy #3:

> *CSO-Deputy #3*: "So now, we're going from local to national. And virtual I think it will always be there, but I think as we're growing, we're moving more towards international. Our footprint is going to be bigger internationally."

As CSO-Deputy #2, CSO #1, and CSO-Deputy #4 explained it, each network type within this typology should be perceived as a critical part of the "global" security network. According to these participants, security networks should aim to reach a level of maturity in which each type of network within the global security network is as efficient as possible and work in symbiosis with the other network types so the whole security network may benefit from each of its individual network's nodes:

> *CSO-Deputy #2*: "If you're looking at the security network as a whole, it would be nice if you had both an information exchange network, you know, working in parallel with, you know, knowledge generation or knowledge capture, I guess that would be a better term ... you want to capture that knowledge and keep it for future purposes. Problem-solving networks are also very good and coordination. Coordination network would probably be something you'd see more around, like a G7 [G7 Summit], or like a major event."

Evaluation of the Findings

The study's findings were consistent to the literature and indicated that to be more efficient in preventing cyber-related incidents, private sector's security practitioners want to receive information or actionable intelligence, and they would like to receive it in near real-time and as frequent as possible. By sharing cyber-threat or threat actor's information between banks or receiving intelligence from the public sector, one financial institution being victimized may assist the others in preventing the same incident of being perpetrated a second time.

Real-time or near real-time two-way communication between stakeholders is critical in cybersecurity or cyber-fraud prevention as successful attempts may lead to significant monetary losses, prevent an incident, and identify bad actors. Participants argued that an effective and efficient way to exchange information and intelligence, maximizing resources, streamlining operations, and improving capabilities to combat cyber-related crimes would be to create joint-venture teams composed of public and private security professionals or fusion centers operational capabilities to increase information sharing between actors. It should also be noted that by having common and easily understood/clearly defined terms of information, data definitions, and classifications for each organization's members in a partnership was identified as a best practice.

The Canadian banking sector has data that could be beneficial for the other sector in identifying threats or common data sets. By combining various types of data sets and information, it would allow identifying relationships, patterns, to identify more actors, and to understand better who is behind such criminal activities to take appropriate preventative, detective, and responsive actions. The virtual platforms facilitate secure communications, but current platforms are still rudimentary, and various platforms are being used to share different types of information with multiple entities.

There is currently a framework in place between banks to share information to prevent crime which is the Bank Crime Prevention and Investigation Framework (BCPIF), but such a framework does not exist to share information and intelligence with the public sector. Financial institutions security professionals do not want to get the public sector's intelligence about classified intelligence techniques or bad actors under secret or top-secret investigation. Private security professionals want to receive timely, specific, and detailed threat indicators to be able to manage better the individual cyber risks they face.

The findings of this research indicate the S-4 Bill eliminated the body of investigations into the law, and changes made under the PIPEDA Act created uncertainty among banking security professionals attempting to suppress crimes while also limiting banks to share information for other crimes than fraud. While managing investigations such as a data breach, participants are having difficulties sharing information with law enforcement due to the necessity of having consent to disclose the information from potential victims as well as for privacy issues. Study participants repeatedly mentioned current laws do not sufficiently allow them to share information with public security actors for crime prevention. In terms of national security, private security professionals believed there should be more clarity about what is considered private and when does privacy become less important than national security. This study showed some private members might not want to share information as it may lead to reputational risks for their organization.

Public and private partners have conflicting missions and objectives; law enforcement and intelligence agencies want to protect the population, protect national security, and to arrest criminals, while the private sector's mission is to increase profits for its shareholders in focusing on preventing crimes, reducing losses, and protecting their customers. Private security professional's perspective on holding security clearances does not have a direct impact on the frequency, the quality, and the type of intelligence they are receiving from the public sector. Study participants demonstrated they have trust in their private security colleagues to exchange information. Trust was built over the years through a process of reciprocity, and the interpersonal connections of security played a role in building that trust level. Study participants also confirmed professional trust in the public sector, but the level of trust to share information is lower than the level of trust they currently have with private stakeholders. Having an effective and common legal framework promotes information sharing and trust between private security members.

This study's findings showed private security professionals have significant responsibilities in protecting a large portion of the financial sector when it comes to cyber-threats. This research study's findings showed each bank must assure its own protection, but the government must protect the industry as a whole. When it comes to sharing information and depending on the type of threat, participants mentioned they must deal with different agencies when dealing with potential national security matters.

National security responsibilities are under the public sector's umbrella, but roles and responsibilities are unclear when it comes to protecting financial institutions against cyber-threats that may come from nation-states. The findings demonstrated that making payment settlements is a critical operation for FI's and cyber-attacks on more than one bank in a short period of time could lead to negative impacts on investors, the customer's confidence in the financial system, the reputation of organizations under attack as well as on the stock markets. Furthermore, Canadian critical infrastructures are highly interconnected and dependent on each other. Thus, critical infrastructure sectors should share information to protect themselves. This study's findings demonstrated financial institutions (Finance sector) should prioritize sharing information with telecommunication companies (Information & Communication Technology sector) to prevent cyber-related crimes as these two sectors have synergies in terms technologies, mobile and Internet products usage, and similar threat actors.

Study participants mentioned it would be imperative to share more information with the public sector than they actually share now as long as there is a legal framework in place to do so. The study's findings demonstrated the public sector holds strategic information deemed essential to the private sector, while the private sector holds critical information and intelligence that could assist the public sector's law enforcement and intelligence agencies in identifying suspects more quickly, making additional connections in ongoing and future criminal investigations as well as in helping the government to increase the Finance's sector resilience maturity level.

Private to private information sharing between financial institutions to prevent crime is working considerably well due to the reliance of the private security professionals on the Canadian Bankers Association BCPIF framework. However, research findings demonstrate that such a public–private information-sharing framework does not exist, thus inflicting a negative impact on the level of information and intelligence that is being shared between the private and the public sector. The majority of this study participants confirmed multiple PPPs projects were attempted over the years, but most of them failed due primarily to the time needed to complete PPP's investigations, lack of legal and governance framework, the fact that both partners were not working together toward the same objectives, the lack of cybersecurity and financial crime expertise as well as the lack of financial and human resources. One PPP project with law enforcement was mentioned by participants as the only example of a successful PPP project over the years.

The primary reason this project was perceived as successful is that it was a secondment PPP project in which financial institutions assumed the costs associated with one financial institution's analyst to work full-time with law enforcement. As for successful international PPP's, the findings suggested partnership initiatives in the United Kingdom and in the United States were believed to be leading examples in this field. These partnerships projects were the UK Joint Money Laundering Intelligence Taskforce (JMLIT) project, and The Financial Services Information Sharing and Analysis Center (FS-ISAC), the National Cyber-Forensic and Training Alliance (NCFTA), and the National Cybersecurity and Communications Integration Center (NCCIC) in the United States.

Moreover, this study's findings showed that information-sharing PPPs between financial institutions and its public sector stakeholders should be categorized as security networks as per Dupont's (2004) definition. The current model of security networks study participants participated in could be categorized as "private" institutional networks operating at the national level. However, these institutional PPPs networks were not operating effectively. Study participants agreed that most network types; information exchange, knowledge-generating, problem-solving, and coordination networks would be necessary at some point depending on the goals and objectives of the networks. Based on Whelan and Dupont's (2017) typology, participants previously relied on the information exchange network at the national level. In the future, information exchange, knowledge-generating, and problem-solving networks will become prominent types of security networks, and these networks will have to be operating at the transnational level. As for coordination networks, participants believed this type of network would be under the leadership of an association such as the Canadian Banking Association and a similar public sector's entity.

References

Canadian Bankers Association. (2015). *Bill S-4—Digital Privacy Act: Remarks by Linda Routledge*. Retrieved from https://cba.ca/Assets/CBA/Documents/Files/Article%20Category/PDF/sub-20150312-bill-s4-en.pdf.

Canadian Bankers Association. (2019). *Members banks*. Retrieved from http://www.cba.ca/memberbanks.

Dupont, B. (2004). Security in the age of networks. *Policing & Society, 14*(1), 76. https://doi.org/10.1080/1043946042000181575.

Public Safety Canada. (2015). *National security*. Retrieved from https://www.publicsafety.gc.ca/cnt/ntnl-scrt/index-en.aspx.

Whelan, C., & Dupont, B. (2017). Taking stock of networks across the security field: A review, typology and research agenda. *Policing & Society, 27*(6), 671–687. Retrieved from https://www.tandfonline.com/doi/full/10.1080/10439463.2017.1356297?scroll=top&needAccess=true.

CHAPTER 7

Conclusions and Implications for Practice and Future Studies on Public–Private Partnerships

The fundamental problem actively sought to be addressed by this research study was why private, and public partnership relationships have been ineffective in monitoring, detecting, and reacting to cyber-related incidents (Bures, 2013; Dunn-Cavelty & Suter, 2009). The purpose of this qualitative phenomenological study was to conduct interviews with private security professionals (corporate and information security) working for Canada's national-level financial banking institutions. The primary research focus was (a) to obtain information to understand better the challenges these private security professionals face in sharing information aimed at preventing cybersecurity incidents with the public sector and (b) to provide recommendations for decision-makers on how best to robust their existing cybersecurity protections. Also, by exploring and describing real-life experiences of private security professionals having experience in sharing information through various PPPs, it allowed determining if the Network Security Governance Framework first proposed by Dupont (2004) and adapted by Whelan and Dupont (2017) is pertinent to explain this phenomenon.

This study addressed the central problem of why private and public partnership relationships have been ineffective in monitoring, detecting, and reacting to these incidents by sharing information and intelligence and it resulted in a thick phenomenological description of financial institution's private security professional's experiences to understand

P.-L. Pomerleau and D. L. Lowery, *Countering Cyber Threats to Financial Institutions*,
https://doi.org/10.1007/978-3-030-54054-8_7

better the challenges these security professionals face in sharing information. Analysis of the collected data rendered 12 major themes; (1) Receiving Timely Information Sharing for Prevention Purposes, (2) Joint-Ventures—Integrated Public–Private Fusion Centers, (3) Mechanisms to Share Information, (4) Lack of Legal Framework for Crime Prevention, (5) Conflicting Organizational Missions & Objectives, (6) Interpersonal Trust Relationships, (7) Unclear Roles, Responsibilities, and Processes in Critical Infrastructure Protection, (8) CyberAttacks on Banks; A Potential Domino Effect, (9) Cross-Sector Critical Infrastructure Information Sharing, (10) Necessity to Increase Cyber-Threat Information Sharing, (11) Governance Model to Share Information; The BCPIF Framework, and (12) Various Types of Security Networks Are Necessary.

The resulting data of this qualitative study included various direct quotes from the interviews with private security professionals working for Canadian financial institutions. This analysis illustrated the perceptions of these security professionals regarding the phenomenon under study. Also, this study provided more information about why information sharing between PPPs actors is not optimal. This analysis allowed the researcher to propose recommendations to decision-makers about what should be done to improve information sharing between public and private actors to reduce the impacts of cyber-threats on financial institutions in the future. The primary limitation of this research study included that from one of the two groups of study participants (CISO group), only one member (CISO-Deputy) participated in the research. It would have been beneficial to obtain more information on the perceptions of IT security professionals about this phenomenon.

This chapter includes the implications that expand on the interpretations of the findings by providing thematic alignment and comparison with the previous literature presented in this study. The primary unit of analysis contributing to the development of the themes were segments of descriptive verbatim conversations from the study participants. Recommendations for practices are presented to apply the study findings to practical use as well as recommendations for future research to add insight and knowledge to the field of study.

Implications

Research Question #1

Theme #1 Receiving Timely Information Sharing for Prevention Purposes

Theme #1 revealed that to deal with cyber-threats and to increase the resilience of the industry, it is critical for banking security professionals to receive information and intelligence in a timely manner. For public–private partnerships (PPPs) to be relevant, the information must be timely. According to study participants, there is a need to move from reacting to traditional attacks by using available data to anticipate and predict the threat that may affect both sectors (Schaeffer & Payne, 2016). Responding to threats cannot be defined in months, weeks, or days as the threat environment requires actions and speed to minimize the impacts (Schaeffer & Payne, 2016). This finding implies that timely information sharing is imperative for financial institutions to focus on prevention. In cybersecurity or in cyber-fraud prevention, security professionals could share a variety of information or datasets (Indicators of compromise) allowing them to take the appropriate actions manually or automatically within their proprietary IT and fraud prevention systems. Participants want to receive actionable intelligence to prevent incidents, and they would like to receive in near real-time. This intelligence may come from the private or the public sector's partners. Receiving timely intelligence allows security professionals to be able to prevent an incident, and if they cannot prevent it, to respond in a timely manner to mitigate losses or the impacts to their organization's stakeholders. Also, when banks are receiving intelligence from the public sector, one financial institution being victimized may assist the others in preventing the same incident of being perpetrated on several occasions within the industry.

These findings are in line with Carr (2016) as she confirmed PPPs should get real-time capabilities, have access to actionable cyber-threat and alert information. Other scholars such as Boes and Leukfeldt (2017) and Borghard (2018) concluded the banking sector does not have the necessary intelligence collection authorities and capabilities to protect its network and infrastructure. These findings are also in line with the evaluation conducted by Public Safety Canada in compliance with the Treasury Board of Canada Policy on Results—involving 48 interviews with government officials working for 11 different governments, academics, and experts—concluding information sharing was done on an ad hoc basis with no mechanisms to share timely and systematic information in real-time between partners (Public Safety Canada, 2017).

The government does possess these necessary authorities and abilities to collect intelligence, but it does not have the banking-specific expertise of the cyber threats affecting the financial industry (San Juan Menacho & Martin, 2018). By assisting one another in the collective pool of mitigating risk and sharing information, organizations can reduce the time it takes to prevent a major event or to detect newly discovered vulnerabilities and then decide the appropriate course of action (Kolini & Janczewski, 2017).

Theme #2 Joint-Ventures—Integrated Public–Private Fusion Centers

A best practice in information sharing is to have law enforcement and private sector banking security professionals working together "side by side" in a fusion center. To become effective, a fusion center is necessary to gather different information and intelligence feeds "holistically" in a centralized function. By working together on a joint project, it promotes the sharing of information to find common denominators or a criminal nexus as well as to share expertise, technological, and analytical tools. The implication of this finding is that depending on the PPP project, people from both sectors may have to "physically" work together in the same location or collaborate through a "virtual" fusion center, where security professionals from both sectors do not necessarily need to be physically sitting in the same location to share information with each other as technology allows them to work together and share information in a collaborative network through virtual capabilities.

A public–private fusion center integrated with financial institutions employees working with the public sector does not exist in Canada. Based on the professional experiences of study participants, creating a fusion center, including law enforcement, intelligence agencies, and financial institution's professionals, would be beneficial to influence the culture of information sharing in cybersecurity and financial crime. This finding coincided with Graphia's (2010) results when she claimed fusions positively affect the nature of professional relationships and minimized subcultural barriers between members. Also, as argued by Bright and

Whelan (2018), very few fusion centers exist, and most of them are focused primarily on national security and law enforcement while financial institutions would be typical private sector members of a fusion center.

Theme #3 Mechanisms to Share Information

The study findings demonstrated that private security professionals use different mechanisms and virtual platforms to share information, threat indicators, and indicators of compromise (IOC) with their private partners and public sector stakeholders. Meeting each other in-person, exchanging information through verbal communications over the phone and by emails are still commonly used between public and private partners even though virtual private platforms are the most appropriate communication mechanism to exchange information securely. Various public–private information-sharing secured virtual platforms are still relatively new and are not used by all members. The Canadian Financial Intelligence Initiative (CFII) is a novel initiative brought forward by the financial institutions to enable information sharing between each other, and study participants confirmed this platform facilitates secure and encrypted communications among themselves. The significance of this finding shows study participants used to rely on various means to share information, and by deciding to implement a secured virtual platform to share threat data among themselves, it increased the security of the information being shared, and it reduced the risks associated with previous methods to share information.

As seen in the cybersecurity literature, intelligence and information systems with technical standards such as MITRE'S (Mitre Corporation) or OASIS Cyber Threat Intelligence (CTI), standardized language such as the Structured Threat Information eXpression (STIX), or standardized exchange mechanisms such as the Trusted Automated eXchange of Indicator Information (TAXII) are used by various organizations to share automated cyber-threat data (Kolini & Janczewski, 2017; Skopik, Settanni, & Fiedler, 2016; United States Computer Emergency Readiness Team, n.d.). This finding implies that encrypted communications through secure virtual platforms could allow to share threat indicators (Fraud & cyber) in a very short timeframe and to automate this information within the banking systems. In line with these results and as confirmed by Quigley, Bisset, and Mills (2017), a consistent approach between critical infrastructure's sectors is to prioritize sharing information through new tools and information-sharing mechanisms such as secure websites.

Recommendations for Practice

The Canadian federal government should enact new laws and develop coordinated processes to facilitate timely notifications and communications with critical infrastructure. These information-sharing processes, consistent with the need to protect national security information and receiving timely information would include the dissemination of classified reports to critical infrastructure entities, such as financial institutions professionals, that would be authorized to receive them to protect their organizations (United States Computer Emergency Readiness Team, 2016). Also, technical communication standards such as STIX and TAXII should be used to share cyber-fraud data as well as cybersecurity threat indicators in an automated fashion.

A fusion center should be created between banks and the public sector to combat cyber-threats and financial crime. Clarke and Knake (2019) described very well why information sharing is so important and the fundamental reason why it is possible for a fusion center to generate value for its participants when they wrote:

> We discussed the value that a single corporation got by pooling the insights of its employees on what might be a spear-phishing email. Now, imagine the value that corporation could get if it shared those insights with its peer companies and in return, received insight from those companies' employees? That might really put the hurt on these companies' common adversaries. Why? Because if the companies are not sharing this information, the adversary is free to use the same email message, from the same account, with the same payload, delivered using the same URL, exploiting the same vulnerability, and communicating back to the same command-and-control infrastructure, across multiple different companies. (p. 58)

The creation of a fusion center would facilitate timely information sharing between both actors. Another recommendation would be to evaluate how to implement multiple local fusion centers across the country. Fusion centers located at the provincial level would facilitate regional collaboration (e.g., Montreal, Toronto, and Vancouver) and one central—federal fusion center—under the responsibility of the government. The

Canadian Center for Cybersecurity, the Canadian Security Intelligence Service, and the Royal Canadian Mounted Police should play critical roles within these fusion centers in working with the banking industry. As recommended by Bright and Whelan (2018) in their study of Australian fusion centers such as the Fintel Alliance project with AUSTRAC, the "hub-and-spoke" model should be prioritized in sharing information for national security and for law enforcement purposes (Chadderton & Norton, 2019). Financial institutions should be included in this fusion center model to assist and to participate in cybercrime investigations. This model has a primary center that acts as a central "hub," while various Joint Analyst Groups (JAGS)—multiagency groups located in major jurisdictions or regional fusion centers—are connected to the central hub (Bright & Whelan, 2018; Pomerleau, 2019). These provincial and federal fusion centers would be a great strategy to implement in order to facilitate communication, information sharing, disruption, and coordination of activities between banks, local and federal agencies (Cozine, Joyal, & Ors, 2014).

A virtual collaborative environment would allow the government, including law enforcement, intelligence agencies, and industry partners the possibility to exchange information on threats and vulnerabilities as they are identified (Rosemont, 2016). To do so, decision-makers from the private as well as the public sector will need to provide direction and concrete guidance (Graphia, 2010). Funding for the creation of fusion centers, resources such as cybersecurity experts from both sectors, implementing a secured architecture and technology such as an encrypted virtual platform will need to be provided.

In focusing primarily on cybersecurity and cyber-fraud intelligence sharing, creating a centralized IOC database where technical and nontechnical information about malware, cyber-incidents such as cyber-attacks, confirmed online fraud incidents, where threat actor's data are stored in a structured format would allow to creating relationship through link analysis, data matching capabilities and to share automated data feeds to members of the PPP (Skopik et al., 2016). Future PPP projects using virtual platforms should make sure that members are using common taxonomy, a governance framework to govern information sharing using new and existing processes. Also, PPP projects should develop engagement and intelligence-sharing strategies that are appropriate for law enforcement agency obligations, allow incident-specific triggers to intelligence sharing, and offer capabilities to share trends identified by members.

On a more technical level, peer-to-peer intelligence sharing mechanisms such as key exchanges and hash validation (public–private key encryption sharing to be in a position to decentralize the data) and various forms of encryption such as homomorphic encryption—securing data in use, data at rest, and data in transit—should be used to share data securely. The use of encryption would secure the information and better protect the entity sharing it with other members. More specifically, advanced analytics, privacy-preserving capabilities, and machine learning capabilities over combined data should be explored further (San Juan Menacho & Martin, 2018).

Recommendations for Future Research

Future research should focus on understanding what systems, technological platforms, alert capabilities fusion centers as well as PPPs such as the NCFTA in the United States or the JMLIT in the United Kingdom currently use to share real-time or near real-time information between public and private partners in a secured manner. This analysis would allow to learn what worked and what did not work well within these PPPs and to compare the alert systems to the one currently offered by the Canadian Cyber Incidence Response Center (Public Safety Canada, 2017).

In terms of information sharing between financial institutions and the public sector in a fusion center setting, it would be recommended to study and compare other legal frameworks such as the ones in the United States, the United Kingdom, and Australia to evaluate what could be applicable in Canada or how these legislations could be adapted to the Canadian reality. In the United States, the provision under the 2001 Patriot Act 314(a) for public to private and 314(b) for private to private information sharing as well as the UK Crime and Court Act 2013 allowing a person (not only a financial institution) to voluntarily disclose information to the National Crime Agency if the disclosure is made for the purposes of the exercise of any NCA function (e.g., criminal intelligence, crime reduction, or the NCA's functions under the Proceeds of Crime Act 2002) should be explored further. A similar analysis should be conducted as well to evaluate what other industries such as the telecommunications industry or other critical infrastructures have in place to share threat indicators in other regions of the world while respecting privacy.

Research Question #2

Theme 4 Lack of Legal Framework for Crime Prevention

The findings of this study illustrated that the actual legal framework is a critical challenge for private security professionals to share information with the public sector and to focus on preventing cyber-threats. Participants confirmed legal hurdles do not allow them to be efficient in preventing crime against financial institutions. Under this lack of a legal framework to share information, participants mentioned privacy issues are commonly associated with (a) getting the consent from victims to disclose their information, customers or the individuals under investigation to share information and (b) the potential reputational risks associated with voluntarily sharing information about vulnerabilities to assist other companies in improving their security posture.

For national security and activities constituting threats to the security of Canada or threats to life and specific articles under the Canadian criminal code, findings demonstrated it is clear for private security professionals that they can provide information to law enforcement without consent of the suspected individuals. However, under current laws, information sharing with the public sector is not permitted for cybercrime prevention, making it more difficult for private security professionals to focus on preventing crimes before they occur. Findings showed previous PPPs were not efficient in sharing information as there was no legal framework in place between the public sector and the private sector. In the survey responses, 90% ($N = 9$) of the participants answered PPPs were "somewhat effective" at the question "How would you rate the effectiveness of the public-private partnerships"?

Also, there is currently a framework in place between banks (e.g., bank to bank) which is the Bank Crime Prevention and Investigation Framework (BCPIF) to share information to prevent crime, but such a framework does not exist to share information with the public sector. Since 2001, the Canadian Bankers Association (CBA) was recognized as an investigation body under the PIPEDA Act. CBA was acting as a designated body through which banks were able to share information with each other to prevent a broad scope of criminal activities. These types of criminal activities included but was not limited to data theft, criminal breach of trust, proceeds of crime, money laundering, terrorist financing, cybercrime, banks robbery, and physical attacks on critical infrastructures (Canadian Bankers Association, 2015). The reform of the PIPEDA Act on June 18, 2015, with the Digital Privacy Act through Bill S-4, restrained how financial institutions can share information regarding criminal activities under the new section 7 (3) (d.2) (Office of the Privacy Commissioner of Canada, 2017). Under the new amendments, the CBA was no longer considered an investigative body since the notion of investigative bodies was effectively abolished. Bank Crime Prevention and Investigation Framework's (BCPIF) participants—most of the participants in this study (CSO)—may now only use personal information "to facilitate the investigation of criminal and dishonest activity including contraventions of the laws of Canada for fraud prevention during an internal investigation within their respective banks, or when it is provided that the fraud is likely to be committed" (Office of the Privacy Commissioner of Canada, 2017).

Privacy and protection of the client's information are critically important for financial institutions. Bill S-4 contained valuable amendments to the privacy law such as the new breach notification and reporting requirements for organizations to notify individuals when their personal information is at risk due to a data breach as well as allowing banks to advise family members or an authorized representative in suspected cases of elderly financial abuse (Canadian Bankers Association, 2015).

However, findings demonstrated it is not clear for private security professionals (even though Bill S-4 may allow sharing with other parties for fraud prevention) if they can share information between the financial institutions and other private organizations (e.g., telecommunications companies to a bank) to prevent cyber-fraud or cybersecurity-related attacks.

The information sharing between banks is working considerably well, even though it could still be improved, but the information does not flow as it should from the private to the public sector or from the public sector to the private sector (banks). These findings have implications for Canadian policymakers as there was a consensus among study participants that the most important challenges private security professionals currently face in private–public partnerships are legal issues associated with information sharing for prevention purposes. Previous scholars confirmed legal challenges in PPPs, but this study is the first research taking into consideration the perceptions of Canadian security professionals working for financial institutions.

The results of this study regarding legal, privacy, and reputational risks challenges are in line with what previous academics confirmed in the literature as the most important obstacles to effective collaboration of public–private partnerships. The issue related to the obligations of disclosure and exposure of private organization's divulging internal vulnerabilities to other members of a partnership project was brought forward as well by Germano (2014) in her study on cybersecurity public–private partnerships. The potential losses of fraud, financial crime, and cybersecurity negative impacts to the reputation of organizations as well as to their customers are critical aspects that have been discussed by many scholars (Baulin, 2019; Chadderton & Norton, 2019; Christensen & Petersen, 2017; Lagazio, Sherif, & Cushman, 2014; Musiał, 2019; Ozkaya & Aslaner, 2019; Sedenberg & Dempsey, 2018; Vroegop, 2017). These findings are also comparable with those of Borchert (2015) when he concluded public and private partners need to address legal hurdles, and the lack of regulatory incentives to engage all members in sharing information.

Theme 5 Conflicting Organizational Missions & Objectives

The results of this study demonstrated that participants believe the public and the private sector have different missions and organizational objectives, which significantly reduce efficiency information sharing. Law enforcement and intelligence agencies want to protect the population, to arrest criminals and deter them while the private sector focuses its effort on crime prevention, on reducing potential losses and on protecting their customers. Despite the fact the objectives of both sectors are legitimate, this situation leads to conflicts between public and private actors.

The results of this research endeavor clearly demonstrated that the public sector places a great deal of emphasis on the importance of security clearances for private security professionals to participate in the public sector's events, projects, and to share information with them. According to the study participants, these security clearances did not allow them to get strategic and actionable intelligence. The experience of the participants in this study also helped to understand that the leadership of both sectors has different organizational culture, chain of command, priorities, definition of success, different accountability, and the decision-making power greatly differs between a law enforcement organization, an intelligence agency and a financial institution's security department. However, these organizations have to learn to work together as study participants confirmed this is the only way to adapt to the rapid evolution of the criminal landscape and mitigate risks.

These findings have implications for future policies as 44% of the participants in the interviews used to work in the public sector either in law enforcement (provincial and federal law enforcement) or for intelligence agencies. These participants were in the best position to witness the differences between both sector's missions, objectives, and the differences in culture in the public and the private sector. These findings also have implications for practice as previous academics studying PPPs have not captured the perspective of professionals who have worked both in the public sector and in a financial institution's security department. These participants confirmed that, in their perspective, a shift in attitude, a change of culture, and a "tone at the top" shared leadership between leaders of both sectors would be needed if policymakers want Canadian PPPs to become effective in preventing cybercrimes.

Throughout the available contemporary (and unclassified) academic/technical journals available on this subject, very few authors focused on the organizational differences between the public and private actors responsible for managing the security of critical infrastructures. As explained by Quigley, Bisset, and Mills (2017) in their review of how Canada manages threats to critical infrastructure, sharing information, and managing crisis gets complicated as intelligence agencies, law enforcement, and private security professionals do not have the same objectives. According to Etzioni (2017), the two sectors are characterized with conflicting values, ideological obstacles, divergent interests or values as the public sector is oriented toward the community and the private sector on its self-interests as a private business. Intelligence agencies want to gather information to build intelligence, law enforcement wants to use the information to prosecute criminals (Quigley, Bisset, & Mills, 2017), and private security professionals want to use the information to protect their organization's critical assets.

The importance of security clearance in exchanging information was a frequent topic in the literature. Quigley (2013) pointed out Canadian private sector professionals participating in a critical infrastructure study claimed that classified briefings are vague, and they often do not provide actionable information. Dupont (2015) stated that anti-terrorist networks are faced with multiple problems preventing professionals from doing their work correctly and sharing information as they should since security clearances became "true data sharing obstacles" (p. 12). This issue was also highlighted by Vroegop (2017) when survey participants in his study indicated that security clearances and potential reputational damages were common obstacles in information sharing. The difficulty in sharing confidential information was also identified as a vital issue in PPPs studied by Dupré (2014) and Graphia (2010), and intelligence-sharing challenges discussed by Maras (2017).

Theme 6 Interpersonal Trust Relationships

Findings demonstrated study participants have trust in their private security colleagues to exchange information to assist them in preventing crime against their respective organization. In the private sector, trust and reciprocity were built over the years. The frequent interactions between study participants through meetings, conference calls, training, and managing incidents played a role in building that trust level in the banking sector. As mentioned by Whelan (2015), two conditions must be met to develop trust; risk and interdependence. For study participants, trusting relationships are being built by taking the risk of being the first one sharing information with another member of the private or public sector. As explained by Clarke and Knake (2019), sharing information does not always benefit you directly in the short term. It only benefits you when, in return, other companies or individuals you previously shared information with also share with you.

This study demonstrated that trust within the private sector was built from the process of sharing information with another entity, and when members see the benefits that have been gained by sharing the information. Having a legal framework (Bank Crime Prevention and Investigation Framework) to share information increases the chances security professionals will share information to assist another member in investigating a crime or in preventing an incident from occurring. As demonstrated, when both information-sharing partners can see the benefits, it motivates them to continue sharing information. In these situations, it created an incentive to keep sharing information to assist other members.

Individually and collectively, the study participants in this research clearly demonstrated they have less trust in the public sector they have with the private security professionals working in the financial industry. Data findings demonstrated that reciprocity in sharing information was key to build trust for participants. Simply put: if you share information with other professionals, the information needs to be shared both ways so that both partners may benefit from sharing it. This data sharing also reduces the risk of both individuals that may be associated with sharing the information as both actors will have participated in the exchange of information. As advanced by Quigley, Bisset, and Mills (2017), when it comes to critical infrastructures, information sharing should be a "two-way street," the private sector should share vulnerabilities with government and the public sector should share intelligence with private organizations.

This study's research findings closely aligned to those of (Costantini, 2016), who concluded that trust between both sectors remain fragile as private sector professionals do not believe they nor the public sector engage in trust-based behaviors. Differences in organizational culture may negatively impact trust within a group (Costantini, 2016). As argued by Costantini (2016) and previously by Koski (2015) and Powley and Nissen (2012), collaborative partnerships such as PPPs depend on factors such as communality, culture, and trust to motivate participation, to manage performance, and achieve success (Koski, 2015). Trust builds over time and particularly in situations where partnership members manage critical and uncertain situations such as crisis or emergency situations (Powley & Nissen, 2012).

Recommendations for Practice

The PIDEDA Act should be amended to allow financial institutions to share information with the public sectors for any criminal activities affecting banks. Cyber-fraud and cybersecurity incidents are often intertwined with other types of criminal activities, and private security professionals should not have to wonder if they are breaching any laws or rely on informal communications when trying to prevent crime and share information with public sector professionals as it was mentioned by one participant:

> *CSO #3*: "I think the pendulum has swung a little too far. I think that basically, it ties the hands of financial institutions on a number of occasions where if you are going to get a blessing from legal, you're not going to get it just because of let-down legislation."

The high-level of maturity in information sharing between banks through the private to private framework (BCPIF) should be an excellent basis to allow future PPP projects to be successful. Future PPP projects should rely on what is currently working and try to expand it to the public sector, as explained by one participant:

> *CSO #4*: "So, I think that if you look at the BCPIF framework, there is a lot of that can be transposed over a triple P framework as well because it is a triple P framework. It is something that has been tested, something that's been true, and a lot of good has come out of it."

Security professionals know that bad actors are not limiting themselves to cybercrime and financial crime. Organized crime is committing a vast array of criminal activities that are not related to each other. Thus, future PPP projects implemented to tackle cyber-threats against financial institutions would undoubtedly have positive impacts to counter other forms of crimes such as major crimes, or the fight against money laundering and terrorist financing. As described by one of the study participants:

> *CSO #2*: "But I do think that we can work more collaboratively with law enforcement to take bad people out of the environment. These bad people aren't just robbing banks; they're doing a number of different things ranging from, you know, drug trafficking, you know, human trafficking, you know, cybercrime, money laundering whatever it is they're doing a whole bunch of stuff. And so, the challenge is the banks can protect themselves, but the bad people aren't actually taken out of the environment. So that's where law enforcement and the public sector could come in."

As cybercrime increases, fraud incidents, data breaches, and insider threat cases are more frequent, it would be the right time to reopen the regulation debate and think about how the government should be interacting with the private sector to share information and to reduce the opportunities for cybercriminals to attack private organizations and its customers (Clarke & Knake, 2019). New legislation should focus on providing legal protections for private companies such as financial institutions to share cyber threat data with the public sector (Schaeffer, & Payne, 2016). Also, it would be appropriate to think about the possibility of having, "outcome-based" regulations that would specifically explain regulated organizations what they need to achieve instead of telling them how to do it (Clarke & Knake, 2019). This could be applicable to industries such as critical infrastructures.

The government will have to implement a legal framework to facilitate information sharing for better protection of critical infrastructures and to find creative ways to remove legal challenges and barriers (Kaplan, Bailey, O'Halloran, Marcus, & Rezek, 2015). Creativity will be necessary to make sure both sectors remained engaged in the partnership, and the public and the private sectors will need to agree to compromise between self-regulation of the partnerships and additional legislation (Borchert, 2015). Thus, strategies of self-regulation and co-regulation should be used to combine the strengths of multi-stakeholders (Tropina & Callanan, 2015) as only focusing on having more government regulations is not the proper way to go forward to improve public–private partnerships (Clinton, 2011). As for security clearances, the government should recognize the value of current private sector secret and top-secret security clearances in the same way as security clearance provided to government employees.

Recommendations for Future Research

Future studies should consider conducting phenomenological qualitative studies to measure the perceptions of public sector professionals—having experience collaborating with financial institutions—regarding the efficiency of PPPs and to get their perspective about current challenges in line with the themes discussed in this study. Law enforcement and intelligence agencies professionals might have a similar perspective than the participants in this study, but they might also perceive the challenges differently than banking security professionals.

Research Question #3

Theme 7 Unclear Roles, Responsibilities, and Processes in Critical Infrastructure Protection

Having clear roles and responsibilities (tactical versus strategic intelligence), a shared language, and management of expectations to avoid misunderstandings and communication issues is vital in managing PPPs (Den Boer, 2019; Public Safety Canada, 2017). Study findings demonstrated that private security professionals understand that national security responsibility is under the public sector. Participants had difficulty identifying where the national security responsibility begins as some of the threats they face could easily be associated with national security matters. How national security is defined may be different from one individual to the other when managing cyber-threats. The protection of financial institutions sensitive data and the transactions financial institutions are monitoring may have a significant effect on national security. When private security professionals are not aware that what they are investigating might be associated with a national security matter, they might not share information with the public sector. As a consequence, when participants don't share the information, they are not getting back intelligence that may assist them in managing risks while at the same time contributing to assist law enforcement or intelligence agencies in fulfilling their national security mandate. Since private security professionals care about the safety and security of the financial industry, most participants want to play an active role in protecting the industry. Study findings clearly demonstrated the power structure of government is extremely fragmented when it comes to critical infrastructure protection. Thus, when the private sector wants to take a greater share of responsibilities at this level, it can create tensions between both sectors.

The implications of this study's findings are important for practice. When it comes to critical infrastructure protection such as the financial industry, roles and responsibilities are not clearly established between the private and public sectors. Information-sharing processes for critical infrastructure protection are not well-established and documented. As concluded by Public Safety Canada, several Governments of Canada's organizations are proclaiming they are the "single point of contact" for the private sector in case of security incident, when in fact, multiple agencies still need to be contacted to make sure the information is processed at the intelligence and operational levels. Since the roles of security actors are not clear and that both sectors do not always agree on their individual responsibilities when it comes to defending against various cyber-threats, the security of the banks is solely managed by each bank's security departments. Furthermore, when it is time to defend against advanced persistent threats and nation-states threats affecting the financial industry as a whole, this study demonstrated that roles and responsibility are not clear even though all participants agreed that threats from nation-states are often associated with national security investigations that are under the public sector's responsibility.

This study's findings indicated there is still a fundamental disjuncture between the expectations of private and public security partners regarding roles, responsibility, and authority in protecting critical infrastructure from cyber-threats as previously identified by Carr (2016). The two reasons are (a) because the government or the public sector is viewed as being responsible and accountable for the response and the provision of national security while critical infrastructures are privatized, and (b) the private sector is under the impression the public sector lacks the knowledge, skills, and flexibility to properly monitor critical infrastructure owners in managing cyber-risks (Carr, 2016; Christensen & Petersen, 2017; Etzioni, 2017; Quigley, Bisset, & Mills, 2017).

Theme 8 Cyber-Attacks on Banks; a Potential Domino Effect

Participants in this study acknowledged that simultaneous attacks on banks could have significant negative impacts on investors, on customers' confidence in the financial system, the reputation of the financial institution's under attack as well as on the stock markets. One of the most important risks is that one or multiple bank's under attack would not be in a position to follow the two steps in a payment process, which are: first clearing and second settlement. The clearing processes consist of (a) transmitting funds, (b) reconciling, and (c) confirming payments between banks, and the settlement process corresponds to the payment obligations between two parties when they are transferring funds between each other (Bank of Canada, n.d.). The scenario of one or more banks being hit by a cyber incident rendering them incapable of carrying out their normal operations is not likely to materialize. In risk management, this scenario would be evaluated as being a low-probability and high-impact incident. However, if this type of incident would occur, the study findings demonstrated such a scenario would create significant collateral damage in the industry. These findings have implications for practice because only one large incident affecting one or more financial institutions or a single third-party dealing with the affected financial institutions would increase the systemic risk to the financial system (Bouveret, 2018).

Theme 9 Cross-Sector Critical Infrastructure Information Sharing

The findings of this study demonstrated private security professionals working for financial institutions believe that financial institutions should share information with other Canadian critical infrastructures as they are highly interconnected and dependent on each other. Among all Canadian critical infrastructures, participants believed financial institutions should share cyber-threat and financial crime information with the Canadian Information and Communication Technology sector, more specifically with telecommunication and internet provider companies. The potential synergies between telecommunications and financial institutions are more important today since banking is predominately done through mobile phones and the use of the Internet.

As national and transnational cyber threat actors may use a mobile phone or the Internet to commit cybercrimes and financial crimes, the importance of sharing information between these companies becomes critical. Data types such as Internet protocol (IP) addresses, proxies, virtual private networks (VPN), geo-localization data, device ID IMEI/MEID numbers to identify mobile phones are only some of the data sets that could be highly beneficial for financial institutions to link threat actors data with telecommunication and internet provider companies. As mentioned previously by CSO #4, collaboration on sim-swapping cases is highly critical to prevent identity theft fraud. By linking these threat actors, more incidents could be prevented. Furthermore, telecommunications companies and financial institutions are playing increasing roles in combatting organized crime and terrorism (Whelan & Dupont, 2017) and these private organizations would be typical private sector members of fusion centers (Bright & Whelan, 2018). Similar operational partnerships have already been implanted in Europe such as the Microsoft's Digital Crime Unit, Europol EC3, and the UK's National Cybersecurity Centre's work with telecommunications providers (Avina, 2011; Dixon, 2019).

Recommendations for Practice

Public–private partnerships main objective should be to increase the resilience of the financial industry. Given the rapid evolution of the cyber threat landscape and a barrage of recent cyber-attacks on banks at the international level, foreign threats to the financial sector in cyberspace should be a priority and conceptualized as a national security challenge. Roles and responsibilities from each federal organization (RCMP & intelligence agencies) and the role of financial institutions regarding national security should be clearly explained and defined to reduce ambiguity. Private security professionals working for banks should be given a special "security or law enforcement" status accorded by the federal government to assist the public sector during incidents and investigations. The potential of private security professional's roles in addressing crime against financial institutions should be further examined (Montgomery & Griffiths, 2016).

The new Canadian Centre for Cyber Security created in October 2018 should become the single authoritative source for cybersecurity operational matters, incident management, and situational awareness (Communications Security Establishment, 2018). The evolution of this new center should be evaluated in order to see the benefits for the private sector and to provide incentives to continue working with the government in improving cybersecurity.

A whole-of-state approach to cybersecurity is necessary to manage critical infrastructure (Garcia, Forscey, & Blute, 2017). By following such an approach in cybersecurity, stakeholders define and establish timelines, accountability mechanisms, and they allocate resources (Garcia et al., 2017). This way, it allows adequate governance, and the roles and responsibilities in cyber prevention and cyber disruption are better understood by individual members.

All measures that can increase resilience to the financial system of Canada should be taken, and public–private partnership should be a preferred vehicle to reach this objective. To tackle cybercrime, integrated PPPs should include members from intelligence agencies, law enforcement, banks, academia, as well as regulators (Chadderton & Norton, 2019; Perianayagam, Nesbitt, & Caplan, 2018). Regulators should be included in PPPs as they currently have little interaction with law enforcement and PPPs investigations. Regulators have primarily concentrated on reporting processes while it would also be highly beneficial for them to consider the value of the information provided by the private sector to the government to prevent crimes (Den Boer, 2019; San Juan Menacho & Martin, 2018).

Recommendations for Future Research

On June 26, 2019, the Bank of Canada announced the creation of the Canadian Resiliency Group (CFRG), replacing the previous Joint Operational Resiliency Management program (JORM)—A public–private partnership initiative of the Bank of Canada focusing primarily on conducting tabletop exercises with potential crisis scenarios to measure how the private and public sectors would react to a crisis—"to ensure collaboration and information sharing among major participants in the financial system to reduce risk and enhance recovery actions in the event of a systemic-level operational incident" (Bank of Canada, 2019). Future studies should focus on evaluating the efficiency of these PPP initiatives in economic terms. In crime prevention, it may be difficult to assess the impacts of crime prevention actions. However, developing the right metrics and success criteria should be a priority to the sustainability of PPP projects. Also, the results of tabletop exercises and the improvement of business continuity key risk indicators in line with crisis management procedures should be evaluated. Additionally, the benefits of sharing information between critical infrastructures such as the telecommunication companies and financial institutions should be evaluated as well to demonstrate the impacts of sharing information to reduce risk, potential losses, and negative impacts to customers of both industries.

Research Question #4

Theme 10 Necessity to Increase Cyber-Threat Information Sharing

This study's results confirmed private security professionals would like to continue to enhance information-sharing capabilities between public and private partners. Participants felt that to be efficient in mitigating cyber-risks against their organizations; they should be sharing more information with the public sector than what they currently share. According to Sullivan and Burger (2017), sharing cyber-threat data for crime prevention without the consent of the data subjects is in the public interest. In these circumstances, the necessity to share information should override existing legal and privacy requirements as long as these practices are "strictly necessary to achieve security objectives" (Sullivan, & Burger, 2017). In a theoretical perspective and as mentioned by Collins (2016), an essential aspect of the securitization process is that it strongly depends on the power and influence (speech acts) of the securitizing actors to convince a relevant audience that an immediate danger threatens a referent object and that extraordinary measures are required. More information should be provided to the population about the "immediate danger" of cyber-threats as well as the reasons why these "extraordinary measures," sharing information for crime prevention, are necessary to mitigate cyber-risks and to protect their personal data and identity. Moreover, findings demonstrated participants are well aware of the risks associated with sharing information. They do not want to share more information for the sake of sharing information as they understand that laws and privacy must be respected.

Participants understood the value of risk-based sharing information with the public sector, and that it was necessary for them to share information to achieve their objectives of preventing crimes and to protect their organizations. They perceived information sharing as a risk management process since it is not possible to completely avoid risks while sharing information. However, in their view, risk-based decisions need to be taken. From their perspective, there is more risk associated with not sharing information than there is risk associated with sharing information to prevent crime. As participants took part in multiple PPP investigations over the years, they went from a "need to know" to a "need to share" mindset which demonstrates how the culture of information sharing evolved over time to adapt to cyber-threats (Maxwell, 2019).

Theme 11 Governance Model to Share Information; Private to Private BCPIF Framework

This study's findings indicated that good governance of partnerships between financial institutions was possible by having a legal and governance framework, procedures to describe what information can and cannot be shared, by whom, and how the information needed to be shared. The BCPIF framework is perceived and understood by study participants as the proper governance mechanism in place to share information between banking security professionals. Such a governance framework was of critical importance for study participants when it comes to sharing information to prevent crime while respecting laws and privacy regulations. This finding has implications for practice since such a framework does not exist to prevent crime by sharing information with the public sector, thus creating a critical gap in intelligence.

Besides, as argued by participants, most PPPs attempted in Canada did not generate the expected results, and one of the potential reasons is because PPPs did not have the proper legal and governance framework in place. Under the BCPIF framework, banks can centralize the information at the Canadian Bankers Association (CBA) level. The CBA can then coordinate with law enforcement while also acting as a governance body to make sure the framework is followed, training is provided, decisions are taken, and issues are reported to an executive committee for decision-making. Also, this governance framework allows to make sure an audit trail exists to demonstrate by whom, what, when, and how the information was shared according to the procedures and applicable laws.

The only project participants identified as being successful was a secondment PPP project in which financial institutions assumed the costs associated with one financial institution's analyst to work with law enforcement. Even though this project was identified as successful by some participants, if success criteria would have been clearly defined, other participants would not have seen this project as successful since this project lasted for years before arrests were made.

Another important implication for practice is that private security professionals recognized four active international PPPs projects as being successful. These PPP projects were located in two different countries; the United States and the United Kingdom. The three active projects in the United States were the NCFTA, FS-ISAC, and NCCIC. The ongoing PPP project in the United Kingdom was the Joint Money Laundering Intelligence Taskforce (JMLIT). Among the participants, the UK JMLIT project was perceived as "world-leading" in the financial crime field (Rosemont, 2016).

Theme 12 Various Types of Security Networks Are Necessary

Findings confirmed participants believed information-sharing PPPs between financial institutions and public sector stakeholders should be categorized as security networks as per Dupont's (2004) definition. Participants mentioned that each level is essential (Local, institutional, international, and virtual), but the current model of security networks are local networks and institutional networks operating at the national level. The majority of study participants confirmed that each type of network within the typology created by Whelan and Dupont (2017) should exist as these networks are mutually exclusive. From the typology of networks, the security networks they used to be part of in the past and still use today is the information exchange networks.

The results of this study demonstrated that each network type within this typology should be perceived as a critical part of a "global" security network and each individual security network should aim to reach a level of maturity in which each type of networks (information exchange networks, knowledge generation networks, problem-solving networks, and the coordination networks) within the "global" security network should be as timely, accurate, and as effective as humanly possible to allow the global network to benefit from each of its individual network's nodes. These results have implications for future research as it is the first time Dupont's (2004) theoretical framework and the Whelan and Dupont's (2017) typology are validated at the practical level with private security professionals working for financial institutions.

Recommendations for Practice

Virtual data-sharing and data analytics capabilities will become essential in managing cybersecurity and financial crime. Thus, financial institutions' data scientists working on creating cybersecurity, fraud prevention and detection models, and rules should be working closely with technical public sector analysts. Both sectors have unique data sets that should be combined and leveraged further to identify cyber threats. By relying on data, it will allow data scientists to identify a large set of known entities and individuals in each respective data holding that are connected to each other in a set of relationships (Schaeffer & Payne, 2016). In looking further into this data, joint teams of public sector analysts and private sector data scientists would be able to detect more hidden relationships.

As previously cited by former U.S. Secretary of Defense Donald Rumsfeld (2001–2006), these partnerships would allow to detect—"known unknown" scenarios (i.e., the things we know that we don't know) and "unknown unknown" scenarios (i.e., things that we don't know we don't know) and try to make inferences in creating future "known known scenarios" (i.e., things that we know we know) so that PPPs members will be able to act upon these scenarios to prevent future cybersecurity incidents (Perera & Higgins, 2017). These teams would become a great example of future knowledge generation networks. When combined with the work of academia, data analytics teams working on machine learning would undoubtedly generate creativity and innovation in the way future PPPs operate.

At the strategic level, future public–private partnerships will require leadership. More specifically, the leadership of public–private entities' executives to take appropriate decisions to allocate resources, transparency in communications, clear roles and responsibilities, and an excellent understanding of the differences of cultural and organizational diversity. The leadership of both sectors needs to recognize that cybersecurity and financial crime management are imperative. Also, additional and dedicated resources should be provided to PPPs as current security professionals cannot fulfill their full-time employment while also trying to implement and operate PPPs.

At the tactical level, it should be possible for employees from the government to do internships with financial institutions' security teams and these internships should also be available for private sector employees as well to work with the public sector's investigation and intelligence teams (Schaeffer & Payne, 2016). Also, more frequent secondments through the establishment of fusion centers and virtual networks would allow professionals from both sectors to learn from each other and to build trust in managing joint investigations. These secondments would allow to educate and develop the talents of both sectors. These secondments would also be a great opportunity for the employees of both sectors working in cybersecurity and financial crime investigation to get to know each other.

Future PPPs should measure results in economic terms for financial institutions to be able to demonstrate financial losses prevented due to PPP activities and how much the financial resources invested in PPPs created additional value for the organizations. The average cost of cybersecurity incidents or fraud cases prevented should be one of the criteria that are measured to demonstrate the value of prevention. As security is generally an essential factor for financial institutions' clients, the customer's level of trust in the security of the organization should also be evaluated. The governance of PPPs should be done by members from both sectors. A potential model would be what Sedenberg and Dempsey (2018) described as a "government-prompted industry-centric" PPP. In this model, organizational units are sector and problem-specific, created in the form of ISACS or fusion centers. Information sharing may be voluntary, and PPPs under this model are usually nonprofits organizations using contractual terms and services (Sedenberg & Dempsey, 2018).

Furthermore, PPPs projects should be agile as PPPs could last for weeks, months, years, or even permanent depending on the common goals established by the leadership of the PPPs. Since threats are multi-jurisdictional, a multi-level governance framework of PPPs and security networks should be implemented to tackle cyber-threats against financial institutions. Security networks should be established at the provincial and at the federal level. Considering that different levels of governments (provincial and federal governments), multiple financial institutions located across the country, and various policing levels (provincial and federal police) will have to work together, a multi-level governance framework should be implemented to provide guidance and oversight of future PPPs. By having multiple regional security networks interacting at the provincial level, and one security network at the national network, it would allow members of these networks to "physically" collaborate between each other and to rely on a virtual network linking all regional security networks to the federal security network to share information through a virtual secured network.

Some Canadian financial institutions are already members of FS-ISAC to share information. However, different levels of security networks will be necessary to implement efficient PPPs in Canada. Security networks working at various levels such as the Financial Services Information Sharing and Analysis Center (FS-ISAC) for tactical real-time information sharing, the Financial Services Sector Coordinating Council for policy coordination and development, and the Financial Systemic Analysis and Resilience Center for managing systemic risks to the financial sector should be examined further to evaluate if this could be applicable in Canada. As the FS-ISAC model is already very successful, public and private actors should evaluate how more security professionals could contribute to data sharing.

Future PPPs should define success criteria to evaluate the results of each project. Key performance indicators and key risk indicators should be developed as PPPs measured results will become incentives for executives of both sectors and policymakers to show the importance of continuing to establish PPP projects. Thus, success criteria should take into consideration the criteria from both the public and private sectors.

Recommendations for Future Research

The knowledge of how to manage activities conducted by network actors is still lacking, and future research should study how security networks are organized to increase effectiveness and efficiency in cybersecurity and financial crime governance (Rondelez, 2018). To measure the effectiveness of future networks, the model developed by Whelan (2015) should be used to evaluate the effectiveness of networks (a) at the organizational level (effectiveness for individual organizations in the network), (b) at the network level (effectiveness for the network), and (c) at the community level (the effectiveness for the overall community in which the network operates).

Additionally, future studies should evaluate the success factors of PPP projects such as the NCFTA, FS-ISAC, the NCCIC, the Fintel Alliance, and JMLIT. What did not work well within these PPP projects should also be evaluated to make sure to avoid replicating what did not work in future PPP projects. The evidence-based cybersecurity research approach in the context of financial institutions should also be prioritized to evaluate common tools and policies used by security networks to achieve goals, to manage cybersecurity incidents, and to investigate cybercrimes against financial institutions as there is an absence of universally accepted metrics to measure security controls and policies (Maimon, Alper, Sobesto, & Cukier 2014; Maimon, Testa, Sobesto, Cukier, & Wuling, 2019; Testa, Maimon, Sobesto, & Cukier, 2017; Wilson, Maimon, Sobesto, & Cukier, 2015).

According to Dupré (2014) as well as Chadderton and Norton (2019), in an effective PPP, various features must be included such as (a) leadership (leadership approach based on coordination), (b) funding (time, resources, and efforts of the involved stakeholders), (c) expected outcome (information sharing, policy priority identification), (d) inclusion rules (profile of the stakeholder), and (e) participation (voluntary, inclusive, and based on trust). Based on the five main reasons (Why, where, how, what, who) to identify key features of PPPs developed by Dupré (2014) and the results of this study, the PPP key feature model presented in Table 7.1 summarize how future security networks between financial institutions and the public sector should work to become effective in preventing cybercrime and protecting Canadian financial institutions. Future research should evaluate public–private partnerships in evaluating each of these key features as well as evaluating the best practices and challenges of every single PPP to compare them between each other.

Summary of Recommendations

Tables 7.2 and 7.3 provide an overview of the most important recommendations for practice and future studies. A total 11 recommendations for future studies (Table 7.2) and of 19 recommendations for practices (Table 7.3) were identified throughout this study. These recommendations are what policymakers and executives from both sectors should prioritize to implement PPPs best practices to focus on prevention, to remove current challenges to share information between both sectors, to improve the effectiveness of PPPs in mitigating cyber-threats against financial institutions, to govern these partnerships, and to increase resiliency.

Table 7.1 Key features of future Canadian public-private partnerships

Why?	*Where?*	*How?*	*What?*	*Who?*
Topic addressed Public-Private partnership in Information Sharing to Prevent Cyber-Threats against Financial Institutions to increase resilience	*Geographical scope* Provincial & National	*Joint leadership system* Provincial and Federal Fusion Centers & Multi-Level Governance/ Government-Prompted Industry-Centric	*Expected outcomes* Increase Resilience in Countering Cyber & Financial Threats (Cyber-Attacks & Financial Crime)	*Participant's profiles* Financial Institution's security professionals, Law Enforcement professionals, Intelligence Agencies Analysts, Regulators
	Interaction strategy: Physical Meetings (co-location) and Virtual Interactions	*Funding*: Analysts and Investigators from Both Sectors Time & Efforts Financial Resources for PPP Project operations Physical Location and Virtual Platforms	*Incentives*: Threat Integrated Approach Reduction of Losses Disruptions of Threat Actors Cyber & Financial Crime Deterrence Efficiency Improvement Customer trust & Loyalty	*Inclusion rule*: Invitation and Individual Initiatives *Participation rules*: Effort Contribution Based and Individual PPP Results

Note Adapted from Dupré (2014)

Table 7.2 Recommendations for practice on private and public partnerships

Recommendations for Future Research	
1. Focus on understanding what systems, technological platforms, and alert capabilities fusion centers are currently using	8. Future research should study how different security networks are organized to increase effectiveness and efficiency in cybersecurity and financial crime governance
2. Study and compare other legal frameworks such as the ones in the United States and the United Kingdom	9. Futures studies should evaluate the success factors of PPP projects such as the NCFTA, FS-ISAC, the NCCIC, and JMLIT
3. Evaluate what other industries such as the telecommunications industry and other critical infrastructures use to share threat indicators	10. The evidence-based cybersecurity research approach in the context of financial institutions should be prioritized to evaluate common tools and policies used by security networks
4. Future studies should consider measuring the perceptions of Canadian public sector professionals regarding the efficiency of PPPs and the challenges	11. Future research on PPPs in information-sharing should consider measuring the perceptions of other experts such as the anti-money laundering specialists working for Canadian financial institutions or public sector employees working in law enforcement or intelligence agencies
5. Future studies should focus on evaluating the efficiency of PPP initiatives in economic terms	
6. Results of tabletop exercises and the improvement of business continuity key risk indicators in line with crisis management procedures should be evaluated	
7. The benefits of sharing information between critical infrastructure (such as the telecommunication companies and financial institutions) should be evaluated to demonstrate the impacts of sharing information to reduce risk, potential losses, and negative impacts to customers of both industries	

Table 7.3 Recommendations for future research on private and public partnerships

Recommendations for Practice	
1. The Canadian federal government should enact new legislation for timely notifications to banks as a critical infrastructure	13. PPPs should be including members from intelligence agencies, law enforcement, banks, academia as well as regulators
2. A fusion center "hub-and-spoke" model should be created between banks and the public sector to combat cyber-threats and financial crime	14. Financial institution's data scientists should be working closely with technical public sector analysts
3. The Canadian Center for Cybersecurity, the Canadian Security Intelligence Service, and the Royal Canadian Mounted Police should play critical roles within these fusion centers with the banking industry	
4. Future PPP projects using virtual platforms should rely on a common taxonomy, and a governance framework to govern information-sharing	15. Future public-private partnerships will require leadership from both sectors & additional dedicated resources
5. Bill S4 and the PIDEDA Act should be revisited and amended to allow financial institutions to share information with the public sectors for any type of criminal activities affecting banks	16. Internships and secondments should be offered to both public and private security professionals as an education tool to develop cyber skills
6. New legislation should focus on providing legal protections for private companies such as financial institutions to share cyber threat and financial crime data with the public sector	17. PPPs should measure results in economic terms
7. Strategies of self-regulation and co-regulation should be used to combine the strength of multi-stakeholders' information-sharing partnerships	18. Governance of PPPs should be done by members from both sectors through a multi-level governance framework of PPPs and security networks
8. The government should recognize private sector secret and top-secret security clearances in the same way as security clearance provided to government employees	

Recommendations for Practice	
9. Public-private partnerships main objective should be to increase the resilience of the financial industry 10. Foreign threats to the financial sector in cyberspace should be a priority and conceptualized as a national security challenge 11. Roles and responsibilities from each federal organization (RCMP & intelligence agencies) and the role of financial institutions regarding national security should be clearly explained and defined 12. Private security professionals working for banks should be given a special status accorded by the federal government to assist the public sector during incidents and investigations	19. PPPs should define success criteria to evaluate the results of each project

The recommendations presented in Table 7.3 are potential actions in line with the modification of the legislation to allow information sharing, the creation of fusion centers, the clarification of roles and responsibility between public and private actors, the mechanism to share information and the governance of security networks.

Conclusion

The problem to be addressed was why private and public partnership relationships have been ineffective in monitoring, detecting, and reacting to these incidents? (Bures, 2013; Dunn-Cavelty & Suter, 2009). Previous academic research in this area has seldomly considered the perceptions of private corporate security professionals leading corporate security and cybersecurity teams. The professional experiences and inputs of these professionals are vital components enabling the public and private sectors to work together and to improve public–private partnerships in the future.

The purpose of this qualitative study was to conduct interviews with corporate security professionals (corporate and information security) working for Canadian financial institutions. The research focus was (a) to obtain information to better understand the challenges these private security professionals face in sharing information aimed at preventing cybersecurity incidents with the public sector and (b) to provide recommendations for decision-makers on how best to improve their existing cybersecurity protections. Understanding the perspectives of private security professionals on public–private partnerships (PPPs) could lead to better collaboration in preventing cyberattacks against financial institutions, increase the overall effectiveness of cybersecurity systems, and the establishment of proper protocols to cooperate with the public sector in investigating actual cybersecurity incidents.

This research study determined that the Network Security Governance Framework first proposed by Dupont (2004) and adapted by Whelan and Dupont (2017) does allow for better understanding of this phenomenon, as well as to identify best practices for future information-sharing PPPs. This study addressed the central problem of why private and public partnership relationships have been ineffective in monitoring, detecting, and reacting to these incidents.

The resulting data of this qualitative study included various direct quotes from the interviews with private security professionals working for Canadian financial institutions. A total of 12 significant themes were identified, allowing to answer the four Research Questions. This analysis illustrated the perceptions of these security professionals regarding the phenomenon under study. Also, this study provided more information about why information sharing between PPPs actors is not optimal. The results of this study are significant for the literature in security as most of the study participants (67%) were working for a Canadian Schedule 1 banks and five of them were working for one of the six largest banks in the country.

A total of 19 recommendations for practices and 11 recommendations for future studies were identified throughout this study. From a practical and theoretical standpoints, these recommendations are what policymakers and executives from both public and private sectors should prioritize in the future to implement PPPs best practices to focus on prevention, to remove current challenges to share information between both sectors, to improve the effectiveness of PPPs in mitigating cyber-threats against financial institutions, and to govern these partnerships to increase resiliency properly.

Stakeholder management starts at the top, and public–private information-sharing initiative will need to dedicate the right people, processes, and technology to these partnerships. Even though previous academics may have confirmed PPPs were in an impasse and there was no way to make them work, this study demonstrated current PPPs are no silver bullet, but study participants recognized how important they would become in the future. Private security professionals are willing to collaborate with the public sector to create efficient security networks that will enable them to achieve common goals and to succeed in reducing cyber-threats against financial institutions. In the short term, both sectors need to engage seriously in dedicating resources and making this happen as it is clear neither sector is capable of achieving it on his own. As claimed by Borchert (2015), in managing private–public partnerships, it takes two to tango.

References

Avina, J. (2011). Public-private partnerships in the fight against crime: An emerging frontier in corporate social responsibility. *Journal of Financial Crime, 18*(3), 282.

Bank of Canada. (n.d.). *Canada's major payment systems*. Retrieved from https://www.bankofcanada.ca/core-functions/financial-system/canadas-major-payments-systems/.

Bank of Canada. (2019). *Banks of Canada announces partnership to improve resilience in financial sector*. Retrieved from https://www.bankofcanada.ca/wp-content/uploads/2019/06/press_270619.pdf.

Baulin, V. (2019). *Group-IB: More than 70% of Russian banks are not ready for cyberattacks*. Retrieved from https://www.group-ib.com/media/banks-readiness/.

Boes, S., & Leukfeldt, E. R. (2017). Fighting cybercrime: A joint effort. *Cyber-physical security*, p. 185. Retrieved from https://www.researchgate.net/publication/306035727_Fighting_Cybercrime_A_Joint_Effort.

Borchert, H. (2015). It takes two to tango: Public-private information management to advance critical infrastructure protection. *European Journal of Risk Regulation (EJRR)* (Issue 2), 208. Retrieved from https://www.researchgate.net/publication/264312240_It_Takes_Two_to_Tango_Public-Private_Information_Management_to_Advance_Critical_Infrastructure_Protection.

Borghard, D. E. (2018). *Protecting financial institutions against cyber threats: A national security issue*. Retrieved from https://carnegieendowment.org/files/WP_Borghard_Financial_Cyber_formatted_complete.pdf.

Bouveret, A. (2018). *Cyber risk for the financial sector: A framework for quantitative assessment*. Retrieved from https://www.imf.org/en/Publications/WP/Issues/2018/06/22/Cyber-Risk-for-the-Financial-Sector-A-Framework-for-Quantitative-Assessment-45924.

Bright, D., & Whelan, C. (2018). On the relationship between goals, membership and network design in multi-agency "fusion" centres. *Policing: An International Journal of Police Strategies & Management*. https://doi.org/10.1108/PIJPSM-05-2018-0070.

Bures, O. (2013). Public-private partnerships in the fight against terrorism? *Crime, Law & Social Change, 60*(4), 429–455. https://doi.org/10.1007/s10611-013-9457-7.

Canadian Bankers Association. (2015). *Bill S-4—Digital Privacy Act: Remarks by Linda Routledge*. Retrieved from https://cba.ca/Assets/CBA/Documents/Files/Article%20Category/PDF/sub-20150312-bill-s4-en.pdf.

Carr, M. (2016). Public-private partnerships in national cyber-security strategies. *International Affairs, 92*(1), 43–62. https://doi.org/10.1111/1468-2346.12504.

Chadderton, P., & Norton, S. (2019). *Public-private partnerships to disrupt financial crime: An exploratory study of Australia's fintel alliance*. Retrieved from https://www.researchgate.net/publication/333619510_PUBLIC-PRIVATE_PARTNERSHIPS_TO_DISRUPT_FINANCIAL_CRIME_AN_EXPLORATORY_STUDY_OF_AUSTRALIA'S_FINTEL_ALLIANCE.

Christensen, K. K., & Petersen, K. (2017). Public-private partnerships on cyber security: A practice of loyalty. *International Affairs, 93*(6), 1435–1452. https://doi.org/10.1093/ia/iix189.

Clarke, A. R., & Knake, K. R. (2019). *The fifth domain; Defending our country, our companies, and ourselves in the age of cyber threats.* Retrieved from https://www.amazon.ca/Fifth-Domain-Defending-Companies-Ourselves/dp/052556196X/ref=sr_1_1?keywords=the+fifth+domain&qid=1565299313&s=books&sr=1-1.

Clinton, L. (2011). A relationship on the rocks: Industry-government partnership for cyber defense. *Journal of Strategic Security, 4*(2), 97–112. https://doi.org/10.5038/1944-0472.4.2.6.

Collins, A. (2016). *Contemporary security studies.* Retrieved from https://www.amazon.com/Contemporary-Security-Studies-Alan-Collins/dp/0198708319/ref=sr_1_1?s=books&ie=UTF8&qid=1542036106&sr=1-1&keywords=contemporary+security+studies.

Communications Security Establishment. (2018). *Canadian Centre for Cyber Security; National cyber threat assessment 2018.* Retrieved from https://cyber.gc.ca/sites/default/files/publications/national-cyber-threat-assessment-2018-e_1.pdf.

Costantini, L. P. (2016). *Perceptions of trust in public-private partnerships for critical infrastructure protection—Implications for civil security, leadership, policy, and management* (Order No. 10259626). Available from ProQuest Dissertations & Theses Global (1882247286). Retrieved from http://search.proquesst.com.proxy1.ncu.edu/docview/1882247286?accountid=28180.

Cozine, K., Joyal, R. G., & Ors, H. (2014). From local to global: Comparing network approaches to addressing terrorism and transnational crime. *Journal of Policing Intelligence & Counter Terrorism, 9*(2), 117. https://doi.org/10.1080/18335330.2014.940817.

Den Boer, E. (2019). *Countering money-laundering through public-private cooperation in the Netherlands; Qualitative, explorative analysis into influences of external, structural—and—cultural conditions on perceptions and attitudes of decision-makers during network formation* (Unpublished master's thesis). University of Leicester.

Dixon, W. (2019). *Fighting cybercrime—What happens to the law when the law cannot be enforced?* Retrieved from https://www.weforum.org/agenda/2019/02/fighting-cybercrime-what-happens-to-the-law-when-the-law-cannot-be-enforced/.

Dunn-Cavelty, M., & Suter, M. (2009). Public-private partnerships are no silver bullet: An expanded governance model for critical infrastructure protection. *International Journal of Critical Infrastructure Protection, 2,* 179–187. https://doi.org/10.1016/j.ijcip.2009.08.006.

Dupont, B. (2004). Security in the age of networks. *Policing & Society, 14*(1), 76. https://doi.org/10.1080/1043946042000181575.

Dupont, B. (2015). Security networks and counter-terrorism: A reflection on the limits of adversarial isomorphism. In M. Bouchard (Ed.), *Social networks, terrorism, and counter-terrorism* (pp. 155–174). New York, NY: Routledge. Retrieved from https://www.researchgate.net/publication/279561796_Security_networks_and_counter-terrorism_a_reflection_on_the_limits_of_adversarial_isomorphism.

Dupré, L. (2014). *EP3R 2010–2013: Four years of Pan-European public-private cooperation*. Heraklion, Greece: European Union Agency for Network Information Security. Retrieved from https://www.researchgate.net/publication/270592099_EP3R_2010-2013_-_Four_Years_of_Pan-European_Public_Private_Cooperation.

Etzioni, A. (2017). The fusion of the private and public sectors. *Contemporary Politics, 23*(1), 53–62. https://doi-org.proxy1.ncu.edu/10.1080/13569775.2016.1213074.

Garcia, M., Forscey, D., & Blute, T. (2017). Beyond the network: A holistic perspective on state cybersecurity governance. *Nebraska Law Review, 96*(2), 252. Retrieved from https://digitalcommons.unl.edu/cgi/viewcontent.cgi?article=3116&context=nlr.

Germano, H. J. (2014). *Cybersecurity partnerships: A new era of public-private collaboration*. New York, NY: The Center on Law and Security, New York University School of Law. Retrieved from https://www.lawandsecurity.org/wp-content/uploads/2016/08/Cybersecurity.Partnerships-1.pdf.

Graphia, R. D. (2010). *An exploratory study of the perceived utility and effectiveness of state fusion centers* (Order No. 3408888). Available from ProQuest Dissertations & Theses Global. (577642738). Retrieved from http://search.proquest.com.proxy1.ncu.edu/docview/577642738?accountid=28180.

Kaplan, M. J., Bailey, T., O'Halloran, D., Marcus, A., & Rezek, C. (2015). *Beyond cybersecurity*. Retrieved from https://www.amazon.ca/Beyond-Cybersecurity-Protecting-Digital-Business/dp/1119026849/ref=sr_1_1?s=books&ie=UTF8&qid=1530879571&sr=1-1&keywords=beyond+cybersecurity.

Kolini, F., & Janczewski, L. (2017). *Two heads are better than one: A theoretical model for cybersecurity intelligence sharing (CIS) between organisations*. Retrieved from https://www.acis2017.org/wp-content/uploads/2017/11/ACIS2017_paper_199_RIP.pdf.

Koski, C. (2015). Does a partnership need partners? Assessing partnerships for critical infrastructure protection. *American Review of Public Administration, 45*(3), 327–342. Retrieved from: http://citeseerx.ist.psu.edu/viewdoc/download?doi=10.1.1.946.1337&rep=rep1&type=pdf.

Lagazio, M., Sherif, N., & Cushman, M. (2014). A multi-level approach to understanding the impact of cybercrime on the financial sector. *Computers & Security, 45*, 58–74. https://doi.org/10.1016/j.cose.2014.05.006.

Maimon, D., Alper, M., Sobesto, B., & Cukier, M. (2014). Restrictive deterrent effects of a warning banner in an attacked computer system. *Criminology, 52*(1), 33. https://doi.org/10.1111/1745-9125.12028.

Maimon, D., Testa, A., Sobesto, B., Cukier, M., & Wuling, R. (2019). Predictably deterrable? The case of system trespassers. In G. Wang, J. Feng, M. Bhuiyan, & R. Lu (Eds.), *Security, privacy, and anonymity in computation, communication, and storage*. Cham: Springer.

Maras, H. M. (2017). Overcoming the intelligence-sharing paradox: Improving information sharing through change in organizational culture. *Comparative Strategy, 36*(3). 187–197. https://doi-org.proxy1.ncu.edu/10.1080/01495933.2017.1338477.

Maxwell, J. N. (2019). *Expanding the capability of financial information-sharing partnerships*. Retrieved from https://rusi.org/publication/occasional-papers/expanding-capability-financial-information-sharing-partnerships.

Montgomery, R., & Griffiths, T. C. (2016). *The use of private security services in policing*. Retrieved from https://www.publicsafety.gc.ca/cnt/rsrcs/pblctns/archive-2015-r041/2015-r041-en.pdf.

Musiał, N. (2019). Cyber risk in financial institutions: A Polish case. In P. Linsley, P. Shrives, M. Wieczorek-Kosmala (Eds.), *Multiple perspectives in risk and risk management*. Springer Proceedings in Business and Economics. Cham: Springer.

Office of the Privacy Commissioner of Canada. (2017). *Applying paragraphs 7 (3) (d.1) and 7 (3) (d.2) of PIPEDA*. Retrieved from https://www.priv.gc.ca/en/privacy-topics/privacy-laws-in-canada/the-personal-information-protection-and-electronic-documents-act-pipeda/pipeda-compliance-help/gd_d1-d2_201703/.

Ozkaya, E., & Aslaner, M. (2019). *Hands-on cybersecurity for finance*. Retrieved from https://www.packtpub.com/networking-and-servers/hands-cybersecurity-finance.

Perera, T., & Higgins, D. (2017). *Theoretical overview of knowns, unknowns, and unknowable risks to property decision makings*. Retrieved from https://www.researchgate.net/publication/320943325_Theoretical_Overview_of_Known_Unknown_and_Unknowable_Risks_for_Property_Decision_Makings.

Perianayagam, A., Nesbitt, R., Caplan, M. (2018). *National approach to cyber intrusion; A comparison of United Kingdom and Canada*. Retrieved from https://globalriskinstitute.org/publications/national-approach-to-cyber-intrusion/.

Pomerleau, P. L. (2019). Public-private partnerships: Port security. In L. Shapiro & M. H. Maras (Eds.), *Encyclopedia of security and emergency management*. Cham: Springer.

Powley, E. H., & Nissen, M. E. (2012). If you can't trust, stick to hierarchy: Structure and trust as contingency factors in threat assessment contexts. *Journal of Homeland Security and Emergency Management, 9*(1). Retrieved from https://pdfs.semanticscholar.org/f74d/2b25ba0868d827c01cfcb7853ad320dee1fd.pdf.

Public Safety Canada. (2017). *Horizontal evaluation of Canada's cyber security strategy*. Retrieved from https://www.publicsafety.gc.ca/cnt/rsrcs/pblctns/vltn-cnd-scrt-strtg/index-en.aspx.

Quigley, K. (2013). "Man plans, God laughs": Canada's national strategy for protecting critical infrastructure. *Canadian Public Administration, 56*(1), 142–164. https://doi-org.proxy1.ncu.edu/10.1111/capa.12007.

Quigley, K., Bisset, B., & Mills, B. (2017). *Too critical to fail: How Canada manages threats to critical infrastructure*. Retrieved from https://www.amazon.ca/Too-Critical-Fail-Manages-Infrastructure/dp/0773551611/ref=sr_1_1?s=books&ie=UTF8&qid=1548361193&sr=1-1&keywords=too+critical+to+fail.

Rondelez, R. (2018). Governing Cyber Security through networks: An analysis of Cyber Security Coordination in Belgium. *International Journal of Cyber Criminology*, 300–315. Retrieved from https://www.cybercrimejournal.com/RondelezVol12Issue1IJCC2018.pdf.

Rosemont, H. (2016). *Public-private security cooperation: From cyber to financial crime*. Retrieved from https://rusi.org/publication/occasional-papers/public%E2%80%93private-security-cooperation-cyber-financial-crime.

San Juan Menacho, V., & Martin, A. (2018). *Cyber governance and the financial services sector: The role of public-private partnerships*. Retrieved from https://osf.io/preprints/socarxiv/ybqgm/.

Schaeffer, C. R., & Payne, F. X. J. (2016). *Public-private information sharing*. AFCEA International Cyber Committee. Retrieved from https://www.afcea.org/signal/resources/CyberWhitePaper_Oct_16_public_private.pdf.

Sedenberg, M. E., & Dempsey, X. J. (2018). *Cybersecurity information sharing governance structures: An ecosystem of diversity, trust, and tradeoffs*. Retrieved from https://arxiv.org/abs/1805.12266.

Skopik, F., Settanni, G., & Fiedler, R. (2016). A problem shared is a problem halved: A survey on the dimensions of collective cyber defense through security information sharing. *Computers & Security, 60*, 154–176. https://doi-org.proxy1.ncu.edu/10.1016/j.cose.2016.04.003.

Sullivan, C., & Burger, E. (2017). "In the public interest": The privacy implications of international business-to-business sharing of cyber-threat intelligence.

Computer Law & Security Review: the International Journal of Technology Law and Practice. https://doi.org/10.1016/j.clsr.2016.11.015.
Testa, A., Maimon, D., Sobesto, B., & Cukier, M. (2017). Illegal roaming and file manipulation on target computers: Assessing the effect of sanction threats on system trespassers' online behaviors. *Criminology and Public Policy, 16*(3), 687–726. https://doi.org/10.1111/1745-9133.12312.
Tropina, T., & Callanan, C. (2015). *Self & co-regulation in cybercrime, cybersecurity & national security*. Cham, Switzerland: Springer International Publishing.
United States Computer Emergency Readiness Team. (n.d). *Information sharing specifications for cybersecurity*. Retrieved from https://www.us-cert.gov/Information-Sharing-Specifications-Cybersecurity.
United States Computer Emergency Readiness Team. (2016). *Sharing of cyber threat indicators and defensive measures by the Federal government under the Cybersecurity Information Sharing Act of 2015*. Retrieved from https://www.us-cert.gov/sites/default/files/ais_files/Federal_Government_Sharing_Guidance_(103).pdf.
Vroegop, R. (2017). *The state of information and intelligence sharing in Canada*. The Conference Board of Canada. Retrieved from http://www.conferenceboard.ca/e-library/abstract.aspx?did=8487.
Whelan, C. (2015). Managing dynamic public-sector networks: Effectiveness, performance, and a methodological framework in the field of national security. *International Public Management Journal, 18*(4), 536–567. https://doi.org/10.1080/10967494.2015.1030484.
Whelan, C., & Dupont, B. (2017). Taking stock of networks across the security field: A review, typology and research agenda. *Policing & Society*, *27*(6), 671–687. Retrieved from https://www.tandfonline.com/doi/full/10.1080/10439463.2017.1356297?scroll=top&needAccess=true.
Wilson, T., Maimon, D., Sobesto, B., & Cukier, M. (2015). The effect of a surveillance banner in an attacked computer system: Additional evidence for the relevance of restrictive deterrence in cyberspace. *Journal of Research in Crime and Delinquency, 52*(6), 829–855. Retrieved from https://journals.sagepub.com/doi/abs/10.1177/0022427815587761.

Definitions of Key Terms

The following definitions are provided to assist readers to understand the research commonly used terms and concepts:

Advance Persistent Threat:	Adversaries possessing a sophisticated level of expertise and significant resources allowing them to achieve their objectives through multiple attack vectors (NIST, n.d.-a).
Bank Crime Prevention & Investigation Framework (BCPIF):	Crime information-sharing framework used by Canadian financial institutions (members of the Canadian Bankers Association) (CBA) leveraging exceptions provided by the Personal Information Protection and Electronic Documents Act (PIPEDA) to share information between each other to prevent crime.
Botnet:	A network of infected machines programmed to send harmful material to other computers connected to the Internet (Olesen, 2016).

P.-L. Pomerleau and D. L. Lowery, *Countering Cyber Threats to Financial Institutions*,
https://doi.org/10.1007/978-3-030-54054-8

Code Injection:	The exploitation of a computer bug that is caused by processing invalid data (Olesen, 2016).
Chief Information Security Officer (CISO):	Information security leader in the organization.
Chief Security Officer (CSO):	Physical and corporate security leader in the organization.
Corporate Security:	A security provision seeking to achieve corporate organizational goals (Walby & Lippert, 2014); for the purposes of this study, corporate security includes physical security as well as information security professionals working for financial institutions.
Critical Infrastructure:	A point, system, or part of an essential function of society, the health, safety, security, and economic and social well-being of the community for which a cessation or destruction would have a significant impact (Curt & Tacnet, 2018; European Commission, 2008); critical infrastructures include physical and cyber-based systems essential to economic and government operations (Guiora, 2014).
Cyber-threats:	The possibility of a malicious attempt to damage or disrupt a computer system or network (Secureworks, 2017).
Cybercrime:	A criminal infraction that uses the computer or network as the source, tool, target, or place of a crime (Service de police ville de Montreal, 2019).
Cybercriminals:	Individuals whose objective is to obtain profit from illegal and criminal activities in cyberspace (Olesen, 2016).
Cyberattacks:	May include denial of service, theft or manipulation of data, damage to infrastructure through a cyber-based

attack that may have significant losses, consequences for national security, the economy or the safety of citizens (Clark & Hakim, 2017).

Cyberterrorism: The use of Web-based information technology to conduct enabling, disruptive, or destructive operations in the digital domain, creating and exploiting fear through violence or the threat of violence (Rudner, 2013).

Cyber-warfare: Offensive computer assaults to damage, destroy, or deter the enemy's infrastructures and networks (Kenney, 2015).

CyboX: The Cyber Observable eXpression, a normalized schema for communication events in the system and network operations (United States Computer Emergency Readiness Team, n.d.).

Data Breach: When a company suffers a security incident resulting in a breach of confidentiality, integrity, or availability of the information it was accountable to protect (European Commission, n.d.).

Data Leakage: Unauthorized transmission of information or data from within an organization to an external recipient (SANS Institute Infosec Reading Room, 2007).

Distributed Denial-of-Service: Flooding a target with Internet traffic, rendering the service or network unavailable to users (Olesen, 2016).

Email Viral Attachment: Viral attachment sent by email copying itself and automatically sending itself throughout the owner's address book; this malware installed by the user is referred to as a "back-door" virus (Olesen, 2016).

Financial Market Infrastructures (FMIs): Systemically important and prominent payment systems to the financial system (Bank of Canada, n.d.-a).

Fraud: Any crime for gain using deception as a principal modus operandi, misrepresentation of the truth, or material fact (Association of Certified Fraud Examiners, 2019).

Fusion Center: State and local governments engaged in collaborative efforts with the private sector to detect, prevent, investigate, and respond to criminal or terrorist activity (U.S. Department of Homeland Security, 2014).

GCHQ: The United Kingdom Government Communications Headquarters.

Governance Structure: How the PPP is organized, how partners cooperate, its rules, and financing (European Union Agency for Network and Information Security, 2011).

Hackers (Black): Individuals involved in activities such as phishing and stalking in targeted cyberattacks that are playing a key role in deploying cyber threats (Olesen, 2016).

Hacktivism: The actions of a group of politically motivated threat agents whose motivation derives from political ideology and social justice that are using propaganda to influence political decision-making (Olesen, 2016).

Identity Theft: All types of crimes in which someone illegally obtains and use another's person personal information involving fraud or deception for economic gain (The United States Department of Justice, 2017).

Indicators of Compromise (IOC): Artifacts related to particular incidents or attacks (e.g., file names, hashed, IP addresses, hostnames) (Sedenberg & Dempsey, 2018).

Internet of Things (IoT): Term describing the trend of more technological devices being connected to the Internet (Mohn, 2018).

ISAC: Consortia endorsed by the federal government to facilitate the protection of critical infrastructure (Wall, 2017).

JMLIT: Joint Money Laundering Intelligence Taskforce (Rosemont, 2016).

Logic Bomb: Malicious code objects that infect a system and lie dormant until triggered by the occurrence of one or more conditions (Stewart, Chapple, & Gibson, 2015).

Malware: Any file programmed to create computer harm (IT Governance Ltd., 2019). Examples of malware are trojan, virus, worm, ransomware, keyloggers (Kammouh, & Cimellaro, 2019).

Man-in-the-Middle Attack: Technical type of attack occurring when a malicious user can gain a position logically between the two endpoints of ongoing communication (Stewart, Chapple, & Gibson, 2015).

National Institute of Standards and Technology (NIST): Voluntary cybersecurity framework consisting of standards, guidelines, and best practices to manage cybersecurity risks (National Institute of Standards and Technology, n.d.-b).

Phishing: Usually through emails, text messages, phone calls, or Internet pages, an attacker pretends to be someone else trying to convince the potential victim

	to disclose information (IT Governance Ltd., 2019; Kammouh & Cimellaro, 2019).
Public & Private Partnership:	An organized relationship between public and private organizations which establishes common scope and objectives, and uses defined roles and work methodology to achieve shared goals (European Union Agency for Network and Information Security, 2011).
Ransomware:	Type of malware demanding payment after encrypting the victim's computer files and rendering them inaccessible (IT Governance Ltd., 2019).
Resilience:	The capacity for essential functions to be restored as quickly as possible (Curt & Tacnet, 2018). To plan, prepare, and reduce the potential impact of events to minimize time to recovery (Curt & Tacnet, 2018).
Social Engineering:	Psychological manipulation techniques used by malicious attackers to breach organization security measures through people interactions (Jaf et al., 2018).
Spear Phishing:	Target phishing attempts against specific individuals or group of people with common characteristics.
State-Sponsored Actors:	Individuals receiving direction, funding, or technical assistance from the leadership of a country to advance national interests (Ablon, 2018).
STIX:	The Structured Threat Information eXpression, a standardized computer language (United States Computer Emergency Readiness Team, n.d.).
SWIFT:	The Society for Worldwide Interbank Financial Telecommunication is the global provider of financial

messaging services financial institutions use to transfer funds electronically (Society Worldwide Interbank Financial Telecommunication, 2020).

Systemic Risk: The possibility that an event occurring at the company level could trigger significant instability or the collapsing of an entire industry or economy (Chen, 2018).

TAXII: A standardized exchange mechanism (United States Computer Emergency Readiness Team, n.d.).

Zero-Day Vulnerabilities: Unknown vulnerabilities considered as unmeasurable due to the less predictable nature of software flaws and undetectable through regular anti-virus, intrusion prevention and detection systems (Wang, Jajodia, Singhai, Cheng, & Noel, 2014).

References

Ablon, L. (2018). *Data thieves; The motivations of cyber threat actors and their use of monetization of stolen data.* Retrieved from https://www.rand.org/content/dam/rand/pubs/testimonies/CT400/CT490/RAND_CT490.pdf.

Association of Certified Fraud Examiners. (2019). *What is fraud?* Retrieved from www.acfe.com.

Bank of Canada. (n.d.-a). *Regulatory oversight of designated clearing and settlement systems.* Retrieved from https://www.bankofcanada.ca/core-functions/financial-system/oversight-designated-clearing-settlement-systems/.

Chen, J. (2018). *Systemic risk.* Retrieved from https://www.investopedia.com/terms/s/systemic-risk.asp.

Clark, M. R., & Hakim, S. (2017). *Cyber-physical security: Protecting critical infrastructure at the state and local level.* Retrieved from https://www.amazon.ca/Cyber-Physical-Security-Protecting-Critical-Infrastructure/dp/3319813757/ref=sr_1_1?s=books&ie=UTF8&qid=1548189513&sr=1-1&keywords=Cyber-+Physical+Security+Protecting+Critical+Infrastructure+at+the+State+and+Local+Level.

Curt, C., & Tacnet, J. (2018). Resilience of critical infrastructures: Review and analysis of current approaches. *Risk Analysis: An International Journal,*

38(11), 2441–2458. Retrieved from https://onlinelibrary.wiley.com/doi/abs/10.1111/risa.13166.

Dupont, B. (2004). Security in the age of networks. *Policing & Society, 14*(1), 76. https://doi.org/10.1080/1043946042000181575.

European Commission. (2008). *Council Directive 2008/114/EC on the identification and designation of European critical infrastructures and the assessment of the need to improve their protection*. Official Journal of the European Union. Retrieved from https://eur-lex.europa.eu/LexUriServ/LexUriServ.do?uri=OJ:L:2008:345:0075:0082:EN:PDF.

European Commission. (n.d.). *What is a data breach and what do we have to do in case of a data breach?* Retrieved from https://ec.europa.eu/info/law/law-topic/data-protection/reform/rules-business-and-organisations/obligations/what-data-breach-and-what-do-we-have-do-case-data-breach_en.

European Union Agency for Network and Information Security. (2011). *Cooperative models for effective public-private partnerships: Desktop research report*. Heraklion, Greece: European Union Agency for Network and Information Security. Retrieved from https://www.google.ca/url?sa=t&rct=j&q=&esrc=s&source=web&cd=2&cad=rja&uact=8&ved=2ahUKEwi3_7zV5ZLgAhXHm-AKHXcwANgQFjABegQICBAC&url=https%3A%2F%2Fwww.enisa.europa.eu%2Fpublications%2Fgood-practice-guide-on-cooperatve-models-for-effective-ppps%2Fat_download%2FfullReport&usg=AOvVaw1QDdCdB5uE2SaoenNYsoeR.

Guiora, N. A. (2014). Homeland security: Definitions and accountability. *International Journal of Human Rights, 18*(2), 241. https://doi.org/10.1080/13642987.2014.889399.

IT Governance Ltd. (2019). *What is cybersecurity?* Retrieved from https://www.itgovernance.co.uk/what-is-cybersecurity.

Jaf, S., Ghafir, I., Prenosil, V., Saleem, J., Hammoudeh, M., Faour, H., & Baker, T. (2018). Security threats to critical infrastructure: The human factor. *Journal of Supercomputing, 74*(10), 4986–5002. https://doi-org.proxy1.ncu.edu/10.1007/s11227-018-2337-2.

Kammouh, O., & Cimellaro, P. G. (2019). Cyber threat on critical infrastructure; A growing concern for decision makers. In P. Gardoni (Ed.), *Routledge handbook of sustainable and resilient infrastructure* (pp. 359–374). New York: Routledge.

Kenney, M. (2015). Cyber-terrorism in a post-Stuxnet world. *Orbis, 59*, 111–128. https://doi.org/10.1016/j.orbis.2014.11.009.

Mohn, E. (2018). Internet of things. *Salem Press Encyclopedia of Science*. Retrieved from http://proxy1.ncu.edu/login?url=https://search.ebscohost.com/login.aspx?direct=true&db=ers&AN=100558386&site=eds-live.

National Institute of Standards of Technology. (n.d.-a). *Computer security resource center.* Retrieved from https://csrc.nist.gov/glossary/term/advanced-persistent-threat.

National Institute of Standards and Technology. (n.d.-b). *Cybersecurity framework.* Retrieved from www.nist.gov.

Olesen, N. (2016). European public-private partnerships on cybersecurity—An instrument to support the fight against cybercrime and cyberterrorism. In B. Akhgar & B. Brewster (Eds.), *Combatting Cybercrime & Cyberterrorism* (pp. 259–278). Retrieved from http://proxy1.ncu.edu/login?url=https://search.ebscohost.com/login.aspx?direct=true&db=edb&AN=117235697&site=eds-live.

Rosemont, H. (2016). *Public-private security cooperation: From cyber to financial crime.* Retrieved from https://rusi.org/publication/occasional-papers/public%E2%80%93private-security-cooperation-cyber-financial-crime.

Rudner, M. (2013). Cyber-threats to critical national infrastructure: An intelligence challenge. *International Journal of Intelligence & Counterintelligence, 26*(3), 453-481. https://doi.org/10.1080/08850607.2013.780552.

Sans Institute Infosec Reading Room. (2007). *Data leakage—Threats and mitigation.* Retrieved from https://www.sans.org/reading-room/whitepapers/awareness/data-leakage-threats-mitigation-1931.

Secureworks. (2017). *Cyber threat basics, types of threats, intelligence & best practices.* Retrieved from https://www.secureworks.com/blog/cyber-threat-basics.

Sedenberg, M. E., & Dempsey, X. J. (2018). *Cybersecurity information sharing governance structures: An ecosystem of diversity, trust, and tradeoffs.* Retrieved from https://arxiv.org/abs/1805.12266.

Service de police ville de Montreal. (2019). *Cybercrime.* Retrieved from https://spvm.qc.ca/en/Jeunesse/Cybercrime.

Society Worldwide Interbank Financial Telecommunication. (2020). *Discover SWIFT.* Retrieved from https://www.swift.com/about-us/discover-swift.

Stewart, M. J., Chapple, M., & Gibson, D. (2015). *CISSP (ISC)2 Certified Information Systems Security Professional Official Study Guide.* Retrieved from https://www.amazon.com/Certified-Information-Security-Professional-Official/dp/1119042712.

The United States Department of Justice. (2017). *What are identify theft and identify fraud?* Retrieved from https://www.justice.gov/criminal-fraud/identity-theft/identity-theft-and-identity-fraud.

U.S. Department of Homeland Security. (2014). *Facilitating private sector engagement with fusion centers.* Retrieved from https://www.dhs.gov/sites/default/files/publications/Facilitating%20Private%20Sector%20Engagement%20with%20Fusion%20Centers.pdf.

United States Computer Emergency Readiness Team. (n.d.). *Information sharing specifications for cybersecurity*. Retrieved from https://www.us-cert.gov/Information-Sharing-Specifications-Cybersecurity.

Walby, K., & Lippert, R. (2014). *Corporate security in the 21st century: Theory and practice in international perspective*. Retrieved from https://www.amazon.ca/Corporate-Security-21st-Century-International/dp/1349466816/ref=sr_1_1?s=books&ie=UTF8&qid=1548066995&sr=1-1&keywords=Corporate+security+in+the+21st+century%3A+Theory+and+practice+in+international+perspective.

Wall, F. A. (2017). *A phenomenological investigation of perceived effectiveness and success among InfraGard New Mexico members alliance* (Order No. 10624097). Available from Dissertations & Theses @ Northcentral University. (1964717485). Retrieved from http://search.proquest.com.proxy1.ncu.edu/docview/1964717485?accountid=28180.

Wang, L., Jajodia, S., Singhai, A., Cheng, P., & Noel, S. (2014). *K-zero-day safety: A network security metric for measuring the risk of unknown vulnerabilities*. Retrieved from https://ieeexplore.ieee.org/document/6529081/authors#authors.

Whelan, C., & Dupont, B. (2017). Taking stock of networks across the security field: A review, typology and research agenda. *Policing & Society*, *27*(6), 671–687. Retrieved from https://www.tandfonline.com/doi/full/10.1080/10439463.2017.1356297?scroll=top&needAccess=true.

Index

A

Academia, 106, 108, 149, 176, 180, 186
Academics, 12, 15, 16, 22, 49, 57, 105, 109, 160, 166, 168, 188, 189
Account takeover, 129
Act, 35, 69, 100, 101, 134, 138, 139, 148, 163, 164, 180
Acted, 150
Actionable information, 95, 168
Act of war, 69
Ad hoc basis, 160
Advance Persistent Threat (APT), 19, 67
Agile, 60, 181
Alerts, 56, 63, 112, 148, 159, 164, 185
Amendments, 31, 134, 166
Analytical tools, 160
Analyzed, 68, 97, 150
Anomalies, 112
Anonymized, 107
Anonymous, 66
Anticipate, 40, 159
Antivirus, 17–19, 104, 113
Approach, 10, 11, 14, 17, 20, 22–24, 40, 41, 53, 55, 56, 60, 94, 97, 99, 100, 102, 111, 123, 133, 176, 183–185
Archaic, 132
Architecture, 163
Arrest, 2, 3, 9, 67, 136, 148, 153, 167, 179
Artificial intelligence (AI), 3
ASIS International, 71
Assemblage, 53, 54, 110
Assessment, 16, 32, 35, 37, 72
Assistance, 34, 51, 57, 72, 100, 151
Attitude, 168
Attribution, 101
Audit, 29, 31, 32, 179
Australia, 58, 87, 90, 100, 105, 148, 164
Australian Fintel Alliance, 104
Automated, 93, 96, 107, 161–163

P.-L. Pomerleau and D. L. Lowery, *Countering Cyber Threats to Financial Institutions*,
https://doi.org/10.1007/978-3-030-54054-8

Automated teller machines (ATM), 66, 67
Avoid, 73, 90, 111, 112, 128, 172, 178, 183
Aware/awareness, 14–16, 36, 49, 55, 57, 71, 100, 136, 177

B

Background, 12, 39, 137
Bad actors, 96, 128, 130, 133, 148, 152, 171
Bait traps, 20
Bank Crime Prevention and Investigation Framework (BCPIF), 98, 127, 133, 134, 146, 147, 152, 154, 158, 165, 166, 169–171, 178
Bank Crime Prevention and Investigation Office (BCPIO), 98
Bank of Canada, 107, 174, 176, 177
Banks, 14, 29, 39, 40, 48, 49, 55, 56, 58, 62–67, 72, 88, 91, 92, 98, 124, 125, 127–130, 133, 134, 136, 137, 141–144, 146, 147, 151–153, 159, 162, 163, 165, 166, 170, 171, 173–176, 178, 186, 187, 189
Banks robbery, 165
Barrage, 48, 175
Barriers, 55, 56, 114, 160, 172
Behind, 3, 61, 89, 130, 152
Benefits, 41, 52, 56, 60, 93, 99, 109, 110, 137, 139, 140, 151, 169, 170, 176, 177, 180, 185
Best practices, 50, 51, 56, 91, 103, 106, 123, 128, 129, 152, 160, 183, 188, 189
Bill S-4, 98, 134, 152, 166, 186
Birthday attack, 6
Black swan, 89
Blame management, 92
Blockage, 133
Blurred, 135
Body/bodies, 97, 98, 134, 152, 165, 166, 178
Botnet, 67, 103
Bottom-up approach, 108
Brand protection, 93
Breach, 4, 61, 65, 68, 71, 72, 98, 135, 166
Breach of trust, 165
Budapest Convention, 71
Building, 10, 20, 38, 56, 58, 59, 92, 99, 111, 139, 153, 169
Bureaucratic model, 102
Business, 3, 4, 32, 38, 48, 57, 58, 60, 61, 67, 68, 73, 89, 95, 96, 100, 102, 106, 109, 111, 114, 129, 168
Business continuity, 177, 185

C

Calls, 9, 10, 12, 22, 39, 87, 131, 169
Canada, 47–49, 51, 68, 72, 87, 89, 91, 95, 97–102, 106, 107, 110, 123–125, 133, 135, 141, 143, 144, 146, 147, 149, 157, 160, 164–166, 168, 173, 176, 178, 182
Canadian Bankers Association (CBA), 98, 107, 124, 125, 134, 146, 147, 154, 165, 166, 178
Canadian Centre for Cyber Security, 100, 176
Canadian Criminal Code, 98, 165
Canadian Cyber Incident Response Center (CCIRC), 107
Canadian Cyber Threat Exchange (CCTX), 106, 107
Canadian federal government, 101, 106, 162, 186
Canadian Financial Intelligence Initiative (CFII), 131, 161

Canadian Security Intelligence Service (CSIS), 4, 72, 101, 132, 141, 163, 186
CanCyber, 107
Capabilities, 2, 3, 14, 15, 32, 37, 48, 49, 56, 65, 89, 92, 101, 106, 108, 111, 145, 152, 159, 160, 163, 164, 177, 180, 185
Capture, 151
Care, 108, 173
Carrying, 174
Central hub, 105, 106, 163
Centralized, 104, 129, 160, 163
Certification, 125
Chain of command, 167
Challenges, 3, 6, 7, 20, 22, 42, 48–50, 55, 58, 60, 88, 90, 92, 94, 96–98, 101, 114, 123, 132, 140, 157, 158, 165, 166, 169, 171, 172, 175, 183, 185, 187–189
Charter of Rights and Freedoms, 96
Chief executive officers, 49
Chief Information Security Officer (CISO), 13, 14, 16, 22, 23, 50, 60, 111, 124, 126, 132, 135, 138, 140, 143, 144, 146, 149, 158
Chief Security Officer (CSO), 50, 60, 124, 126–151, 166, 170, 171, 175
Civic duties, 109
Civil actions, 93
Clarity, 153
Classified briefings, 95, 168
Classified information, 95, 137
Clearing, 65, 174
Code injection, 67
Collaboratively, 34, 171
Collateral damages, 89, 174
Collective agenda, 110
Collective defense, 130
Co-location, 149, 184
Combat, 39, 47, 71, 103–105, 129, 152, 162, 186
Combined, 164, 180
Command-and-control, 162
Commercial incentives, 91
Commitments, 110, 112
Common, 2, 4, 6, 12, 16, 18–21, 33, 52, 55, 56, 61, 63, 96, 125, 128–130, 144, 152, 153, 160, 162, 163, 181, 183, 185, 186, 189
Common good, 139
Common obstacles, 94, 169
Communality, 170
Communications Security Establishment (CSE), 48, 100, 101, 141, 176
Community, 34, 58, 68, 92, 95, 102, 112, 168, 182
Companies, 2, 11, 14, 16, 33, 40, 47, 49, 51, 58, 59, 62, 67–69, 71, 73, 88–90, 92–94, 96, 102–104, 106–109, 111, 133, 136, 144, 154, 162, 165, 166, 169, 171, 175, 177, 185, 186
Competitive interests, 93
Complex, 5, 6, 50, 53, 54, 91, 107, 110–112, 146
Complicated, 89, 95, 168
Comprehensive view, 97
Compromised bank, 66
Conceptualized, 48, 175, 187
Conference, 22, 38, 169
Confidence, 59, 72, 90, 96, 139, 143, 154, 174
Confidential, 70, 72, 94, 113, 128, 169
Confirming, 66, 70, 174
Conflicting missions, 153
Conflicting objectives, 153
Conflicting values, 58, 168

Conflicts, 42, 124, 167
Consensus, 40, 113, 166
Consent, 59, 98, 132, 133, 135, 153, 165, 177
Consistent approach, 99, 161
Context, 11, 14, 23, 24, 51, 55, 58, 88, 95, 183, 185
Contextual information, 99
Continuing, 37, 182
Contraventions, 98, 135, 166
Cooperation, 39, 55, 56, 60, 72
Coordination, 34, 39, 53, 90, 97, 100, 105, 110, 150, 151, 155, 163, 179, 182, 183
Core banking systems, 65
Co-regulation, 172, 186
Corporate security, 49, 61, 111, 123, 125, 188
Corporate social responsibility (CSR), 61, 104, 109
Correlate, 112
Cost-effective, 14, 61, 89
Costs, 11, 19, 20, 38, 41, 48, 68, 72, 73, 110, 147, 155, 179, 181
Counter, 38, 130, 171
Counterintelligence, 39
Counterterrorism, 39
Country, 15, 35, 39, 41, 47, 60, 64, 66, 67, 70–72, 87, 90, 91, 93, 96, 97, 99–101, 103, 108, 110, 132, 136, 141, 142, 145, 148, 149, 162, 179, 181, 189
Covert, 36
Creativity, 172, 180
Crime, 2, 9–11, 15, 16, 47, 56, 58, 59, 66–73, 88, 96, 98, 99, 102, 104, 111, 113, 129, 130, 132–135, 139, 141, 142, 144, 146, 152–154, 160, 162, 164, 165, 167, 169–171, 175, 176, 178–182, 184–186
Crime prevention, 127, 134, 136, 153, 158, 167, 177
Crime task force, 105
Criminal, 3, 10, 12, 16, 19, 21, 30, 48, 52, 57, 62, 65–67, 70–72, 87, 96, 98, 102, 103, 128–130, 133, 136, 137, 141, 146, 152–154, 160, 164–168, 170, 171, 186
Criminal actions, 93
Criminal networks, 70
Crisis, 56, 58, 89, 107, 108, 168, 170, 176, 177, 185
Criteria, 69, 181, 182
Critical assets, 91–93, 96, 168
Critical infrastructure, 33–35, 37, 38, 42, 47, 48, 51, 52, 55, 56, 58, 60, 63, 72, 87–95, 98–103, 105, 107, 109, 113, 114, 127, 133, 141, 142, 144, 154, 162, 164, 165, 168, 170–174, 176, 177, 185, 186
Criticality, 29, 89
Critical systems, 90
Critical theory, 53
Cross-border domino-effect cyber-attacks, 66
Cross-Sector, 127, 158
Cross-site scripting (XSS) attack, 6
Culture, 53, 56, 94, 102, 108, 133, 160, 167, 168, 170, 178
Customer experience, 109
Customers, 16, 23, 31, 48, 59, 63, 64, 67, 68, 73, 91, 92, 96, 102, 106, 109, 110, 132, 135, 136, 143, 144, 153, 154, 165, 167, 171, 174, 177, 181, 184, 185
Cyber-attack, 3–5, 7, 8, 11, 29, 30, 37–40, 42, 47–52, 62–67, 69–74, 87–93, 96–98, 100–102, 107, 108, 111, 114, 136, 143, 153, 163, 175, 188

Cyber behavior, 41
Cyber-connected infrastructure, 42
Cybercrime, 2–4, 7, 11–14, 18, 19, 22, 23, 38, 48, 49, 55, 56, 62, 67–71, 73, 92–94, 96, 99–106, 111, 113, 142, 163, 165, 168, 171, 175, 176, 183
Cybercriminals, 2, 3, 14, 29, 30, 41, 49, 62, 66, 68, 70, 71, 89, 96, 128, 171
Cyber-dependent crimes, 10, 15–17, 71
Cyber-ecosystem, 41
Cyber-enabled criminal activity, 2
Cyber espionage, 68
Cyber exploitation, 93
Cyber extortion, 68
Cyber-fraud, 128, 130, 152, 159, 162, 163, 166, 170
Cyberheist, 65
Cyber hygiene, 14, 36
Cyber-incident, 4, 37, 61, 67, 70, 73, 88, 107, 109, 112, 163, 174
Cyber Observable eXpression (CyboX), 113
Cyber-perpetrator, 2
Cyber-related, 4, 30, 37, 40, 42, 68, 71, 128, 133, 151, 152, 154, 157
Cyber resilience, 100
Cybersecurity, 2–4, 7, 11–17, 19, 20, 22, 23, 31–41, 47, 49–54, 56, 60, 61, 63, 65, 66, 71, 88, 90, 91, 94, 96, 99–103, 107–111, 123, 125, 132, 135, 152, 154, 157, 159–163, 167, 170, 175, 176, 180–183, 185, 186, 188
Cybersecurity governance, 60
Cyber-security knowledge, 111
Cybersecurity landscape, 106
Cybersecurity posture, 100
Cybersecurity standard, 91, 100
Cyberspace, 2, 7, 10–13, 15, 23, 30, 37–42, 48, 53, 60, 103, 175, 187
Cyber-terrorism, 69, 71, 90, 103
Cyber-threat awareness, 2
Cyber-threats, 4, 13, 36, 37, 40, 47–50, 52, 56, 62, 63, 72, 91, 93, 97, 100, 103, 104, 106, 107, 124, 127, 129, 130, 133, 141, 142, 145, 151, 153, 158–162, 165, 171, 173–175, 177, 178, 180, 181, 183, 186, 189
Cyber-vulnerabilities, 3, 4, 41
Cyber-warfare, 69, 101

D

Data analytics, 109, 180
Data at rest, 164
Data breach, 4, 11, 13, 14, 19, 20, 33, 64, 67, 73, 135, 152, 166, 171
Data exchange protocols, 113
Data holding, 180
Data in transit, 164
Data in use, 164
Data leakage, 67
Data retention, 96
Data scientists, 180, 186
Datasets, 112, 128, 130, 152, 159, 175, 180
Data-sharing, 37, 96, 107, 131, 168, 170, 180, 182
Data-sharing platform, 40
Data systems, 5, 32, 39
Data theft, 62, 165
Dated, 137
Deceptive techniques, 47
Decision-makers, 50, 51, 105, 123, 124, 157, 158, 163, 188
Denial-of-service (DoS), 5, 62
Denominators, 160
Dependency, 59, 72

Dependent, 41, 42, 144, 154, 174
Desecuritization, 54
Designated body, 165
Detect, 17, 32, 49, 51, 65, 112, 133, 137, 160, 180
Deter, 38, 49, 67, 69, 92, 136, 167
Deterrence initiatives, 40
Device ID, 175
Differences, 62, 71, 102, 108, 112, 136, 168, 170, 180
Digital networks, 72
Digital Privacy Act, 98, 166
Digital security, 1, 2
Direct cost, 73
Disagreements, 55, 114
Disclosure, 128, 164, 167
Disjuncture, 48, 173
Disruptions, 2, 34, 69, 93, 102, 163, 176, 184
Dissemination, 13, 22, 162
Distributed Denial-of-Service (DDoS), 4, 5, 11, 13, 63, 66, 67
Divergent interests, 56, 58, 168
Diversity, 56, 180
Documented, 95, 110, 173
Domino, 127, 143, 158
Drastic, 133
Drive-by download attacks, 5
Drug trafficking, 62, 171

E

Early warning, 40
Eavesdropping attack, 6
Economic terms, 177, 181, 185, 186
Ecosystem, 12, 22, 66, 71, 90, 108
E-evidence legislation, 98
Effectiveness, 10, 12–14, 16–19, 22, 23, 41, 50, 96, 112, 165, 182, 183, 185, 188, 189
Efficiency, 51, 54, 136, 167, 172, 177, 182, 184, 185
Efficient, 13, 22, 23, 34, 51, 57, 60, 92, 99, 114, 132, 140, 146, 147, 151, 152, 165, 177, 182, 189
Elderly, 166
Electronic crime, 105
Electronic transfers, 65
Elements, 7, 30, 36, 58, 59, 91, 134, 137, 139, 149
Emails, 3–5, 15, 36, 62–64, 66, 67, 74, 124, 125, 145, 161, 162
Email viral attachment, 67
Emergency, 54, 95, 98, 113, 133, 134, 161, 162, 170
Emergency Management Act (EMA), 98
Empirical evidence, 23, 70
Employees, 3, 14, 16, 17, 19, 23, 62–64, 66–68, 73, 100, 109, 111, 129, 160, 162, 172, 181, 185, 186
Enable, 5, 29, 48, 50, 59, 113, 128, 132, 133, 139, 146, 161, 189
Encryption, 3, 113, 164
Engaged, 70, 172
Enhance/enhancing, 36, 38, 39, 41, 92, 95, 98, 104, 108, 112, 145, 177
European Cybercrime Center (EC3), 103–105, 175
European Union Agency for Network and Information Security (ENISA), 103, 110
European Union Directive on Network and Information Security, 96
Events, 13, 15, 16, 19–22, 52, 54, 88, 89, 92, 112, 113, 130, 143, 151, 160, 167, 177
Evidence, 12, 13, 19, 22, 60, 64, 96, 185
Evidence-Based Cybersecurity (EBCS) Approach, 11–14, 20, 22, 23

Exception, 133, 146
Exchange, 53, 55, 91, 98, 103, 104, 113, 128, 131, 132, 139, 146, 150–153, 155, 161, 163, 164, 169, 170, 179
Execution, 52, 57
Executives, 33, 34, 90, 92, 93, 95, 100, 133, 178, 180, 182, 183, 189
Exfiltrate, 61
Expectations, 3, 16, 48, 56, 59, 172, 173
Experiences, 12, 14, 15, 50, 51, 96, 108, 125, 134, 137, 157, 160, 167, 172, 188
Experiments, 13, 18–20
Expertise, 35, 40, 49, 111, 142, 154, 160
Exposure, 18, 72, 167
Extent, 52, 70, 91, 145
Extenuating, 133
Extraordinary measures, 55, 177

F

Fear, 1, 58, 59, 69, 94
Federal, 30–35, 37, 41, 42, 49, 51, 90, 91, 93–95, 97, 100, 101, 105, 111, 125, 141, 147, 150, 162, 163, 168, 175, 181, 182, 184, 187
Feeds, 129, 160, 163
Fiduciary, 109
Financial abuse, 166
Financial industry, 39, 49–52, 58, 60, 90–93, 97, 99, 101, 105, 107, 126, 130, 132, 140–145, 151, 160, 169, 173, 175, 187
Financial institutions, 2, 3, 13–20, 22, 23, 29–32, 39, 40, 47–52, 62–68, 91–93, 97, 98, 101, 104, 106, 107, 109–112, 114, 123–125, 127–133, 136, 138, 139, 141, 143, 144, 146, 147, 150, 152–155, 157–168, 170–189
Financial market infrastructures (FMIs), 101, 107
Financial sector, 13, 29–31, 39, 40, 42, 48, 49, 63, 66, 73, 91, 97, 108, 141, 153, 175, 182, 187
Financial Services Information Sharing and Analysis Center (FS-ISAC), 39, 40, 97, 149, 155, 179, 182, 185
Financial stability, 91
Financial systems, 14, 29–31, 39, 40, 92, 97, 143, 154, 174, 176, 177
Fintel Alliance, 105, 163, 182
Five Eyes Partners, 100
Flexibility, 60, 88, 174
Floor, 92, 150
Flow, 166
Focus, 3, 10, 12, 19, 23, 37, 40, 41, 49, 52, 53, 57, 71, 91, 97, 99–102, 104, 107, 111, 123, 136, 137, 157, 159, 164, 165, 167, 171, 177, 183, 185, 186, 188, 189
Foreign jurisdiction, 96
Forensic investigations, 89
Formality, 138
Fostering, 114
Fragile, 59, 170
Fragmented, 141, 173
Fraud, 13, 30, 62, 63, 67, 68, 98, 105, 128, 129, 134, 147, 152, 159, 161, 163, 166, 167, 171, 175, 180, 181
Fraudulent financial transactions, 31
Frequency, 42, 137, 153
Fundamental, 19, 31, 36, 48, 57, 88, 135, 157, 162, 173

Fusion center, 39, 40, 109, 110, 127, 129, 158, 160–164, 175, 181, 184–186, 188

G
Game-changer, 142
GCHQ, 104
Geo-localization data, 175
Geopolitical goals, 101
Global, 2, 4, 7, 13, 19, 29, 30, 33, 39, 40, 48, 53, 66, 92, 93, 101, 103, 111, 113, 151, 179
Global network, 180
Gold mine, 145
Good governance, 178
Governance, 52, 53, 60, 127, 131, 135, 146, 154, 158, 163, 176, 178, 179, 181, 182, 184–186, 188
Governance structure, 109, 110
Government, 15, 19, 24, 30, 31, 33–35, 37–39, 41, 42, 47–49, 51, 54, 56, 58, 59, 63, 64, 67, 71, 72, 87–95, 97–104, 106–114, 130, 133, 136, 137, 141–143, 147, 150, 153, 154, 160, 162, 163, 170–174, 176, 181, 186, 187
Government-prompted industry-centric, 181, 184
Greater, 6, 38, 42, 53, 57, 90, 127, 173
Growing pains, 148
Guardians, 12, 13
Guidance, 39, 100, 163, 182

H
Hackers (Black), 2, 6, 13, 15, 20, 49, 64–67, 70, 72, 128, 129
Hacking, 63, 67, 68
Hacktivism, 69, 72, 103
Hacktivists, 30, 66
Harm, 15, 30, 73, 90, 91, 93
Hash, 6, 63, 164
Haystack, 130
Hidden, 3, 5, 6, 180
High-valued targets, 90
Holistically, 7, 129, 160
Homeland security, 41, 42, 47, 58, 110
Homomorphic encryption, 113, 164
Honeypots, 20–22
Hostile, 107
How, 11, 15, 41, 49–51, 53–55, 59, 61, 64, 71, 91, 95, 97, 98, 100–104, 106–108, 114, 123, 132, 133, 135, 137, 138, 140, 144, 146, 147, 149, 151, 157, 162, 164–166, 168, 171, 173, 176, 178, 179, 181–183, 185, 188, 189
Hub-and-spoke, 163, 186
Human, 12, 14, 15, 22, 36, 54, 59, 60, 73, 74, 91–93, 107, 139, 154
Human error, 36
Human trafficking, 62, 105, 171
Hurdles, 165, 167
Hybrid, 58
Hypothetical, 143

I
Identify, 13–15, 19, 23, 33, 34, 38, 40, 56, 61, 65, 67, 88, 89, 96, 107, 129, 130, 152, 175, 180, 183, 188
Identity deception, 67
Identity theft, 32, 67, 68, 175
Ideological obstacles, 58, 168
Immediate danger, 55, 177
Impasse, 189
Imperative, 20, 58, 99, 145, 154, 159, 180

Impunity, 96
Incentives, 56, 59, 60, 94, 114, 167, 169, 176, 182
Incidence response, 108, 164
Incident management, 100, 109, 176
Indicators of Compromise (IOC), 61, 112, 132, 159, 161, 163
Indirect cost, 73
Industry, 2–4, 14, 19, 22, 24, 31, 33–36, 39, 47, 48, 70, 72, 73, 89, 90, 97, 104, 107, 108, 126, 131, 141, 144–146, 153, 159, 163, 164, 171, 173, 174, 177, 185, 186
Ineffective, 9, 48, 50, 123, 157, 188
Inferences, 180
Inflicting, 154
Influence, 12, 15, 21, 38, 54, 55, 58, 90, 108, 110, 133, 134, 160, 177
Information assurance, 57
Information Sharing and Analysis Center (ISAC), 108
Information sharing mechanisms, 51, 99, 162
Infrastructure, 21, 23, 29, 30, 33–35, 42, 47, 49, 54, 66, 67, 69–72, 74, 89, 90, 93, 103, 143, 159, 162
Inherent, 14, 89
Innovation, 11, 35, 64, 109, 110, 112, 180
Insecure, 5, 15, 132
Insider threats, 3, 36, 68, 171
Insight, 103, 142, 158, 162
Institutional, 29, 39, 40, 52, 53, 93, 150, 155, 179
Integrated, 39, 103, 127, 149, 158, 160, 176, 184
Integrated teams, 103
Intellectual property, 38, 72
Intelligence, 30, 37, 48, 49, 57, 60, 61, 63, 87, 93–96, 98–102, 104, 107–110, 113, 114, 123, 127–130, 137, 138, 142, 148, 151–154, 157, 159–161, 163, 164, 167–170, 172, 173, 178, 181
Intelligence agency, 87, 95, 96, 101, 103, 125, 126, 130, 131, 136, 141, 153, 154, 160, 163, 167, 168, 172, 173, 175, 176, 184–187
Intelligence hubs, 39
Interconnected, 52, 87, 93, 144, 154, 174
Interdependence/interdependencies, 34, 91, 92, 169
Interdisciplinary, 13, 53
Interference, 68, 72, 107
Internal controls, 31, 32
International, 22, 33, 35, 38, 40–42, 48, 49, 51–54, 56–59, 64, 65, 72, 99–103, 105, 110, 113, 151, 155, 175, 179
International agreement, 71
International boundaries, 3
International Relations, 53
Internet, 1, 4, 21, 31, 39, 62, 67, 68, 71, 72, 102, 104, 144, 154, 175
Internet banking, 144
Internet Crime Complaint Center (IC3), 11, 105
Internet-enabled threats, 1
Internet of things (IOT), 90
Internet protocol (IP), 5
Internet Service Providers (ISP), 145
Interpersonal relationships, 53, 58
Intertwined, 1, 170
Interviews, 18, 49–51, 70, 111, 123–127, 142, 157, 158, 160, 168, 188
Intranet threats, 36

Intrusion detection system (IDS), 15, 71, 112
Intrusion prevention system (IPS), 112
IP addresses, 5, 63, 96, 175
IT security, 17, 20, 32, 71, 103, 158

J
Joint Analyst Groups (JAGS), 163
Joint Money Laundering Intelligence Taskforce (JMLIT), 104, 105, 148, 149, 155, 164, 179, 183, 185
Joint Operational Resilience Management (JORM), 107, 176
Joint project, 106, 160
Joint task forces, 110
Joint-venture, 127, 129, 152, 158
Jurisdictions, 40, 67, 90, 96, 110, 163

K
Key performance indicators, 182
Key risk indicators, 177, 182, 185
Knowledge, 2, 51, 53, 59, 61, 68, 88, 96, 98, 103, 108, 150, 151, 155, 158, 174, 179, 180, 182
Knowledgeable, 128
Knowledge-sharing, 61
Known, 33, 34, 36, 39, 53, 54, 66, 180
Known known scenarios, 180
Known unknown, 180

L
Lack, 7, 11, 55–58, 60, 71, 88, 95, 98, 111, 114, 127, 132, 134, 143, 145, 154, 158, 165, 167, 174
Latent, 68
Law enforcement, 3, 10–12, 38, 49, 60, 64–67, 70, 71, 73, 92, 93, 95, 96, 99, 101–103, 105, 107, 108, 110, 125, 126, 129–131, 133, 135–137, 141, 147, 153–155, 160, 161, 163, 165, 167, 168, 171–173, 175, 176, 178, 179, 184–186
Laws, 22, 31, 32, 42, 49, 52, 66, 94, 98, 102, 128, 134, 135, 146, 152, 153, 162, 165, 166, 170, 178, 179
Lawyers, 103, 105, 134
Leadership, 56, 57, 61, 91, 100, 112, 155, 167, 168, 180, 181, 183, 186
Legacy infrastructure, 65
Legal framework, 60, 93, 99, 114, 127, 132–134, 145, 146, 153, 154, 158, 164, 165, 169, 172, 185
Legislations, 31, 32, 93, 97, 105, 110, 133, 135, 164, 170–172, 186, 188
Legislative gateway, 105
Leveraged, 11, 15, 180
Limitation, 108, 110, 134, 158
Link analysis, 163
Logic bomb, 67
Logs, 15, 31, 112
London Blue, 67
Losses, 4, 11, 48, 49, 62, 64, 68, 72, 73, 88, 109, 111, 127, 128, 136, 152, 153, 159, 167, 177, 181, 184, 185
Loyalty, 51, 59, 61, 73, 112, 184

M
Machine learning, 109, 164, 180
Machine-readable intelligence, 92
Machines, 5, 18, 131
Major crimes, 171

Malicious attachment, 66
Malicious code, 32
Malware, 5, 6, 11, 13, 15, 18, 19, 36, 62–64, 66–68, 72, 103, 107, 163
Malware attack, 6
Malware Information Sharing Platform (MISP), 107
Mandates, 141, 173
Mandatory disclosure, 96
Man-in-the-middle attack, 67
Matching, 163
Materialize, 174
Mature, 65, 139
Maturity, 151, 154, 170, 179
Mean time to contain, 68
Mean time to identify, 68
Meeting, 112, 128, 131, 161, 169, 184
Memorandum of Understanding (MoU), 104
Metrics, 105, 177, 183
Microsoft Malicious Software Removal Tool, 18
Microsoft Windows Defender, 18, 19
Militarized approach, 39
Military-styled tactics, 39
Mindset, 93, 178
Misidentification, 136
Misunderstanding, 95, 138, 172
Mitigate/mitigation, 11, 13, 14, 23, 34, 39, 40, 62, 88, 97, 101, 108, 112, 127, 138, 146, 159, 168, 177
Mitre, 113, 161
Mobile, 144, 154, 175
Model, 12, 14, 52, 57, 96, 105, 108, 109, 127, 140, 146, 149, 150, 155, 158, 163, 179–183, 186
Modus operandi, 64
Monetary, 29, 128, 152
Money, 12, 29, 63, 65, 66, 70, 72, 93, 144
Money laundering, 62, 104, 141, 165, 171
Money mules, 65
Montreal, 18, 64, 124, 125, 162
Moral duties, 109
Motivates/motivations, 60, 62, 89, 94, 102, 110, 139, 169, 170
Multi-agency, 163
Multi-dimensional, 130
Multi-disciplinary, 105
Multiple entities, 152
Mutual interests, 38, 56
Myopic view, 48
Myriad, 22, 111

N

National, 1, 10, 13, 30, 32–35, 37–39, 41, 51, 54, 87, 89, 91, 96, 99, 100, 102–104, 108, 111, 123, 125, 136, 150, 151, 155, 157, 175, 179, 182, 184
National Crime Agency (NCA), 104, 164
National Cyber-Forensic and Training Alliance (NCFTA), 106, 149, 155, 164, 179, 182, 185
National Cybersecurity and Communications Integration Center (NCCIC), 106, 149, 155, 179, 182, 185
National Institute of Standards and Technology (NIST), 11, 35–37, 60, 110
National security, 30, 33, 37, 38, 41, 47, 48, 51, 53, 60, 61, 72, 88, 89, 95, 97, 100, 109–112, 135, 141, 142, 149, 153, 161–163, 165, 172–175, 187
Nation-state, 2, 13, 30, 38, 41, 62, 64, 99, 106, 142, 143, 153, 173
Near-real-time, 127

Need, 1, 10, 13, 42, 50, 52, 54, 57, 61, 65, 69–71, 89, 91, 103, 109, 112–114, 128–130, 132, 133, 135, 136, 138–141, 151, 159, 160, 162, 163, 167, 169, 171–173, 178, 180, 189
Needle, 130
Need to know, 140, 178
Need to share, 94, 114, 133, 178
Networks, 4–6, 10, 14–21, 29, 31, 32, 34, 36, 37, 39, 40, 49, 53, 54, 57, 59, 61–64, 67, 69–71, 73, 87, 91, 92, 94, 99, 100, 103, 105, 107, 112, 113, 128, 130, 139, 150, 151, 155, 159, 160, 168, 179–182
Network Security Governance Framework, 50, 53, 123, 157, 188
Neutral, 106
Neutralizing, 106
Nexus, 160
Nimble, 147
Nodes, 47, 52, 151, 180
Non-profits, 73, 181
Non-technical, 163
NVivo, 51

O
OASIS, 113, 161
Online environment, 70
Open society, 72
Open source software, 107
Operational, 14, 16, 29, 31, 34, 36, 38–41, 49, 61, 62, 89, 103, 104, 129, 146, 148, 152, 173, 175–177
Organizational pathologies, 94
Organizational setting, 59
Organizational structures, 41, 58, 71, 94
Organized crime, 62, 70, 71, 102, 129, 130, 143, 171, 175
Outcome, 14, 15, 18, 53, 59, 183
Outcome-based, 171
Own, 4, 32, 37–39, 47, 51, 54, 89, 93, 136, 141, 142, 148, 153, 189

P
Paradigm, 12, 53, 110
Partnerships, 34, 35, 37, 40–42, 48, 52, 55–61, 91, 103–105, 111, 112, 114, 148, 152, 155, 167, 170, 172, 175, 178, 180, 183, 186, 189
Password attack, 6
Patriot Act, 105, 164
Patterns, 7, 107, 130, 152
Payload, 63, 162
Payments and settlements, 91
Payments systems, 65, 66, 143
Peer to peer, 40
Peer-to-peer intelligence, 40, 131, 164
Pendulum, 170
Perceived, 2, 49, 53, 60, 88, 102, 128, 130, 138, 145, 146, 151, 154, 178, 179
Perceptions, 49, 50, 55, 56, 111, 124, 133, 136, 158, 166, 172, 185, 188, 189
Perimeter threats, 36
Permanent, 108, 181
Perpetrators, 63, 67, 71, 89
Personally identifiable information (PII), 63, 135
Perspectives, 7, 50–53, 55, 57, 58, 88, 101, 111, 128, 134, 136, 137, 142, 143, 149, 153, 168, 172, 177, 178, 188
phenomenological study, 157
Phenomenology, 50

Phenomenon, 11, 50, 55, 123, 124, 157, 158, 188, 189
Phishing, 3, 5, 15, 36, 66, 67
Phones, 1, 125, 131, 144, 161, 175
Physical attacks, 89, 165
Physical harm, 69
Pillars, 36, 38, 41, 137
Pinpoint, 140
PIPEDA Act, 98, 152, 165, 166
Pluralism, 112
Police, 9, 10, 19, 57, 100, 103, 108, 137, 147, 182
Policing, 10, 12, 56, 103
Policing levels, 181
Policy/policies, 11–15, 17, 18, 22, 23, 32, 36, 38, 40, 52, 54, 60, 97, 101, 114, 160, 168, 182, 183, 185
Policymakers, 23, 49, 90, 166, 168, 182, 183, 189
Pooling, 162
Power structure, 51, 141, 142, 173
Practical, 158, 180, 189
Predict, 159
Predominately, 175
Prevent, 6, 16, 17, 20, 32, 51, 52, 62, 65, 93, 95, 97, 98, 105, 112–114, 127, 128, 132, 133, 135, 137, 138, 144, 146, 151, 152, 154, 159, 160, 165, 166, 170, 175, 176, 178, 180, 184
Preventative measures, 3
Preventing, 11, 17, 18, 30, 41, 49–51, 59, 72, 94, 98, 100, 101, 103, 123, 128, 132, 133, 139, 151–153, 157, 159, 165, 168, 169, 178, 183, 188
Principles, 37, 57, 90, 112
Priority/priorities/prioritize, 33, 34, 38, 48, 55, 61, 95, 110, 136, 154, 162, 167, 175, 177, 183, 187, 189
Privacy, 1, 19, 58, 73, 95, 96, 98, 113, 132, 133, 135, 146, 153, 164–166, 177, 178
Privacy-preserving, 164
Privacy rights, 95
Private corporate security professionals, 49, 188
Private platforms, 131, 161
Private security, 56, 103, 104, 111, 139, 153, 169
Private security professionals, 49–51, 95, 96, 111, 123, 124, 133, 134, 137–141, 152–154, 157, 158, 161, 165–170, 172–177, 179, 180, 186–189
Private-to-private, 131, 139, 154
Private to private partnerships, 58
Proactive, 40, 51, 56, 57, 93, 97, 102, 104, 111, 137
Probability, 15, 16, 19, 21, 49, 66, 70, 89
Problem-solving, 53, 150, 151, 155, 179
Procedures, 36, 57, 60, 62, 63, 95, 102, 110–112, 129, 177–179, 185
Proceeds of crime, 164, 165
Process/processes, 7, 11–13, 19, 20, 23, 50, 54, 55, 60, 65, 67, 87, 89, 91, 93, 101, 108, 111, 127, 128, 131, 132, 135, 137, 139, 153, 158, 162, 163, 169, 173, 174, 176–178, 189
Profits, 30, 47, 48, 60, 69, 70, 91, 106, 107, 109, 153
Progressively, 146
Prohibition, 134
Prominent, 155
Promptly, 127
Proprietary, 70, 96, 111, 128, 159
Prosecute criminals, 96, 168

Protect, 3, 19, 32, 38, 47, 49, 50, 52, 58, 60, 66, 73, 88, 90–93, 96, 97, 99–101, 103, 105, 109, 111, 113, 134, 136–138, 141, 142, 153, 154, 159, 162, 164, 167, 168, 171, 177, 178
Protection, 19, 32, 33, 35, 36, 38, 47, 50, 52, 57, 61, 70, 88, 90, 99, 102, 113, 114, 123, 127, 134, 141, 153, 157, 158, 166, 171–173, 186, 188
Provincial, 49, 90, 100, 125, 141, 147, 162, 163, 168, 181, 182, 184
Proxies, 142, 175
Public good, 53, 88, 109
Public interest, 3, 96, 177
Public police, 111
Public policy, 110
Public-private partnerships (PPP), 37, 50–52, 55–61, 88, 90, 91, 94, 96, 97, 102–108, 110, 111, 113, 114, 124, 125, 128, 130, 133, 136, 138, 142, 147–150, 154, 155, 157–160, 163–172, 175–189
Public Safety Canada, 48, 87, 99, 100, 102, 107, 141, 159, 160, 164, 172, 173
Public sector, 11, 48–52, 56, 58, 59, 94, 96, 102, 104, 107, 109–111, 123, 128–134, 137–142, 145, 146, 148–150, 152–155, 157, 159–174, 176–181, 183, 185–189
Public to public partnerships, 59

Q

Quality, 23, 57, 58, 93, 128, 137, 153
Quick, 127, 132
Quickly, 38, 39, 47, 128, 129, 154

R

Ransomware, 4, 6, 62–64, 67, 68, 143
Rapidly, 4, 11, 32, 39, 60, 90, 91, 103, 109
Real-life, 157
Real-time information-sharing, 97
Reason, 11, 36, 55, 63, 69, 88, 90, 92, 111, 133, 146, 147, 154, 162, 174, 177, 178, 183
Reciprocation, 58
Reciprocity, 94, 114, 139, 140, 153, 169
Recommendations, 41, 50, 51, 60, 71, 90, 95, 102, 105, 123, 124, 157, 158, 162, 164, 170, 172, 175, 176, 180, 182, 183, 185, 188, 189
Reconciling, 174
Recover, 68
Refined, 19, 137
Regulators, 108, 176, 184, 186
Regulatory framework, 110
Relationship, 9, 48, 50–53, 56, 58, 59, 70, 72, 89, 99, 110, 114, 123, 127, 130, 139, 140, 142, 152, 157, 158, 160, 163, 169, 180, 188
Reliance, 22, 57, 72, 154
Reopen, 171
Repeatedly, 153
Reporting, 7, 11, 32, 128, 137, 166, 176
Reputation risks, 60, 136
Resilience/resiliency, 34, 37, 40–42, 47, 51, 58, 60, 61, 92, 97, 103, 108, 129, 141, 146, 154, 159, 175, 176, 183, 184, 187, 189
Resources, 5, 35, 40, 49, 55, 60, 61, 66, 71, 90, 100, 102, 110, 113, 142, 152, 154, 163, 176, 180, 181, 183, 184, 186, 189

Respond, 38, 51, 66, 91, 109, 112, 127, 137, 159
Responsibility/responsibilities, 37, 47, 48, 51, 53, 56, 60, 71, 87–89, 91, 100, 101, 103, 104, 108–110, 127, 141, 142, 153, 158, 162, 172, 173, 175, 176, 180, 187, 188
Results, 15, 18, 19, 32–34, 56, 60, 68, 70, 73, 88, 96, 142, 150, 160, 161, 166, 167, 177–187, 189
Right, 54, 57, 69, 109, 110, 113, 129–131, 134, 135, 137, 140, 142–144, 146, 147, 149, 171, 177, 189
Ring, 102, 129
Risk, 2, 11, 13, 14, 16, 19, 23, 34–36, 39, 42, 47–49, 52, 57, 59–63, 71, 73, 88, 89, 96, 101, 108–112, 132, 133, 136, 137, 140, 141, 152, 153, 160, 161, 165, 166, 168–170, 173, 174, 177, 178, 185
Risk appetite, 109
Risk assessment, 30, 37
Risk management, 34, 35, 89, 93, 99, 174, 178
Risk mitigation, 3, 37
Rogue, 142
Roles, 5, 30, 34, 38, 47, 48, 56, 70, 71, 73, 101–103, 106, 109, 127, 139–142, 153, 158, 163, 169, 172–176, 180, 186–188
Root cause, 129
Royal Canadian Mounted Police (RCMP), 62, 87, 100, 131, 141, 163, 175, 186, 187
Rudimentary, 131, 152

S

Scholars, 12, 13, 16–18, 21, 22, 50, 58, 61, 70, 73, 114, 159, 166, 167
Scope, 32, 68, 111, 165
Second factor identification, 145
Secondment model, 105
Secret, 105, 137, 138, 152, 172, 186
Secure emails, 131
Secure environment, 104
Securely, 113, 131, 161, 164
Secure websites, 99, 162
Securitization, 54, 55, 177
Securitization Theory, 54
Security actors, 54, 55, 58, 153, 173
Security assemblages, 54, 57
Security clearances, 94, 95, 137, 138, 153, 167–169, 172, 186
Security controls, 4, 68, 183
Security information and event management (SIEM), 112
Security Network Framework Theory, 52
Security networks, 52, 53, 57, 94, 96, 127, 150, 151, 155, 158, 179, 181–183, 185, 186, 188, 189
Security of Canada Information Sharing Act, 97
Security posture, 23, 141, 165
Security Studies, 53, 55
Security threat briefing, 95
Security tools, 12, 17, 18, 23
Select, 49, 140
Self-interests, 58, 168
Self-regulation, 172, 186
Self-reported data, 73
Sensitive, 5, 6, 36, 56, 70, 93, 94, 96, 98, 100, 103, 128, 173
Server, 5, 6, 21, 62, 145
Shared responsibility, 47, 54, 90, 142
Shareholder interests, 109
Short term, 169, 189

Silos, 130
SIM cards, 66
Sim-swapping, 145, 175
Simultaneous, 143, 174
Sit, 127, 145, 150
Situational awareness, 31, 40, 100, 176
Slippery slope, 135
Social chaos, 72
Social control, 101
Social engineering, 5, 6, 14, 63, 64, 67, 68, 74
Social networking platform, 104
Societal, 90
Society for Worldwide Interbank Financial Telecommunication (SWIFT), 48, 63–65, 67
Sociotechnical, 53
Sophisticated, 19, 64, 70, 90, 103
Spear-phishing, 5, 62, 64, 162
Speech acts, 55, 177
Speed, 54, 99, 128, 159
SQL injection attack, 6
Stakeholders, 34, 42, 52, 53, 56, 58, 87, 99, 105, 108, 127, 138, 140, 148, 150, 152, 153, 155, 159, 161, 172, 176, 179, 183, 186, 189
Standard Operating Procedures (SOP), 128
Standards, 16, 31, 33, 35–37, 60, 90, 108, 113, 161, 162
Standard transport protocol, 113
State, 19, 48, 53–55, 59, 62, 65, 69, 72, 88, 89, 91, 93–96, 101–103, 105, 107, 112, 113
State-actors, 101, 130
Stimulate, 103
Stock price, 68, 69, 143
Strategic, 34, 37, 40–42, 51, 101, 103, 130, 138, 139, 148, 154, 167, 172, 180
Strategic dimension, 59
Strategies, 10, 17, 34, 37–41, 52, 56, 62, 87–89, 99–102, 163, 172, 186
Streamlining, 152
Strengthening, 12, 13, 38, 114
Strengths, 38, 172, 186
Structure, 47, 58, 71, 94
Structured data, 106
Structured Threat Information eXpression (STIX), 107, 113, 132, 161, 162
Subcultural, 160
Success, 57, 145, 167, 170, 182, 185
Success criteria, 177, 179, 182, 187
Successful, 2–4, 7, 11, 12, 60, 92, 145, 147–149, 152, 154, 155, 170, 179, 182
Supervisory control systems and data acquisition (SCADA), 91
Suppress, 134, 152
Suspicious activity, 31–33, 87
Sustainability, 177
Symbiosis, 151
Synergies, 109, 144, 154, 175
Systematic, 12, 160
Systemic, 97, 143
Systemic approach, 92
Systemic-level, 177
Systemic risk, 91, 97, 174, 182
System logs, 5, 113
System-related limitations, 8
System trespassers, 19–22
System trespassing, 19–22

T

Tabletop, 107, 176, 177, 185
Tactical, 71, 97, 103, 172, 181, 182
Tango, 189
Targets, 5, 12, 13, 20, 21, 29, 30, 41, 62–64, 66, 69, 72, 89, 93, 145, 146

Tarnish, 140
Taxonomy, 163, 186
Technical, 2, 3, 11, 12, 32, 34–36, 40–42, 49, 63, 65, 70, 71, 90, 92, 100, 103, 111–113, 161–164, 168, 180, 186
Technical boundaries, 8
Technical skill sets, 39
Technology, 3, 10, 23, 35, 36, 42, 53, 57, 62, 69–71, 87, 90, 93, 112, 113, 129, 149, 154, 160, 163, 175, 189
Technology as an instrument, 62
Technology as a target, 62
Telecommunications, 104, 106, 133, 144, 154, 164, 166, 175, 177, 185
Tensions, 173
Terms, 12, 23, 31, 40, 69, 97, 125, 135, 139, 141, 142, 148, 151–154, 164, 181
Terrorism, 55, 72, 89, 95, 101, 103, 133, 141, 175
Terrorist financing, 55, 104, 141, 165, 171
Themes, 51, 113, 127, 158, 172, 188
Theoretical frameworks, 52, 180
Threat landscape, 35, 48, 61
Timeframe, 124, 132, 161
Timeliness, 57
Tipping, 143
Tolerance, 109
Tool, 6, 10–14, 17–19, 22, 23, 39, 63, 89, 90, 99, 107, 112, 113, 131, 146, 162, 183, 185, 186
Top-down approach, 96
Top-secret, 137, 138, 152, 172, 186
Toronto, 124, 125, 162
Trail, 179
Training, 16, 42, 169, 178
Transaction, 2, 29, 31, 33, 62, 65, 92, 140, 144, 173
Transmitting, 6, 174
Transnational, 11, 53, 155, 175
Transparency, 59, 180
Triggers, 99, 164
True name fraud application, 129
Trust, 55, 56, 58, 59, 73, 90, 99, 102, 114, 127, 138–140, 143, 153, 158, 169, 170, 181, 183, 184
Trust-based behaviors, 170
Trusted, 5, 40, 56, 59, 139, 140
Trusted Automated eXchange of Indicator Information (TAXII), 107, 113, 132, 161, 162
Two-way, 94, 132, 140, 152, 170
Typologies, 53, 103, 150, 151, 155, 179, 180

U

Umbrella, 97, 134, 141, 153
Unanimous, 132
Unauthorized disclosures, 32, 36
Unclear, 17, 127, 141, 142, 153, 158
Unequivocal, 132
United Kingdom (UK), 35, 56, 67, 87, 104, 105, 133, 148, 155, 164, 175, 179, 185
United States (US), 10, 11, 30, 34, 37, 38, 40–42, 58, 63, 64, 67, 87, 93, 96, 100, 105, 106, 113, 129, 130, 133, 148, 155, 161, 162, 164, 179, 185
Unknown unknown, 180
Unstructured data, 106

V

Value, 4, 15, 56–58, 69, 89, 137, 138, 162, 168, 172, 176, 178, 181
Various, 11, 15, 18, 21, 36, 47, 50, 58, 60, 61, 63, 64, 67, 69, 90, 92, 93, 95, 98, 102, 104, 106, 107, 110, 112, 113, 124, 127, 130, 131, 141, 149, 152, 157, 158, 161, 163, 164, 173, 181–183, 188
Vectors, 8, 14, 107, 130
Vehicle, 53, 131, 176
Verbal, 1, 131, 161
Verbatim, 158
Versatile, 36
Vetting, 137
Victimization, 11, 16, 68
Victims, 2, 5, 11, 14, 15, 52, 64–67, 69, 74, 102, 113, 128, 132, 143, 153, 165
Virtual, 1, 52, 53, 104, 129, 131, 132, 150–152, 160, 161, 163, 179–182, 184, 186
Virtual private networks (VPN), 15, 175
Voluntarily, 164, 165
Voluntary disclosure, 96
Vulnerabilities, 2, 3, 5, 13, 16, 23, 36, 40, 42, 52, 62, 65, 67, 74, 88–90, 94, 104, 106, 110, 111, 128, 132, 136, 146, 160, 162, 163, 165, 167, 170

W

WannaCry, 64
Weakness, 74, 136
What, 7, 15, 23, 30, 42, 49–52, 54, 55, 57, 58, 61, 66, 70, 71, 92, 98, 101, 105, 110, 112, 114, 124, 128, 129, 131, 135, 137–140, 142, 143, 146–151, 153, 158, 162, 164, 166, 171, 173, 177–179, 181, 183, 185, 189
When, 3, 6, 7, 12, 17, 32, 34, 38, 41, 42, 54, 56, 61, 67–69, 73, 88, 91, 93–98, 102, 109, 111, 128, 134–137, 139, 141–148, 150, 153, 159, 160, 162, 166, 167, 169, 170, 173, 174, 178–180
Whole, 30, 36, 141, 151, 153, 171, 173
Whole-of-state, 176
Whom, 178, 179
Wire frauds, 64

Y

Yara rules, 107

The manufacturer's authorised representative in the EU is Springer Nature Customer Service Centre GmbH, Europaplatz 3, 69115 Heidelberg, Germany. If you have any concerns regarding our products, please contact ProductSafety@springernature.com

Printed and bound by CPI Group (UK) Ltd, Croydon, CR0 4YY
22/09/2026
02221058-0002